DEBT AND REFUGE

Stanford Studies in Middle Eastern and Islamic Societies and Cultures

DEBT AND REFUGE

Syrian Farmworkers and the Politics of Displacement in Lebanon

China Sajadian

STANFORD UNIVERSITY PRESS
Stanford, California

Stanford University Press
Stanford, California

Library of Congress Cataloging-in-Publication Data
Names: Sajadian, China author
Title: Debt and refuge : Syrian farmworkers and the politics of displacement in Lebanon / China Sajadian.
Other titles: Stanford studies in Middle Eastern and Islamic societies and cultures
Description: Stanford, California : Stanford University Press, 2026. | Series: Stanford studies in Middle Eastern and Islamic societies and cultures | Includes bibliographical references and index.
Identifiers: LCCN 2026008623 (print) | LCCN 2026008624 (ebook) | ISBN 9781503647602 cloth | ISBN 9781503647862 paperback | ISBN 9781503647879 ebook
Subjects: LCSH: Agricultural laborers, Foreign--Lebanon | Foreign workers, Syrian—Lebanon | Refugees—Lebanon | Refugees—Syria | Debt—Lebanon
Classification: LCC HD1537.L4 S25 2026 (print) | LCC HD1537.L4 (ebook)
LC record available at https://lccn.loc.gov/2026008623
LC ebook record available at https://lccn.loc.gov/2026008624

Cover design: Martyn Schmoll
Cover photo: China Sajadian
Typeset by Newgen in Brill 10.5/14.4

The authorized representative in the EU for product safety and compliance is: Mare Nostrum Group B.V. | Doelen 72 | 4831 GR Breda | The Netherlands | Email address: gpsr@mare-nostrum.co.uk | KVK chamber of commerce number: 96249943

For Mateu, Sol, Oriol, and my parents

Who built the seven gates of Thebes?
The books are filled with names of kings.
Was it the kings who hauled the craggy blocks of stone?

—Bertolt Brecht, "A Worker Reads History"

Contents

Note on Translation and Transliteration

This book follows a simplified version of the *International Journal of Middle East Studies* (IJMES) transliteration system for rendering both Modern Standard Arabic and colloquial dialects. Diacritics are used to denote the letters ʿayn (ʿ) and hamza (ʾ), and double consonants indicate the Arabic shadda. Long vowels are represented largely in accordance with IJMES standards. For proper names, honorific titles, and Arabic terms now common in English usage, I have omitted diacritical marks and adopted standard spellings (e.g., Beirut, Bekaa).

Two principal dialects appear throughout this book: Lebanese Arabic, particularly that of the Bekaa Valley, and Syrian Arabic, especially the northeastern dialect. Wherever possible, I have sought to capture the nuances of Arabic as it was spoken to me in daily life, remaining attentive to the regional inflections that give local speech its texture. I quote people at length not only to convey the substance of what they said but also to evoke the poetic character and rhythm of their voices—their cadence, musicality, and play of parallelism and alliteration. My aim throughout is to make Lebanese and Syrian vernacular speech accessible to English-language readers while preserving its unique syntax and expressive force. All translations from Arabic are my own.

Most of my Syrian interlocutors spoke *shāwi* Arabic, which refers to a cluster of dialects spoken across eastern Syria (mainly Deir ez-Zor, Raqqa, and al-Hasakah) and western Iraq. Some of its distinctive characteristics include the use of /g/ for *qāf*, the pronunciation of the second-person feminine suffix -k as -ch (e.g., *ʿindich* for *ʿindik* to express "you have"), as well as a lexicon rich with loanwords from Kurdish. Linguistically classified within the Mesopotamian Arabic dialect area, many of these features attest to its historical association with nomadic and semipastoral communities across the Euphrates basin. For speakers today, especially those displaced from Syria's eastern countryside, *shāwi* Arabic carries a strong sense of tribal identity and rural rootedness within the region's broader linguistic landscape.

Readers unfamiliar with colloquial Arabic may notice the frequent use of Abu ("father of") and Imm ("mother of") in personal names. These are known as *kunyas*, or teknonyms—names that identify a person through their relationship to a child, most often the eldest son (for example, Abu Sharif, Imm Brahim). *Kunyas* are especially common when addressing elders, serving at once as expressions of respect, social belonging, and familiarity. While *Umm* is closer to the standard IJMES transliteration, in everyday eastern Syrian and Lebanese dialects, "Umm" is pronounced "Imm."

Except for public figures and well-known individuals, all personal names that appear in this book are pseudonyms. In some cases, I have slightly modified biographical details to protect the anonymity of my interlocutors.

FIGURE 1. Lebanon and Syria. Map by Oriol Vallès Codina.

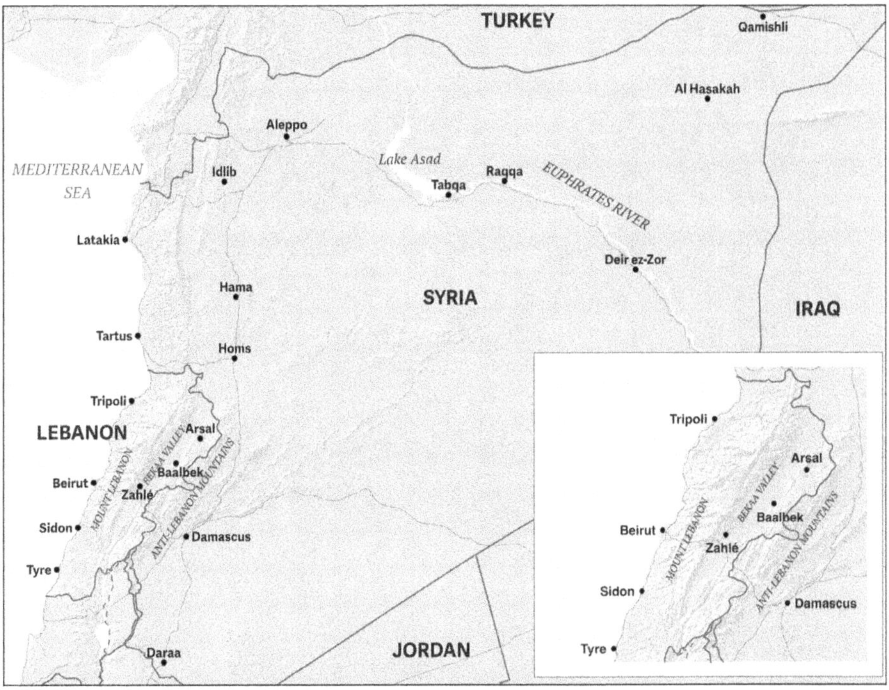

DEBT AND REFUGE

PROLOGUE

IT WAS MARCH 2019, THE MIDDLE OF POTATO PLANTING SEASON IN Lebanon's Bekaa Valley. I was perched on a rickety semiautomatic planter hitched to the back of a bright red 1974 Massey Ferguson tractor. On either side of me sat Rawia and Marwa, who were hunched over two metal carousels that rotated clockwise as the tractor lurched forward. Their job was to repeatedly drop potatoes into the carousels' rusty chambers. The air hung heavy with condensation that left our hair and clothes damp. We were only halfway through a ten-hour double shift, and our feet were completely numb from the cold.

"*Wallāh mallayna min hūn*," Rawia sighed, as she grabbed a handful of potatoes and deftly plopped them, one by one, into each carousel chamber. The phrase could be translated as "I swear, we're tired of being here" or "We're fed up with this place," but literally referred in Arabic to a sense of being bored—a fitting reference to the day's work.

Rawia and Marwa were among eight women from their camp who were hired that day to plant for one of the largest potato processing and distribution companies in Lebanon. Though the semiautomatic planter was designed for two workers, we had managed to squeeze together onto the plywood bench affixed to the back, periodically switching spots to distribute the work among the three of us. The mechanical precision of planting work kept our gaze downward, but our flowing conversations helped pass the time. Usually, these conversations revolved around what we would eat after work, Rawia's new romantic interest, or the latest gossip in the camp. But, on that particular day, we talked about the war in Syria.

Three days earlier, the Kurdish-led Syrian Democratic Forces had raised victory flags in Baghuz, the last stronghold of the Islamic State in Syria, marking the defeat of its five-year caliphate. Rawia, Marwa, and their families were among the countless Syrians who sought refuge in Lebanon years earlier when their villages in the countryside of Raqqa were embattled and eventually occupied by the Islamic State. Yet, for all the official fanfare about the region's "liberation" and Bashar al-Asad's proclamations beseeching refugees to come home, Rawia was especially uncertain about her family's prospects of return.

Uncertainty was something Rawia shared with the one and a half million Syrians like her who fled to Lebanon throughout the Syrian conflict. Considered one of the largest migration crises of the twenty-first century, the 2011 Syrian uprising's tragic devolution into a protracted war has seen hundreds of thousands killed, millions displaced, and countless others detained or disappeared. At the time of this conversation with Rawia in 2019, much of Syria's infrastructure and food system remained in shambles, the Syrian pound had devalued tenfold, most Syrians struggled to find the resources to rebuild their homes, and many others remained in exile, fearing military conscription or arrest. For these reasons, among others, many Syrians remained reluctant to return, even as a popular backlash against them was mounting across Lebanon.

Yet Rawia's predicament, and that of many Syrian farmworkers like her, was rather distinct from the conventional picture of Syrian refugees in several important ways. Unlike many of their exiled compatriots, she and her family were not newcomers to Lebanon, nor were they political dissidents. Though they were registered with the UN High Commissioner for Refugees, her family's experiences of displacement long predated their refugee status, as they had migrated seasonally to Lebanon as farmworkers for years before the war began. And as I came to learn, Rawia remained uncertain, even outright pessimistic, about her future prospects for one reason above all else. Her family was thousands of dollars in debt to their *shawīsh*, the patron-moneylender who brokered their jobs in agriculture and ran the camp where they lived. And despite her desires to find true love and leave the camp, her indebted family continually deferred her marriage—and, thus, her transition to feminine adulthood—because they critically depended on her wages as a farmworker.

What was the connection between these conditions—Syrian farmworkers' deeply historical presence in Lebanon, their mounting debts, and interfamilial struggles about women's labor and life transitions? I became immersed for nearly two years in the Bekaa Valley, the long agricultural plateau that flanks Lebanon's eastern border with Syria, in order to find answers to this question. As I worked every day with different teams of farmworkers across the valley, most of my days looked very much like the scene I just recounted. Staring into the creaking wheel of a semiautomatic potato planter, following the repetitive motions of Rawia's pink-rubber-gloved hands, straining to hear her words over the rattling tractor engine, our shoes sodden from treks through muddy fields together at dawn—it was here in this seemingly marginal, bucolic place that I learned what displacement and refuge meant to Syrian farmworkers like her.

Over time, it became clear to me that Lebanon's refugee crisis was about much more than the war in Syria. By laboring with Syrian farmworkers in their daily lives—not only in the fields but also in their homes, caring for their children, cooking meals, and sleeping side by side in their tents each night—the more enduring and mundane aspects of displacement came into view. What struck me most were the distinctly *agrarian* roots of these farmworkers' displacements, conditions that ultimately exceeded the strict confines of their refugee status. Displacement was deeply present, for example, in Rawia's struggles with her parents over when to get married, in how piece rates were set during harvests, and in disputes between camp residents and their *shawīsh* over the proper accounting of their wages. Displacement also endured in her family's attachments to ideals of state provisioning, in their reckonings with Syria's land reforms, and in the silences and occasional dark humor that surrounded histories of rural dispossession and debt on both sides of the Lebanese-Syrian border. Displacement, in other words, was a process of navigating many fraught and often contradictory attachments to people, places, and promises. These attachments, as well as their paradoxes, are the subject of this book.

FIGURE 2. Potato planting in the Bekaa Valley.

FIGURE 3. Close-up of a semiautomatic potato planter.

That cloudy day with Rawia and Marwa, as we fed potatoes into the creaking machine, bored, hungry, and shivering from the cold, came to embody for me a different way of engaging with the dramatic events that were unfolding around us. The scene was unremarkable, even dull—a far cry from the spectacular imagery of violence that filled headlines at that time and, until today, characterizes how Lebanon, Syria, and other parts of the Middle East appear in most people's media feeds. Planting potatoes may, indeed, seem like a strange place to begin a story about forced migration. Yet it was precisely through such labor that I began to understand the sheer longevity of Syrian refugees' predicaments, along with the ordinary routines that ran deep within this ostensibly exceptional wartime situation. In their stark monotony, these workdays invited another orientation entirely, one very much akin to the view from the back of a potato planter. It was not the distant gaze that witnesses suffering from afar, but a persistently lowered one, attentive to the repetitive rhythms of hands in motion, to the bodily tedium of labor, and to the weight of familial obligations that tied women like Rawia to their work, day after day.

Debt and Refuge is based on nineteen months of continuous fieldwork that I spent immersed in the everyday lives of Syrian refugee-farmworkers in Lebanon's Bekaa Valley. The core of this research took place from June 2018 to December 2019, while two summers of preliminary research in 2016 and 2017 helped lay the foundations for it, and a follow-up trip in 2022 brought it to a close. But the seeds of this project developed while I was living in Beirut from 2012 to 2013, a period of monumental popular upheaval and deepening violence in Syria. At the time, I was working as a researcher for the United Nations Relief and Works Agency, the UN body chiefly responsible for Palestinian refugees. As I witnessed scores of Syrians, including Syrians of Palestinian origin, camped outside of the main headquarters in Beirut beseeching the UN to assist them, I tried to make sense of how this tiny postcolonial country of 4.5 million people, still recovering from the legacies of its own civil war from 1975 to 1990, could accommodate 1.5 million Syrian refugees alongside the hundreds of thousands of Palestinian refugees already living there.

The Bekaa Valley—known locally for its fertile land that sustains Lebanon's oldest vineyards, as well as olive trees, fruit orchards, vegetables, and wheat (and further north, hashish fields)—was, by that time, making international headlines as the major frontline for Syrians seeking refuge in Lebanon. Media feeds were saturated with images of Syrian women, children, and their tarpaulin tents. These images ranged from the harrowing to the tritely sentimental, reproducing a now-familiar repertoire of humanitarian iconography, most of them variations on the same genre of feminized victimhood and suffering.

The sight of tarpaulin tents across the valley was nevertheless unmistakable: they were everywhere, clustered in wheat fields and orchards, pitched in empty lots and junkyards, some even tucked away in people's private backyards. Still, what immediately caught my attention whenever I visited was not really the tents themselves. It was rather the labor that quietly bustled around them: women in colorful dresses riding on the backs of trucks, bent over in vineyards as they weeded with hoes, laying out seasonal vegetables to dry in front of their tents, and hanging laundry with children in tow. One might say that my pathway to Rawia and her family—to writing this book—began there: with an impulse to look past the spectacle of this "refugee crisis" to grasp its deeper historical roots, beginning with the work of women that endured so subtly yet persistently in the background.

That was back in 2012, a time that now feels remote in its sense of dynamism and quiet hopefulness—before the cascading impacts of another decade of violence, dispossession, and loss made living with "crises" (in the plural) a crushingly routine condition for the region's impoverished majority. This is not to say that times were necessarily easy in 2012, nor that signs of more difficult times to come were not already present. Spending most of my days and nights in working-class neighborhoods, camps, and small villages across Lebanon, I remember very well the tension and uncertainty that reigned in that period: the violent clashes, the car bombs and targeted assassinations, the rounds of political accusation, the stark inequalities. Yet I also recall moments of solidarity: evenings that culminated in friends from Shatila, Damascus, and Beirut's suburbs breaking out into revolutionary songs, and how Lebanese villagers in the Bekaa fondly remembered the Syrian border-town residents who hosted them throughout the devastating July 2006 war with Israel.[1]

By the time I returned to Lebanon in 2016, this spirit of solidarity from those early years of Syria's popular uprising had steadily waned in the face of violent state repression, the further militarization and fragmentation of Syria's opposition movements, and a looming economic crisis on both sides of the border. As I navigated this darkening reality, I embarked on this project with many questions, prepared—as any anthropologist must be—for my expectations and intuitions to be unsettled. A concern with agriculture remained central throughout, but my deeper encounters with *shawīsh* camp residents like Rawia marked a turning point. Working with them on a daily basis confronted me with two interrelated predicaments that I had not fully anticipated: the central role of women's unpaid reproductive labor within Lebanon's agricultural system and the pervasiveness of farmworkers' indebtedness, both of which carried a historical durability that demanded deeper investigation. When considered together, they brought to light dimensions of their mobility that legal or humanitarian framings could not capture, such as how waged work, childrearing, and debt obligations conditioned when and how different family members could move throughout days, weeks, and seasons—and, crucially, how they planned for return. This ultimately laid the groundwork for the project's central feminist stake: to rethink the terms of this "refugee crisis" by reconceptualizing debt and refuge as struggles over *social reproduction*, routed through and rooted in generations of agrarian displacement.[2]

Six years have passed since I concluded the core period of my fieldwork, and I write in the wake of many transformations that refract this account in new ways. Lebanon and Syria alike have endured food shortages, staggering inflation, and the rapid devaluation of their currencies amid a regional economic crisis that took a drastic turn for the worse from 2020 onward. Israeli military bombardments have killed and displaced thousands across Lebanon since 2023, paralleling a genocidal war in Gaza that has inflicted an unspeakable human toll. And in December 2024, the Asad family's fifty-four-year regime fell with unexpected swiftness. Its collapse initially sparked hope for change among many Syrians, but ensuing waves of violence and the sheer scale of destruction have left the country's future in doubt. Today, millions of displaced people across the region struggle with the questions of if, when, and for how long they might return home.

Every ethnographer is faced at some point with the uncanny feeling of becoming a historian of the recent past, not least when writing about a region that has witnessed such profound losses and transformations in the span of just a few years. In making sense of what has changed since I first embarked on this research, I often recall that cold March morning in the Bekaa: the sensation of dampness in my hair, the smell of soil, Rawia's gloved hands bobbing up and down, the strange dissonance of talking about war and speculating about the future set to the deafening tune of a tractor engine. As we sat together on that plywood bench, the significance of the news in our midst seemed, for a moment, to collapse into the more immediate effort of keeping pace with the work before us. So much has happened since then, but banal working days like that do carry on. Understanding how and why this labor has endured across the thresholds of crisis is no simple matter: it is one of the main questions that I set out to answer in the coming pages.

Syrians' predicaments are often understood to be an extreme case of displacement, and in many respects, they are: half of Syria's population was forcibly displaced throughout the war, and one-sixth of the world's refugees are Syrian. Lebanon, likewise, is arguably an exceptional case: it hosts the highest number of refugees per capita in the world, and at the height of the war, refugees made up one-quarter of the country's entire population. Yet, in many other respects, the conditions through which Syrians have struggled to secure their livelihoods in Lebanon are remarkably resonant with those of workers elsewhere, particularly their dependence on debt. Such predicaments are not only confined to the countryside or war-torn regions: virtually every person depends on debt to survive today, whether in the form of home mortgages, student loans, credit card bills, or the everyday favors that flow between friends and family.

At a time of unprecedented backlash against displaced people across the globe, I invite readers to pay close attention to these farmworkers' stories and to consider their larger reverberations. While situated in specific places and times, Syrian farmworkers' lives are at once a mirror and a window, offering broader lessons for thinking about refuge—about the labor that makes it possible, the forms of debt that sustain it, and how those responsibilities are distributed in today's violently partitioned yet vitally interconnected world.

Introduction
FROM WORKERS TO REFUGEES

THIS BOOK TELLS THE STORY OF HOW SYRIAN FARMWORKERS WENT into debt as refugees in Lebanon. Its major aim is to reframe the politics of mass displacement through the lens of debt—two issues that are intimately related yet rarely considered together. Debt, in this context, refers not only to the economic obligations Syrians incurred and the sums of money they owed, but also to the morally significant social relationships that sustained them and their aspirations. Whether these debts were to patrons, employers, neighbors, or intimate kin, they revealed the tense continuum between coercion and interdependency that characterizes the pursuit of refuge today. Set against the long eve of Lebanon's sovereign debt crisis and key phases of the war in Syria, *Debt and Refuge* is ultimately about the binding and displacing power of debt in times of extraordinary political upheaval and uncertainty.

The places from which I examine these issues are seemingly marginal—Lebanon's Bekaa Valley and Syria's northeastern Jazīra region[1]—but the ethical and political questions they raise are globally consequential. The United Nations High Commissioner for Refugees estimated recently that over 123 million people around the world are living in conditions of forced displacement, which is the highest number on record since World War II.[2]

These numbers look much larger if we include labor migrants. Between 1970 and 2012, the number of transnational migrants worldwide doubled to 232 million.[3]

Mainstream media debates and political leaders routinely juxtapose refugees and migrant workers against each other, and the rhetorical power of such distinctions is well known: between those who are deemed deserving or undeserving of asylum, those who are said to be freely migrating as opposed to those who are forced to, and those whose conditions are cast as economic as opposed to political.[4] A closer look reveals that their structural circumstances are often shared, from the violence of criminalization, stigmatization, and racism to the dislocating effects of economic insecurity. Regardless of their status, few can truly be said to be "choosing" migration, and the process by which one moves or stays put is rarely a linear path. As in Rawia's case, refugees and migrants are often the *same people*: workers in search of refuge in places to which they have long-standing ties.

While the need for refuge is usually associated with those fleeing acute wartime conditions, such emergencies are always embedded within more protracted struggles for income, shelter, and food. This is especially so in agrarian contexts. A Syrian friend once described this to me as the cruel dialectic between the spectacular "bloody war" and the mundane "economic war" that trails in its wake. The latter, he insisted, is the one that is truly catastrophic, because its root causes are harder to pinpoint and it never seems to end. This is rendered all the more difficult when the bloody war is said to be over and refugees' lingering material predicaments cease making the news. A key aspect of that economic war, as my friend understood it, is the crushing weight of debt.

Debt is central to the politics of displacement because it is the means by which many ordinary people make ends meet in the face of compounding crises, insufficient wages, slashed public spending, and rising global inequalities. Despite their distinct legal statuses and diverse conditions of mobility, those differentiated as "labor migrants" and "refugees" are both increasingly dependent on debt to secure their basic needs and aspirations, whether it be to smugglers to reach their destinations or local moneylenders for shelter when they arrive. To whom they go into debt may vary widely, and the conditions of such debts are certainly not all the same. But the broader historical dynamics and material conditions that have pushed many people across borders and into debt throughout the world are deeply intertwined.

As Syrian farmworkers' predicaments make apparent, debt is among the most common yet least visible forces governing people's mobility today, particularly in the countryside. Debts have the power to force people to move, as in the case of foreclosure from an unpaid mortgage, but debts can also keep people firmly stuck in place, as in the case of countless farmworkers like Rawia who are bound to seasonal calendars of debt-based labor recruitment. In a world of shrinking state provisions and declining real wages, debt shapes how ordinary people move because it is vital to their survival.

One of the central contentions of this book is that Syrians' growing dependence on debt fundamentally unsettles the distinction between "free" labor migrants and "forced" political refugees, as well as the idea of a refugee crisis itself. Whether displaced people are decried as a "threat" by xenophobic leaders or deemed "deserving" of protection by progressives, the idea of a refugee crisis remains powerful because it conveys a sense of urgency in a world defined by unprecedented migratory movements. An implicit assumption running through much of these debates is a liberal-humanitarian understanding of "crisis" as an acute emergency, one rooted in fraught Cold War–era distinctions between refugees and labor migrants.

Debt and Refuge, in contrast, analyzes crisis not simply as a humanitarian disaster but rather as a recurrent condition within our global food system. This is a crisis that has been endured disproportionately by subsistence farmers like Rawia's family who must migrate in search of waged work, a worldwide phenomenon that accelerated dramatically in the 1990s era of expanded free trade, market-led development, and globalized production. Viewing Syrian farmworkers' predicaments in light of their commonalities with other displaced workers reveals how the war in Syria was not only a rupture but also an amplification of material predicaments that had long characterized many Syrians' lives. More than a catastrophic event or acute emergency, displacement for these farmworkers was a multigenerational, protracted crisis of social reproduction that preceded the Syrian conflict by decades.

DISPLACEMENT AS A CRISIS OF SOCIAL REPRODUCTION

Importantly, I almost never heard Syrian farmworkers refer to themselves as "refugees" (*lājiʾīn*) nor "displaced persons" (*nāziḥīn*) throughout my research. These two terms—and their politicized juxtaposition—remain extremely salient within regional Arabic media, Lebanese policymaking and public life, and humanitarian discourse. Politicians' use of the latter term has often been interpreted, rightly, as indicative of Lebanon's "disassociation policy" toward refugees and "an attempt to circumvent any obligations and privileges owed to these individuals by virtue of their refugeehood."[5] Yet the rarity of these two terms in the everyday lives of agriculturalists I met was telling. Though registered with the United Nations High Commissioner for Refugees (UNHCR), farmworkers usually referred to themselves as workers (*ʿummāl* or *shaghīla*), Bedouin (*ʿarab*),[6] or simply Syrians (*Sūriyyīn*), while their employers and other Syrians often referred to them as "girls" (*banāt*). The stakes of such distinctions were clearly more than semantic; these different terms indexed a much longer history of labor that continually chafed against the urgencies of the wartime present: namely, how the most backbreaking and lowest-paid work in Lebanon's agricultural system has been increasingly carried out by young women like Rawia from eastern Syria since the 1990s.

Two radical traditions of politically engaged research—critical agrarian studies and feminist social reproduction theory—proved essential to this research, because they brought to light the less visible relationships of labor and debt through which Syrian refugee farmworkers have striven to rebuild their lives amid enormous uncertainties. As an interdisciplinary field broadly concerned with the political economy of rural life, agrarian studies centers a critical understanding of the shifting dynamics of capitalist accumulation in agriculture across different contexts, including granular, on-the-ground class relations and struggles over land and labor.[7] Social reproduction theorists, in turn, study the conditions through which capitalist relations are renewed across different domains, making visible the extent to which these relations rely upon unpaid labor and gendered and racialized inequalities on local, regional, and global levels.[8] Both of these traditions of scholarship have shown how debt has become a key factor in the contemporary politics of labor migration and familial life.[9]

Through a feminist agrarian perspective, this book makes a case for fundamentally rethinking the Syrian "refugee crisis" as an intertwined crisis of social reproduction, debt, and mobility, one that remains inseparable from the dynamics of rural dispossession that pushed many Syrians to migrate across borders before the war began. In contrast to "crisis" in the humanitarian sense, *this* type of crisis—agriculturalists migrating seasonally abroad, squeezing women's labor, and taking on debts to sustain rural households throughout decades of economic liberalization—is not usually accorded urgency nor visibility. Yet across the world, what has long been in crisis is displaced workers' capacities to secure a stable livelihood and to find refuge, that is, a safe and durable place to call "home" in which their social relationships, needs, and aspirations can flourish.

Reframing crisis in these terms invites a deeper consideration of the agrarian roots of Syrian farmworkers' indebtedness, beginning with their rural origins as poor subsistence farmers and pastoralists in Syria's northeastern Jazīra region. The Jazīra, as the coming pages will show, was once the heartland of the Syrian Ba'th Party's ambitious plans for agrarian development and the site of the iconic Soviet-funded Euphrates Dam project.[10] As humble shepherds from low-ranking tribal clans (*'ashā'ir*) known as *shawāya*, Rawia's grandparents' generation were positioned as ideal subjects of rural uplift during Syria's heyday of state-led agrarian reform in the 1960s and early 1970s, which promised to transform them into self-sufficient peasants on state-owned farms.[11]

Such ideas of prosperity and development, however, have existed in tension with eastern Syrians' long, fractured histories of displacement, especially as Syria's state-led economy began to liberalize in the 1990s and 2000s. Emblematic of what agrarian scholars refer to as "dispossession by displacement," this was marked by a growing need for cash among rural Syrian households, which pushed unprecedented numbers of women and teenagers into seasonal waged work in Lebanon to supplement their incomes or secure their families' basic needs through labor brokers called *shawīsh*.[12] Many *shawīsh* were enterprising Syrian labor migrants who had built up the necessary capital to recruit workers across borders.[13] The expansion of this labor brokerage network was also driven by competitive pressures within

Lebanon's market-led agricultural system, as hiring low-paid Syrian workers helped reduce the costs of production.

Understanding these layered histories of agrarian transformation and class differentiation is important because it helps explain how Syrian farmworkers were first drawn into migration, as well as how they ultimately ended up going deeper into debt throughout the war. Like most other migrant workers around the world, Syrian farmworkers' wages and labor conditions were, and continue to be, well below Lebanese living standards. Syrian labor migrants were historically able to endure such low wages because they were sustained by a cross-border economy of seasonal mobility, where the bulk of household maintenance and subsistence work was carried out by their female kin in their home villages.[14] As Syria became engulfed in a protracted and devastating conflict, *shawīsh* headmen scaled up their camp operations to accommodate growing numbers of refugees from all over the country throughout the year, which included both newcomers and former migrant families.

It was in this context of protracted immobility, coupled with demand for their cheap labor, that Syrian farmworkers went into debt throughout the war. One of the chief struggles many farmworkers faced was the rising cost of living in Lebanon, as their wages were insufficient to support their displaced families year-round. Unable to return to Syria on a seasonal basis as they once had, many began to incur debts to *shawīsh*, who offered sources of income and housing in the absence of alternatives. Already well established in Lebanon, many *shawīsh* built up temporary migration infrastructures to create long-term refugee camps, in which they lent cash, offered shelter, brokered work opportunities, and served as a focal point for humanitarian services.

Approaching debt ethnographically in light of its everyday nuances and social contingencies, the coming chapters attend carefully to the conflicting moral, economic, and emotional attachments that bound Syrians to *shawīsh* camps in this period of deepening economic uncertainty and political instability. These attachments were formed in and through the temporal pressures of household debt, marked by a constant balance between immediate reproductive needs, seasonal labor obligations, and longer-term aspirations, all of which were compounded by the rapid devaluations of the Syrian and

Lebanese currencies. For many precarized rural Syrians facing the challenges of meeting their daily subsistence needs in exile, *shawīsh* camps provided a vital source of welfare, offering not only affordable housing and services but also a sense of moral community and baseline security.

Against this backdrop, households in these camps became gendered battlegrounds of conflicting reproductive needs and aspirations, as Syrian men faced a growing wave of criminalization across Lebanon and were often out of work as a result. These challenges deepened the burdens of their female kin's paid and unpaid labor obligations, including—as in Rawia's case—deferring young women's marriages in families that depended on their wages. Paradoxically exploitative and life sustaining, this debt-based camp system was simultaneously a site of labor discipline that constrained feminized workers' mobility and a vital refuge for criminalized men in the absence of alternatives.

Looking at the lives of displaced people through the prism of labor and debt ultimately reveals the contradictory faces of *refuge* itself. Refuge, as I define it here, refers to the daily work of sustaining life in the face of an uncertain future. It speaks to the basic human propensity to make home, find community, and forge spaces of stability in even the most destabilizing times and, equally so, to the dilemmas associated with being stuck in place. More than a legal status or humanitarian predicament, refuge is most fundamentally a struggle to secure one's conditions of social reproduction in times of displacement—including the pressures of debt to meet those needs.

These labors of reproduction are also sites of intergenerational inheritance and future aspiration: they are made up of the daily processes by which people grapple with their kin about their obligations to one another, set against the burdens of what previous generations have lost, gained, or passed on to them. Such forms of reproductive labor may be devalued or rendered invisible, but they are not at all marginal to the shifting dynamics of capitalism. On the contrary, they are capitalism's most acute inflection point, for it is this unpaid and underpaid labor—provisioning families, procuring food, household budgeting, rearing children, planning for the future—that ensures survival in a world where the "freedom" to move or stay put remains an ideal reserved for the privileged few.

BEYOND THE MIGRANT-REFUGEE DIVIDE: A FEMINIST AGRARIAN PERSPECTIVE

Though varying across space and time, the modern humanitarian refugee regime can be distilled down to a basic idea: displacement has an ideal *end* that finds resolution in the provision of long-term refuge, asylum, resettlement, or safe repatriation. That most refugees' lives do not conform to this linear progression is evident to many: the vast majority are not resettled in the Western countries that govern this refugee regime.[15] Most remain in various states of political limbo in countries that can hardly afford to accommodate them, like Lebanon. A staggering 85 percent of today's refugees are hosted by non-Western countries.[16] One need only look to multiple generations of Palestinian refugees across the Middle East, Afghans in Pakistan and Iran, or Somalis in Kenya to understand what the anthropologist Liisa Malkki meant when she memorably referred to refugees as a "Third World problem."[17]

It is well known that the refugee, as a juridical category and subject of displacement, was born out of the tumult of World War II. Yet in the interwar period, the categories of the "refugee" and the "migrant" were, in fact, quite fluid. Until the 1940s, refugees were treated as a special category of economic migrants and their resettlement was oriented around ensuring that they found gainful employment.[18] The 1951 Convention Relating to the Status of Refugees in many ways represented the decisive moment in which the economic needs of refugees became subordinate to the threat of political persecution, thus formalizing what many now recognize as the migrant-refugee distinction.[19] Along with the UN High Commissioner for Refugees and the 1967 Protocol, the 1951 convention remains the current institutional framework through which forced displacement is governed internationally and defines the "refugee" as follows:

> One who owing to a well-founded fear of being persecuted for reasons of race, religion, nationality [as belonging to a "people"], membership of a social group or political opinion is outside the country of his nationality [as membership of a state] and is unable or, owing to such fear, is unwilling to avail himself of the protection of that country; or who, not having a nationality and being outside the country of his habitual residence . . . is unable, or, owing to such fear, is unwilling to return to it.[20]

The absence of economic conditions in this definition reflects the shifting Cold War rivalries that emerged after World War II. Given the Soviet Union's often limited and fraught participation in the making of these international norms, this transnational governing framework evolved over time into one increasingly designed to accommodate expressly "political" refugees fleeing across the Iron Curtain from the socialist East and South to the capitalist democracies of the West.[21]

Noting these historical and geopolitical legacies of the migrant-refugee divide, scholars have long argued that this dichotomy overlooks the complex structural and historical conditions that compel people to migrate, artificially separating the "economic" and "political" and the "free" from the "forced."[22] Indeed, as far back as the early 1990s when refugee studies was consolidating as a specialized field of research, anthropologists began writing *against* treating refugees as a bounded subject of expert knowledge and humanitarian politics.[23] Taking these different strands of scholarship together, one might say that from the very inception of "refugees" as a topic of anthropological inquiry, we have sought to break the category apart. And yet, more than three decades later, this struggle against refugee exceptionalism remains very much on the table. In the face of today's unprecedented ecological, economic, and political displacements, many are asking how the intersecting predicaments of displaced people can be understood beyond the politics of humanitarianism and the many well-established critiques of it.

This book sets out to do so by turning readers' attention to the local, regional, and globalized dynamics of agriculture, which necessarily brings into view histories and relationships that far exceed the traditional purview of humanitarian governance. My aim in taking such an approach is not to develop a more precise definition of a "refugee" or "migrant," nor to reprise the conditions that seemingly differentiate them. On the contrary, it is an invitation to think beyond our inherited frameworks and dominant lines of inquiry, which so often uphold the refugee as an exceptional figure, paradigm, or abstraction outside of history, rather than as ordinary living people whose struggles they share with workers elsewhere.[24]

Reframing displacement through an agrarian lens draws attention to a ubiquitous yet often unremarked global condition: the unprecedented mass migration of small farmers in search of waged work within and across borders over the past several decades.[25] These migrations are a product of multiple factors, including the uneven implementation and subsequent liberalization of land reforms in formerly state-led economies like Syria; the slashing of public institutions and labor protections under the dictates of the International Monetary Fund and the World Bank; and the imposition of free trade agreements that have disproportionately benefited US and European markets and multinational corporations in the supply of fertilizers, seeds, technical support, and machinery, which render agriculture in places like Syria and Lebanon ever more difficult for those who cannot afford these products.[26] These policies came on the heels of decades-long struggles across decolonizing states to chart independent paths of national development, with varying levels of success. Agrarian scholars refer to this as the "neoliberal food regime," the effects of which are globally integrated but highly unequal.[27]

Across the postcolonial world, the manifestations of these global transformations are manifold: subsistence farmers' growing reliance on waged work and off-farm migration, rising demand for flexible and inexpensive labor across multiple sectors that relegate workers to precarious conditions, mass indebtedness, compounding ecological crises, the proliferation of ongoing conflicts that separate farmers from their land and means of subsistence, and the growth of urban peripheries and low-income communities in what Mike Davis famously dubbed our "planet of slums."[28] In the Middle East, such experiences of economic insecurity triggered waves of popular struggle and revolutionary movements—of which the 2011 Syrian uprising was a critical part—as well as the devastating militarized conflicts that followed in their wake.[29] Such a historical perspective shows that neither displaced people nor their "hosts" are monolithic subjects, but rather are highly differentiated according to the multiple inequalities and rural-urban disparities that deepened throughout these global transformations. Indeed, for many of the world's workers, displacement is rarely an *event* of uprooting but rather an ongoing and often protracted struggle to secure a stable livelihood across borders in the face of compounding crises.

A critical agrarian perspective also upends the conventional image of refugee camps as spaces of humanitarian provision ostensibly on the margins of economic life. This speaks to Ruth Wilson Gilmore's incisive claim that the apparent "marginality" of rural spaces is a trick of perspective: camps, borders, and hinterlands are not margins but interfaces that bring into view the concrete social relations and struggles that comprise them.[30] While *shawīsh* camp residents in Lebanon were undoubtedly grappling with poverty and various forms of structural violence, their work was central to a labor-intensive agricultural system struggling to maintain profitability under the pressures of market competition, compounded by the reverberating effects of war and a brewing financial crisis. As seasonal migration infrastructures were remade into long-term sites of refuge across Lebanon, *shawīsh* camps were a specific manifestation of a much larger global trend toward humanitarian austerity, namely, how growing networks of privatized aid provision and labor recruitment have increasingly taken up the responsibility for accommodating displaced people in the face of slashed public budgets and diminishing state capacities.

A political economy lens likewise sheds critical light on the role of borders in the lives of displaced Syrians. While seemingly marking the boundaries between nation-states, borders are not lines on a map but mechanisms of social control that filter and differentiate based on who or what is crossing them.[31] Borders may be porous in some ways and militarized in others, but this incoherence is a strategy of governance in itself. Scholar-activist Harsha Walia refers to this as "commodified inclusion," wherein the value of border-crossers' labor is cheapened and precarized by the militarization of border crossing, the threat of deportation, and the structural vulnerabilities that stem from their noncitizen status.[32] The border, as such, is elastic—it does not "end" when it is crossed but rather continuously traverses the lives of noncitizen workers through mechanisms that contain their mobility and curtail their abilities to unionize, strike, or otherwise advocate to improve their working conditions.[33] The pressures to pursue gainful work across borders and the constraints that this places on workers' mobility also keep their families divided, often shifting the burden of household provisioning and care onto feminized labor and pushing families into debt.

These points are often lost in mainstream humanitarian accounts of Syrian refugees' conditions, where their "exclusion" from formal political and economic rights is perceived to be the essence of their predicament. Viewing Syrian refugees as workers coping with a loss of seasonal mobility, thus, turns the paradigm of refugee exclusion on its head, shifting the focus, rather, to how they are *included*.[34] While the war in Syria represented a rupture in the sense that Syrians' mobility across the Lebanese-Syrian border was subjected to unprecedented levels of state surveillance and criminalization, it was also a reconfiguration of the border's long-standing role in regulating their labor, often with deeply gendered effects. Such considerations help resituate refugees' predicaments within a wider range of scholarship on farmworkers and labor migrants—parallels that are vital to understanding the politics of displacement but are too rarely engaged in research on refugees and forced migration.[35]

Finally, challenging the migrant-refugee divide is a gendered question. *Debt and Refuge* builds from the pioneering work of Marxist feminist scholars like Silvia Federici who argue that crises of displacement are, at their core, crises of social reproduction, expressed in the privatization of caregiving and other forms of reproductive work; a globalized, gendered division of labor; and rising rates of household debt.[36] Among Syrian farmworkers and beyond, mobility operates within a shifting continuum of waged and unwaged work, which means that within any given household, family members' conditions of mobility may differ considerably within and across borders, even as their livelihoods are mutually interdependent.[37] Insofar as Syrian farmworkers were compelled by a lack of independent means and the compounding conditions of war to seek long-term refuge in *shawīsh* camps, this predicament ultimately deepened the burdens of feminized work in the fields and in the home. As Syrian farmworkers became dependent on credit wages to secure their basic livelihoods, these debt obligations were buttressed by the flexibility of family labor—especially that of women, teenagers, and children—inside and outside of the home. Gendered and generational norms regarding the difference between "girls' work" and "men's work" played a key role in reinforcing these dynamics.[38] That northeastern Syrian tribal women and girls overwhelmingly comprise the lowest rungs of Lebanon's agricultural system bears similarity to undocumented migrants in other contexts whose ethnicity, race, gender, and lack of citizenship are a form of "conjugated oppression" in agriculture.[39] It is also symptomatic of how low-paid migrant workers often hail from regions that are stigmatized and minoritized *within* their national contexts in linguistic, ethnic, religious, or racialized terms.[40]

Most of the predicaments examined here are not unique to Syrians nor the region. It thus bears reiterating that one of the larger contributions of this book is to locate the Middle East squarely within the comparative field of critical agrarian studies, where the study of Latin America, South and East Asia, and sub-Saharan Africa is much more robust.[41] In its close ethnographic attention to rural lifeways and the politics of social reproduction, it is also inspired by a long tradition of research on gender and family life in the Middle East—scholarship that has often been narrowly relegated to the domain of women's studies despite its enduring relevance to the politics of migration, labor relations, and class politics.[42] While my work focuses on northeastern Syrians, it was indeed the rich ethnographic literature on Palestinian women in refugee camps—particularly that of Rosemary Sayigh who analyzed these refugees' rural roots as subsistence farmers—that pushed me toward the discipline of anthropology in the first place and helped inspire this project.[43]

GUEST OF THE *SHAWĪSH*: ON PLACE AND METHODS

Tracing the dynamics of inequality among rural Syrians and Lebanese was an essential part of this research, and the Bekaa Valley proved to be an especially generative place from which to explore these dynamics ethnographically. On one level, I aimed to unravel any simple rendering of "Lebanese" and "Syrians" as territorially bounded or self-evidently distinct national groups by foregrounding their internal diversity and complex relationships to each other. On another, I wished to avoid romanticizing or essentializing village life by taking seriously the deep hierarchies that shape commercial agriculture in Lebanon—and asking difficult questions about how they came to be.

Like borderlands elsewhere, the Bekaa is a place of extraordinary contrasts and contradictions, at once sleepily pastoral and deeply cosmopolitan. It is a narrow plateau nestled between two mountain ranges that extends seventy-five miles, forming Lebanon's eastern border with Syria. The distinct topographical features of the Bekaa, with snow-capped mountain peaks towering over sprawling agricultural plains, have allowed this valley to serve as the region's breadbasket since antiquity. Accounting for half of the total agricultural area of Lebanon, the Bekaa is cultivated throughout the year with vineyards, fruit orchards, vegetables, olives, legumes, and cereals for domestic consumption and export. Its hot, dry high season extends from May until October, bookended by a brief spring and fall, which gives way to a frigid, often snowy winter slack season from December to March.

Many parts of the Bekaa look and feel like far-flung places, but its central hub in Chtoura is just over an hour from Lebanon's bustling capital, Beirut—less if one is driving very quickly, as I learned too well during many heart-stopping rides in the shared minivans that congregate there. A long-standing site of transit between the coastal cities of the Levant and Syria's agricultural interior, the Bekaa was historically connected to Damascus and its hinterlands and was annexed to what became the state of Lebanon less than a century ago.[44]

"Syria and Lebanon are one," a local Lebanese landlord once told me in an impromptu history lesson as we sat in the auto repair shop he owned in a western Bekaa village. "The French came and decided that the Bekaa would be part of Greater Lebanon," he went on while his Syrian employees changed the tires on a local *shawīsh*'s pickup truck. "Before that, we were

FIGURE 4. The Bekaa Valley and the Anti-Lebanon Mountains.

part of Syria." These sentiments mirrored official Syrian state discourse that framed the Bekaa Valley as an "open border" between two "brotherly" countries of historic Greater Syria (Bilād al-Shām).[45] Syrians, for their part, often asserted to me with pride that they "built" Lebanon. In some cases, this was a jingoistic reference to the Syrian military's contentious presence in Lebanon that lasted for three decades.[46] In a deeper sense, though, it was a reference to the millions of Syrians who have migrated seasonally to Lebanon since the 1960s to perform virtually every back-breaking job deemed too low-paid and precarious for Lebanon's citizens.

Syrian farmworkers' employers include a diverse group of people whose social circumstances vary greatly depending on their access to land, labor, and capital and their position within the agricultural production process. The three main employers featured in this book are landowners, contract farmers (*ḍammān*), and *shawīsh*. Given the immense variation within and between these groups, I chose to approach them not as coherent "classes" but rather in terms of their dynamic social relations across space and time. Much of my fieldwork took place on the large landed estates of several wealthy Lebanese landlord families, a type of property referred to as *iqṭāʿ*.[47] These landlords rented out parts of their properties on a seasonal or annual basis to Lebanese *ḍammān*, whose responsibilities usually included all aspects of cultivation and marketing and sometimes the cost of irrigation works as well.[48] For landlords, renting to *ḍammān* was a strategy of minimizing the risks associated with agricultural production and maximizing returns in a period when the value of land rents was rising.

By following the life histories of Lebanese employers and their workers who cultivate a variety of seasonal vegetables on these estates for domestic markets and regional export, I ultimately sought to understand the divisions of labor that currently predominate in the Bekaa: Lebanese *ḍammān* who hire Syrian labor brokers (*shawīsh*), who recruit and give shelter to Syrian refugee farmworkers. As the next chapter shows, contract farming is a risky venture reserved only for those who have the capital to remain competitive, as they rely on imported machinery and inputs in order to maintain profitability in Lebanon's unregulated, market-led agricultural system. After 2011, this work was rendered all the more risky amid the reverberating economic and political uncertainties wrought by the Syrian conflict, including disruption of overland trade routes. One way they sought to cut production costs was by hiring low-paid Syrian farmworkers from camps run by *shawīsh*.[49]

The majority of my research revolved around the inner life of Rawia's camp, which was run by a *shawīsh* named Abu Sharif, who had recruited workers for jobs in weeding, harvesting, and planting on a variety of family farms and large estates across the Bekaa since the 1990s. In Arabic, "*shawīsh*" means someone vested with authority to enforce security, but in vernacular terms refers to brokers who run camps of varying sizes for Syrian farmworkers. Some *shawīsh* are Lebanese, but most of them, like Abu Sharif, are enterprising Syrian labor migrants with long-standing migratory ties to Lebanon. Running a camp for three hundred people, he was responsible for arranging shelter, agricultural work opportunities, and services for the residents. Though registered as refugee camps with the UNHCR, *shawīsh* camps like his are still locally referred to by their prewar name, *warash banāt* ("girl workshops") or *warshāt*.[50]

I was first introduced to Abu Sharif through his employer, a Lebanese engineer who oversaw the *iqṭāʿ* estate of a wealthy landlord family. Given the deeply hierarchical nature of agricultural work in Lebanon, it could not have been otherwise. Gaining access to these spaces meant submitting to the very hierarchies of labor, class, and kin that I was seeking to understand. With patience, I was eventually welcomed into this world as a friend, daughter, and sister.

Tellingly, it was through the idiom of fictive kinship that my long-term participation in Abu Sharif's camp was eventually secured, the start of countless meals, sleepovers, and working days spent there over the course of over a year. "We've shared bread and salt," Abu Sharif told me, evoking the power of commensality. "You are our sister and our daughter, from us and within us [*minna u fīna*]." Emblematic of the profound hospitality of eastern Syrians, the camp residents were constantly fighting over who would host me on a given night. "You are welcome to sleep in any tent you like," he insisted. "You're under my care" (*inti bi-amāntī*). Through this proprietary concept of *amāna*—which connotes security, entrustment, protection, and care—Abu Sharif invited me to become an honorary member of this camp community, over which he presided as a protective patriarch. "They are all like family. We don't make distinctions."

Despite Abu Sharif's often grandiose references to paternal authority, I learned quickly that a far more complex set of inequalities structured the camp's political economy. His camp functioned through an elaborate credit-debt system, in which newly arrived Syrian refugee workers went into debt to him for the cost of their tent, their yearly rent, and other daily expenses in exchange for seasonal work in agriculture. Much like the thousands of other *shawīsh* camp residents across the Bekaa Valley, Abu Sharif's workers were recruited each day to perform the most exhausting and least remunerated tasks within Lebanon's food system.

Through the multiple seasons I spent there, many men and women in Abu Sharif's camp became dear friends, especially Rawia and her family. They generously hosted me in their tents, as we woke up before dawn for morning shifts practically every day. I spent the spring with them weeding vineyards; the summer harvesting peas, onions, potatoes, and green beans; the fall harvesting grapes and olives; the winter chasing the odd job gathering wood or planting potatoes; and long evenings preparing meals, making *mouneh* (food preserves), and looking after their children. This highly immersive approach gave me deep insight into the latent axes of household inequality that were rarely articulated explicitly. Given the importance of seasonal contracts within this camp's debt system, my long-term involvement in the camp helped me understand the subtle repertoires through which these debt obligations were contested and negotiated at the interfamilial level, including how families made plans to leave the camp or return to Syria.

Alongside this work, I conducted interviews with Lebanese landlords, contract farmers, distributors, truck drivers, syndicate activists, municipal leaders, and humanitarian representatives. I also regularly joined several other Syrian work teams, including various teams of "free workers" (*shaghīl ḥurr*), who were considered "free" by virtue of the fact that they did not have a *shawīsh* middleman brokering their work opportunities or living arrangements. Though I had the occasional opportunity to conduct lengthy interviews in the comfort of an office, most of these conversations unfolded within the less formalized rhythms and routine interruptions of people's daily work obligations, from agricultural fields to distribution markets, to the passenger's seat of trucks, to the din of children's cartoons blaring over evening meals in the camp. When working in the fields, I was considered a volunteer and never paid, which meant that I was under no strict obligation to work and could come and go as I pleased. Workers nevertheless seemed to greatly appreciate my presence, whether it was to help supplement their output when working on a piece rate or simply to "entertain" them (as they often put it) with conversation and singing together during long, tedious workdays.

There were a few important aspects of my positionality and situatedness that made this research possible. As an Iranian American woman raised in the United States, I was treated as a not-quite-foreigner and not-quite-local in Lebanon. Far from the classic ethnographic trope of "suspicion,"[51] I experienced a remarkable level of kindness, care, and generosity as I moved across different spaces. Because of my fluency in the Lebanese dialect and obviously Middle Eastern appearance, I was often initially taken to be Lebanese or Lebanese American in casual conversations with those who did not already know me, though I always made sure to clarify my status as a graduate student researcher from the United States.

As an Iranian, I was treated as a Shiʿa Muslim and was thus held to certain standards of feminine propriety and piety that I imagine are not usually expected of "Western" researchers. Yet, given my US upbringing, I was occasionally invited to exclusively masculine spaces, such as evening gatherings in the *shawīsh*'s guesthouse. The tacit grammars of kinship mattered greatly in such settings, and the fact that I was married and became pregnant with my first child during the last six months of my fieldwork brought me closer to the mothers I knew, which opened some spaces to me, and limited others.

I was also deeply conscripted into the networks of credit and debt that I set out to study. My status as a privileged guest meant learning how to receive hospitality while reciprocating through gestures and material goods that were respectful to the terms of each encounter.[52] Indeed, a significant part of my experience as an ethnographer was deciphering the etiquettes of reciprocity and camaraderie by carefully observing what counted as an appropriate gift or favor in any given context. A gift too small or infrequent risked offense. A favor returned too quickly risked appearing transactional, and one too slowly, ungracious. And a gift too large risked transgressing the boundaries of friendship or decorum by making it impossible to reciprocate.

Finally, in reflecting on how I gained access and permission to do this research, it bears emphasizing that my interest in agriculture was often viewed as relatively apolitical and uncontentious by landlords and other powerful figures I met, at least compared to many other researchers who came to Lebanon to learn about Syrian refugees. Much to my surprise, my probing questions about wages, farm size, labor history, rent, and property were seen by elites and experts as mostly innocuous technocratic matters, which meant that Lebanese landlords and *ḍammān* were receptive to my research and allowed me to work freely alongside their Syrian employees. By contrast, among my Syrian and Lebanese friends with a background in labor organizing and left-wing politics, the political significance of such questions were self-evident—and my desire to grasp their nuances within the broader sweep of rural class struggles was a source of endless conversation between us.

With Syrian farmworkers, I believe that laboring together so consistently day after day helped foster trusting relationships and conversations that would otherwise have been impossible. My genuine interest in their labor conditions conveyed my sense of solidarity with them, and it was in these terms that they grasped my intentions for this research. I realized this from the way that members of Abu Sharif's camp earnestly introduced my research to others and went out of their way to connect me with their family members and farmworkers from other camps. My interest in agriculture also elicited lively discussions about a whole range of topics that I had not initially set out to study, including the nuances of the "*shāwi*" Arabic dialect, the rules of marriage and bridewealth, the Euphrates Dam project, and the politics of eastern Syrian tribal clans. Agriculture, it turned out, was an enormously generative topic, precisely because it was how virtually everyone I knew in the Bekaa spent their days and made plans for the future.

LEBANON'S BORDER REGIME

The Lebanese-Syrian border is not simply the setting where this research took place; this is also a story about the border's changing role in Syrians' lives, including Lebanon's fraught position within the globalized terrain of border regimes relative to Western states. In its contemporary treatment of Syrians, Lebanon is not especially different from the United States and the European Union insofar as its immigration policies aim to criminalize "undesirable" people on the move, while keeping its borders open enough to extract value from the underpaid labor of noncitizen workers when that labor is needed and rendering them disposable when it is not. Yet the scale and scope of Lebanon's ongoing obligations as a refugee host country are of an entirely different magnitude, one wholly incomparable to any Western nation. Along with Türkiye and Jordan, Lebanon is one of the key countries of "externalization," which refers to a set of policies by states, international organizations, and private companies—largely driven by the interests of Western nations—to place the obligation for hosting refugees squarely upon countries that directly border political conflicts or regions of "transit" in exchange for aid and technical assistance.[53] This was a responsibility that most of Lebanon's political elites never fully endorsed and to which many remain deeply hostile.

One of the most significant yet often overlooked consequences of this Western-led consensus toward externalization is how the scale and scope of these responsibilities have exacerbated social inequalities in host countries, particularly in terms of labor conditions, gender relations, and access to land. These inequalities stem from long-term structural and historical dynamics that are largely invisible to the short-term demands of humanitarian refugee relief. But as in the case of Lebanon and other states whose share of refugee populations far exceed those of most Western states, it is only through a deeper historical perspective that one can grasp the tensions that run through its position as a host country and the on-the-ground relationships through which those obligations have taken shape.

Before 2011, Syrian labor migrants to Lebanon were permitted to spend six months at a time as temporary residents in Lebanon within a de facto policy of "open borders" that vacillated between mobility and criminalization depending on the fluctuating demands of Lebanon's economy.[54] This was buttressed by the 1993 bilateral Agreement for Economic and Social Cooperation and Coordination that allowed citizens of both countries to move visa-free across the border as part of Lebanon's post-civil-war transition.[55] Throughout this period, Syrian labor migration remained mostly seasonal and temporary, and it was quite uncommon for Syrians to settle with their families in Lebanon long term.

When the Syrian popular uprisings began in March 2011, this de facto open border policy initially remained in place. Months of nonviolent protest in the face of relentless state repression eventually gave way to an increasingly militarized and multisided conflict from 2012 onward, plunging Syria into devastating rounds of violence as foreign-funded militias flooded the country. Countless Syrians had no choice but to flee across the border, while others with long-standing migratory ties to Lebanon found themselves immobilized there year-round. Lebanon, a tiny country already facing a protracted crisis of governance and infrastructural problems stemming from its own fifteen-year civil war, certainly did not fit the ideal picture of a host country. It nonetheless received more refugees than all the European Union member states combined in that period, as displaced Syrians quickly amounted to one-quarter of Lebanon's population.[56]

The early years of Lebanon's approach to hosting refugees have often been linked to the idea of hospitality, and it is easy to see why: in the absence of a centralized state response and capacity for coordination, it was often average Lebanese people who first gave refuge to Syrians.[57] And like any private, informal arrangement, what it meant to "host" Syrians varied widely. Many Lebanese villagers in the Bekaa offered rooms in their homes, half-finished apartments in buildings they owned, or tracts of land in their backyard for Syrians to pitch a tent for free. Others saw the influx of Syrians as an opportunity to charge often exorbitant rents in a growing housing market.[58] Though these everyday relationships between Syrians and Lebanese were often understood by Syrians and Lebanese alike as expressions of moral duty, they were an obviously insufficient substitute for a coordinated state-led refugee response, and their privatized nature often subtly reproduced and deepened the inequalities that existed among Syrians and Lebanese before the war began.[59]

Famously described as a "policy of no policy," Lebanon is not a state party to the 1951 Convention Relating to the Status of Refugees nor its 1967 protocol.[60] It also does not consider itself an asylum country, a position that builds upon a controversial memorandum of understanding signed by the UNHCR and the government of Lebanon in 2003.[61] Further, Lebanon rejects the principle of local "integration" or "resettlement" of refugees, which can be traced back to clauses within the 1926 Lebanese Constitution prohibiting settlement (*tawṭīn*) of Lebanese nonnationals.[62] This means that, in practice, refugees and asylum seekers are treated in Lebanon like any other foreign national and are thus required to have government-issued residence permits. At the same time, Lebanon has also ratified several of the major international human rights agreements, which bind Lebanon to the basic principles of refugee protection.[63] This includes the norm of non-refoulement, considered "the cornerstone of international refugee law in that it prohibits refugees from being returned or expelled to places where their lives or freedoms could be threatened."[64]

Beyond these legal conditions, the relationships and institutions that comprise Lebanon's refugee regime cut across multiple domains, from transnational humanitarian organizations to state security and border policies, to village mayors and municipalities, to employment networks, to neighborhoods and households. These relationships have never cohered into a central governance strategy, despite many efforts to coordinate via what came to be known as the Lebanon Crisis Response Plan. Unleashed in 2015, this was a loose framework of negotiation and planning among Western donor states, UN agencies, the Lebanese government, and over one hundred local and international nongovernmental organizations to harmonize the terms of humanitarian intervention and aid allocation for accommodating Syrians.[65]

The amount of aid Lebanon has received for this is substantial, ranging from $900 million to $1.1 billion annually since 2013.[66] The relative marginality of all this work to the everyday lives of Syrian farmworkers was nevertheless quite remarkable, given the outsized presence of these humanitarian organizations in most media and scholarly discourses about Syrians' predicaments. Other than the ubiquitous UNHCR logo that adorned their tarpaulin tents, the UN and NGOs were scarcely visible and rarely mentioned in farmworkers' daily talk, except as it concerned basic infrastructural amenities (such as refilling water tanks and desludging their outhouses), monthly installments of cash and food aid that sustained their livelihoods, and, for some, the dim prospect of being offered resettlement in Europe.

Rather than humanitarian aid, the issue that remained most definitive in my conversations with Syrian farmworkers was their changing conditions of mobility as workers and the decimation of their livelihoods back in Syria. Above all, they lamented their inability to migrate freely across the Lebanese-Syrian border on a seasonal basis as they once had, for it was during these seasonal returns that they managed to survive by availing themselves and their families of the relatively lower cost of living and public services in Syria.[67] Meanwhile, within Lebanon, their movement was curtailed by a growing wave of criminalization against Syrian men, which made it difficult for them to pursue gainful employment outside of agriculture. In this context of unprecedented internal and cross-border constraints, it was the maddening uncertainty of when and how they and their loved ones could move that sent them deeper into debt and kept many bound to *shawīsh* camps in the absence of stable alternatives.[68]

Understanding these changing conditions of Syrians' mobility was key, because the period of my fieldwork paralleled a distinctive phase of the Syrian conflict and a deepening financial crisis on both sides of the Lebanese-Syrian border. After years of political stalemate, Lebanon's caretaker government was formed in mid-2018.[69] Meanwhile, the Asad regime and its international allies had violently recaptured much of Syria's embattled territories, as active combat became confined largely to the Turkish-Syrian border region of Idlib. Claims that the Syrian war was, by the standards of active combat and violence, "over" loomed large throughout this period, generating unprecedented pressure on Syrians to repatriate, as Syrians became convenient scapegoats for Lebanon's mounting financial and infrastructural crisis. As these claims went, Syrian refugees were "stealing" Lebanese jobs, hoarding aid and opportunities, draining the Lebanese economy, and many were perfectly able to return but were merely "posing" as refugees.[70]

The crackdown on Syrians was a culmination of an earlier set of nativist policies imposed in 2015 by the Lebanese Council of Ministers, including bolstering border security and limiting the scope and conditions of legal employment for non-Lebanese nationals.[71] Those who could not meet these requirements—which was the position of the vast majority of Syrians—were henceforth required to secure a Lebanese citizen-sponsor (*kafīl*).[72] Registered refugees were also required by the Lebanese government to sign a document certifying that they will not seek employment in Lebanon. Yet, as was plainly obvious to everyone, including Lebanese officials, Syrians continued to work in jobs that are essential to the functioning of Lebanon's economy, particularly female farmworkers and their children.

This was not the first time that Syrians became a subject of moral panic in Lebanon. The status of Syrian labor in Lebanon has vacillated between invisibility and hypervisibility for decades.[73] By the early 2000s, Syrians made up an estimated 20 to 40 percent of Lebanon's total workforce.[74] This fact remained largely unremarked in public discourse until the assassination of Prime Minister Rafiq al-Hariri in 2005, ushering in a wave of popular campaigns against Syrian workers. Lebanese scholars and activists have linked such periods of anti-Syrian rhetoric to a broader "culture of diversion" among Lebanon's ruling elite, where responsibility for the country's internal economic, social, and political problems have been routinely deflected onto those cast as "foreigners."[75]

The growing backlash against Syrians brought to light another key facet of Lebanon's refugee crisis: Syrians living there were not a homogeneous collectivity, but rather were deeply differentiated according to class, regional origin in Syria, gender, prewar migratory connections to Lebanon, and legal status.[76] Many were, as they came to be known, *maksūr*, literally meaning "broken" but referring to Syrians lacking up-to-date residency paperwork and work permits. This encompassed many different types of predicaments that vary according to when a Syrian entered Lebanon and whether they were registered as refugees with the UNHCR. There were those like Abdullah, who we will meet in the next chapter, who had the misfortune of entering Lebanon after 2015 and thus was considered to be working illegally. On the other end of the spectrum were some well-established Syrian workers who secured, through prewar connections, a Lebanese *kafīl* that allowed them to work legally and, in principle, move more freely across the border. And there were others who were not registered or recorded as refugees with the UNHCR but remained in legal limbo in exile to avoid military conscription, among other reasons.

The war ultimately amplified these inequalities and fault lines among Syrians, while also giving rise to new ones. For some well-established Syrian labor migrants like Abu Sharif and other *shawīsh*, the war was initially an opportunity to make a profit and rebuild savings, as they expanded their camp operations to accommodate Syrians' long-term need for refuge. Meanwhile, for middle-class Syrians like Abdullah, many of whom had led relatively stable lives before the war, displacement in Lebanon was an experience of steep class demotion. As Abdullah put it, "We moved backward" (*raj'na la-wara*). His protracted exile brought him, and many other middle-class Syrians like him, into an often uneasy proximity with their historically poorer rural counterparts in the Jazīra region, the latter of whom comprise the majority of *shawīsh* camp dwellers and whose life stories are the focus of the coming chapters.

THE LONG EVE OF LEBANON'S SOVEREIGN DEBT CRISIS

As is always the case with fieldwork, from the very moment that I set out to commit this research to paper, the ethnographic present became past. But for those familiar with the Lebanese context, this was painfully true. Though I did not fully realize it then, I now know in retrospect that I was witnessing the long eve of Lebanon's sovereign debt crisis, as a deepening trade deficit, currency instability, capital flight, mass popular uprisings, and growing anti-Syrian sentiment were a prelude to the dramatic collapse of Lebanon's economy right after I finished my fieldwork in 2020. Narrated with the clarity of hindsight, a significant factor that runs throughout this book is the dialectic between the microlevel dynamics of Syrians' mounting debts in everyday life and the incipient macrolevel conditions of Lebanon's debt crisis that were unfolding at the time of my research.

Though often narrowly cast as a problem of "local" corruption, Lebanon's economic crisis was of a global provenance, including an international consensus toward market-led development and the imposition of austerity measures that have undercut the productive basis of its economy and increased its dependence on low-paid noncitizen workers.[77] Like many parts of Latin America, Africa, and the Caribbean under structural adjustment in the 1980s and 1990s, Argentina in the early 2000s, and Greece in the aftermath of the 2007–8 financial crisis, it is important to note that public debt crises, policies of economic liberalization, and processes of displacement go hand in hand. Austerity measures—including the slashing of public welfare, liberalization of public institutions, regressive taxation, and labor demobilization—often shift the burdens of social reproduction onto private relationships and push households into debt. As Syrian farmworkers' struggles demonstrate most acutely, such processes have powerful effects in everyday life; they render communities, households, and individuals more precarious and require them to reorganize their sources of livelihood and forms of interdependency, exacerbating many preexisting forms of inequality.[78]

Austerity also pushes people to rise up. Toward the end of my fieldwork, I had the extraordinary opportunity to bear witness to a series of large-scale popular protests across Lebanon that began on October 17, 2019. At their height, these protests brought close to a third of the country's population to Lebanon's streets.[79] Though protesters' grievances were diverse, they were a response to long-standing infrastructural problems, rising rates of unemployment and costs of living, widespread corruption, and the Lebanese government's abject failure to form a unified representative coalition. One of the galvanizing slogans of the protests was "All of them means all of them" (*kilun yaʿni kilun*), a powerful invocation of popular unity in a political landscape long dominated by different sectarian political parties and factions.[80]

Though the Lebanese lira had been pegged to the US dollar since the 1990s, its value began to plummet rapidly on the black market as the protests continued throughout the fall of 2019. In 2020, Lebanon's debt crisis took a drastic turn for the worse, exacerbated by the COVID-19 pandemic, a devastating chemical explosion at the port of Beirut, and the Lebanese state's faltering governance. By 2023, the lira had lost an estimated 99 percent of its value. Given Lebanon's dependence on imports, the past several years have been marked by staggering inflation that makes even the purchase of basic goods increasingly prohibitive for those, like Syrian farmworkers, who are paid in lira rather than dollars.[81] Lebanon now not only has the unenviable status as the country hosting the highest number of refugees per capita globally and among the world's highest debt-to-GDP ratios, but also is considered to have experienced one of the most dramatic declines in living standards on global record since 1850.

My goal in the coming pages is to explore these crisis conditions through the lens of agricultural life. This is a historically informed ethnographic approach that necessarily extends our frame of vision beyond the acute urgencies of the present and, I hope, will help readers understand them anew. *Debt and Refuge* is organized into four chapters that take the reader on a somewhat chronological journey through my fieldwork as it unfolded from mid-2018 until I left Lebanon in December 2019, followed by my family's brief return to Lebanon in 2022. It starts with the larger scale of regional agricultural systems, moves to the smaller scale of *shawīsh* camps, and then zooms in on the inner workings of farmworker families' households.

The first half of the book historically locates the rural politics of displacement on each side of the Lebanese-Syrian border, including the rise of contract farming in Lebanon and the wartime expansion of the *shawīsh* labor brokerage system. Whereas the first two chapters chart how the uneven aftermaths of land reform, the subsequent liberalization of Syria's economy, and demand for low-waged labor in Lebanon pushed Syrians to migrate since the 1970s, the second two chapters delve deeper into the other side of this process: the binding power of debt in the face of compounding economic crises and political uncertainty. Each chapter is woven with ethnographic vignettes and images of labor that evoke the rhythms of displaced farmworkers' daily lives, from the calculation of work shifts to the intense physical exertion of farm work, to stealthy acts of gleaning, to the tacit joys of sneaking cigarette breaks in the fields.

Set against the backdrop of Lebanon's autumn 2019 protests and its mounting public debt crisis, the book culminates by following the distinct trajectories of multiple women who sought to refuse their debts through the limited means available to them. Rather than self-directed expressions of individual "resistance," these contentious acts were fraught battlegrounds of competing interdependencies, inextricable from the value of their paid and unpaid labor across different domains. It concludes by situating Syrian farmworkers' struggles in the larger context of Lebanon's sovereign debt crisis and the multiple lines of transnational solidarity that these struggles evoke: from where we get our food to the manifold factors that compel people to migrate or stay in place.

For readers who have come to this book out of interest in refugees, I hope to make a convincing case for why forced migration is fundamentally an agrarian question of land, labor, capital, and social reproduction—one that can be addressed most rigorously using tools of critical political economy and feminist analysis. And for those who are reading out of an interest in farmworkers and agrarian politics, I hope to make a case for why the politics of war, displacement, and refuge matter greatly to the everyday lives of agriculturalists—and, thus, the future of our food systems.

This is, above all, a work of ethnography that seeks to remain faithful to the complexity and moral texture of human life. It is politically engaged but resists the pull to be reductive or flatly prescriptive. It depicts a diverse range of people who, by virtue of their location within larger economic and political struggles and structures, may strive to act ethically, fall short of doing so, or inflict harm. Doing the "right" thing, in other words, is a process of working through multiple contradictions. Some people have more power to change those conditions than others, but the role of any given social struggle in transforming them is neither predetermined nor set in stone. How ordinary people navigate these contradictions in their pursuit of refuge for themselves and others is, ultimately, the story that follows.

One
ENDURING CRISES

THE SUN WAS JUST BEGINNING TO RISE AS JAMIL AND I STOPPED TO catch our breath on a lookout point perched above the Bekaa Valley plains. The sprawling fields of wheat and potatoes looked like a massive green and brown checkerboard, extending eastward to the foothills of the snow-capped mountain range that forms Lebanon's eastern border with Syria. As I surveyed this breathtaking landscape, I glimpsed momentarily how this valley appeared from the perspective of the Salam family, the landlords of these fertile plains. Jamil, an agricultural engineer who meticulously cared for this property on the family's behalf, had taken me up into the foothills of Mount Lebanon precisely for this purpose. Though we had bonded for days over our shared love of agriculture, I sensed his slight annoyance that I kept steering the conversation back to the Syrians who worked there. "We don't hire refugees," Jamil told me insistently.

In the foreground of our panoramic view, plumes of smoke rose from a bonfire next to a large orchard of leafless plum trees in their winter dormancy. A few men were pruning each tree's stray branches with lopping shears and axes. Several dozen women in colorful dresses were crouched on the ground around them, gathering the pruned branches with their hands, which they lined up in neat rows between the trees. Working methodically row by row, they scooped up the unwieldy bundles in their arms and carried them to the bonfire, ambling carefully so as not to drop anything or trip on a wayward branch.

"And who are they? Are they from Syria?" I asked.

"They're from Abu Sharif's camp. I guess mostly from Raqqa," Jamil replied coolly, keeping his gaze fixed above them toward the horizon. "Abu Sharif, the *shawīsh*, brings them here. I call him each day and tell him how many girls (*banāt*) I need for whatever job, and then he brings them in his truck."

"But aren't they refugees?" I pleaded.

Jamil grinned. "You foreigners always come here looking for a story about Syrian refugees," he quipped, playfully indignant though sincere. "It's we, the *Lebanese*, who are the victims. *We're* the ones taking care of them. . . . And anyway, the war in Syria is over. So why aren't they returning home?"

A number of possible responses came to my mind. First, the war in Syria was not actually over. I thought about my Syrian friends from the besieged countryside of Damascus who lived in constant fear of military conscription, detention, or worse, if they were to return. And then, there was the Syrian economy. I thought of a recent conversation with my friend from Raqqa, who was ready to return to Syria but quietly lamented that the Syrian pound was so devalued that he couldn't fathom finding the resources to rebuild his home. Not only this, his debts to his employer and neighbors, from whom he had borrowed thousands of dollars to pay for an unexpected surgery and his wife's ongoing fertility treatments, were mounting.

I recognized immediately the resonances between Jamil's confident pronouncements of the war's end and the growing backlash against the one-and-a-half million Syrians who had sought refuge in Lebanon throughout the war. At the time of our conversation, this backlash had become a full-fledged right-wing movement calling for Syrian refugees' mass repatriation, backed by powerful political figures like Lebanese Minister of Foreign Affairs Gibran Bassil. Still, I couldn't disagree with Jamil that the Lebanese people were in an extraordinarily difficult situation. With over one-quarter of their entire population composed of Syrian refugees, this tiny war-torn country was tasked with a responsibility that, ultimately, no Western state was willing to take on.

Jamil introduced me to Abu Sharif later that day, and over the course of the year, I became deeply acquainted with the dozens of Syrians and Lebanese who worked together on the Salam family's estate. Reflecting on this conversation with Jamil in hindsight, it is hard to imagine how these men, women, and children whom I now know so well must have appeared to me on that first day: as nameless workers in a landscape viewed from above. Beyond this radical shift in perspective, this conversation with Jamil stayed with me for several reasons. It managed to condense into one frame a series of puzzles that shaped the entirety of my fieldwork in Lebanon from 2018 to 2019.

I was struck by Jamil's incisive observation that foreigners—by which he meant the droves of journalists, humanitarian workers, and researchers like me who had come to Lebanon to study the "Syrian refugee crisis"—were largely uninterested in the predicaments of the Lebanese who host them. In his own way, Jamil was giving credence to a well-established anthropological observation: naming something as a "crisis" limits our concepts of who and what matters in particular moments.[1] By claiming that Lebanese were the "real" victims, he was provocatively reversing the humanitarian terms of worthiness, calling into question the very idea that Syrians' predicaments should be framed as a refugee crisis at all.

More striking was Jamil's refusal to refer to Abu Sharif's workers as refugees, but instead simply as "girls" (*banāt*).[2] Jamil was undoubtedly aware that they were registered with the United Nations High Commissioner for Refugees, as he was the person chiefly responsible for recruiting them on a daily basis to work in various seasonal jobs on the estate. But like many Syrians with long-standing migratory ties to Lebanon, these workers perhaps seemed unremarkable to him as refugees because their gendered presence in the landscape evoked a sense of continuity with prewar life: a familiar and mostly taken-for-granted component of everyday agricultural labor. By calling them "girls," Jamil was obliquely referring to their status as labor migrants and, in turn, the *shawīsh* labor brokerage system in which their kin had been recruited as farmworkers long before the war began.

Lebanon, as a nonsignatory to both the 1951 Refugee Convention and its 1967 Protocol, has undoubtedly fallen short of international standards of refugee protection and inclusion in its treatment of Syrians.[3] But it was clear from the historical depth of these Syrian farmworkers' presence in the land that the stakes of accommodating them concerned much more than Lebanon's transnational legal obligations as a host state. As I dove deeper into the life trajectories of these farmworkers—often disclosed to me between bursts of hard labor in the fields and the unrelenting demands of household work—I learned how refuge was, for them, a fraught process of maintaining, renegotiating, and building upon decades-long labor relations between Lebanese and Syrian agriculturalists.

This chapter critically reframes Lebanon's refugee crisis through an agrarian political economy lens. Against a strictly humanitarian concept of crisis as an acute emergency, I draw attention to the protracted forms of crisis that often appeared natural, familiar, and barely remarkable in the lives of Syrians and their employers. At one level, my goal is to probe the limits of the term *refugee crisis* in making long-term, intergenerational predicaments and labor conditions intelligible.[4] At another, it is to go beyond merely critiquing the humanitarian *discourse* of crisis to understand the less visible, structural, and embodied expressions of crisis in daily life: namely, the recurrent crises of social reproduction that have long been characteristic of rural livelihoods on both sides of the Lebanese-Syrian border.[5] How might this protracted concept of crisis, understood not as an exception but rather as a recurrent material condition, reshape the terms of displacement? How can the journey of displacement be understood in terms of its enduring qualities, rather than as a path "out" of crisis that necessarily progresses toward refuge, resettlement, or return?

As the long-standing presence of Syrian "girls" in the landscape suggests, many rural Syrians were compelled to migrate across borders long before their mass displacement by war. Particularly in Syria's northeastern Jazīra region, rural villagers became increasingly dependent on seasonal waged work in the wake of Syria's agrarian reforms in the late 1960s and early 1970s, which expanded with the liberalization of Syria's state-led economy from the 1990s onward. From cost-cutting to the laborious seasonal work of making household food preserves, Syrian women have long borne the brunt of these pressures, squeezing their paid and unpaid labor in times of dearth to secure their households' basic needs. The war in Syria amplified these predicaments, as farmworkers and their families found it difficult or impossible to seasonally return to their villages. Many of these families sought refuge in *shawīsh* camps to meet their rising costs of living in Lebanon year-round, ultimately going into debt at unprecedented rates throughout the war.

An agrarian perspective not only conveys the historical depth of Syrians' relationships to Lebanon as seasonal migrants; it also provides insight into the diverse and differentiated experiences of their Lebanese hosts. Following the life history of a contract farmer (*ḍammān*) who employed Syrian workers, I will chart how Lebanese peasant-smallholders faced their own crises of rural reproduction in a highly liberalized, market-led agricultural system lacking state protections, particularly from the 1970s onward. Most Lebanese smallholders were progressively displaced, as many went into debt, others mortgaged their lands, many exited agriculture entirely, and those with sufficient capital to remain competitive became contract farmers. By the 1990s, this gave rise to the dominant mode of cultivation found in the Bekaa Valley today: Lebanese *ḍammān* who pay rent to landlords like the Salams, take on the risks of cultivation and marketing, and hire low-waged Syrian farmworkers through camps run by *shawīsh* like Abu Sharif.

Importantly, these agrarian histories were rarely accorded urgency or referred to as "crises" in everyday talk throughout the war. Because of their deeply embodied connection to agricultural labor, these histories were more often expressed in the homely details of everyday life—a woman's work gloves, for example, or the shape of her chest after she stuffed it secretly with grape leaves to take home to her family. Such enduring crises were particularly apparent in daily struggles over the burdens of household debt—in the field, within the home, and across the border—and how feminized labor was remunerated, if at all. Though farmworkers' deepening debts were rarely *named* as a crisis, they were perhaps the most ubiquitous condition of their lives, shaping their everyday working conditions, where they lived, and, perhaps most importantly, how they made plans for return.

CHASING CRISES

"Informal tented settlements" was how Carlos, a foreign UN representative, described *shawīsh* camps when I first met him. He exuded that distinctive combination of mission-driven optimism and battered resignation that I knew well from my own experience working for the UN some years earlier.

A voracious reader who had considered pursuing a PhD, he was familiar with anthropologists' critiques of humanitarianism and had arranged personally to meet with me at a bar to learn more about my work in these camps.

"The kind of research you are doing is very important," he told me, taking a sip from his beer, straining to make himself heard over the pounding electronic music. "We need this kind of long-term perspective, but we're constantly chasing crisis after crisis."

Having served in his post in Lebanon for three years, he had one year left in his four-year rotation. With his tenure coming to an end, he was frustrated with a gnawing sense that he was working against time. As he saw it, the Lebanese state's refusal to develop a "holistic plan" for governing Syrian refugees was forcing humanitarian organizations to simply "chase crises."

"What kinds of crises?" I shouted over the thumping bass.

"The Lebanese state has no plan. They want Syrians to go back. They're in destruction mode. Right now, they're destroying the camps in Arsal. And before that, it was Deir el-Ahmar. And before that, Riyaq.[6] That's all I've done since I came to Lebanon: chasing crises and trying to minimize the damage."

He was referring to a series of mass evictions and housing demolition orders against Syrian camps carried out by the Lebanese Armed Forces. These evictions were part of a larger backlash against Syrians that had deepened throughout Lebanon's ballooning economic crisis, including the tightening of border entry and exit requirements, the imposition of nighttime curfews, flying checkpoints, and, starting in late 2018, mass closures of Syrian-run businesses.[7] At the time we met, the Lebanese Armed Forces had just demolished two dozen Syrian refugees' homes in the northeastern Bekaa Valley town of Arsal. These homes were made of concrete rather than wood and tarpaulin; the Lebanese Armed Forces claimed that the semipermanence of these structures violated Lebanon's housing codes because they were located on agricultural land. Syrian refugee advocates, including humanitarian workers like Carlos, were quick to point out that housing codes were rarely enforced in Lebanon. In their view, this was an obviously thinly veiled tactic of intimidating refugees and preventing their long-term settlement.

I was reminded of several different conversations I'd had with Syrian farmworkers who had experienced evictions over the past several years.

Unlike the high-profile evictions in Riyaq, Deir al-Ahmar, and Arsal, these evictions failed to garner headlines or humanitarian attention. I sensed that this was because these farmworkers were evicted not by the Lebanese Armed Forces but by their landlords. They were evicted because they or the *shawīsh* of their camps simply could not afford to pay their rent any longer. I tried to think of a way to ask Carlos what he thought about these less spectacular evictions. But before I could say anything, Carlos was already deep into an impassioned diatribe against the Lebanese government.

> We try so hard to work with the Lebanese, but they keep putting up new barriers and dragging their feet. They refuse to allow Syrian refugees to construct anything that remotely resembles a permanent structure. No bricks are allowed in the camps. But the wood beams and tarp are a fire hazard. Many children have died in fires. One tent catches on fire, and the whole camp goes up in a blaze, like the one in Bar Elias. How many more camps will burn to the ground before the Lebanese government accepts that Syrians need to build something more durable? That they're here to stay, at least for now?

The conversation later digressed to the work of *shawīsh* like Abu Sharif: "I have to work with so many of those guys to coordinate aid to the camps," Carlos grumbled, craning his neck to make sure I could hear him. "Some of them are okay. But most of them are totally corrupt. It's a pity. We try to speak directly to the people in the camps—the women, the children—but the *shawīsh* always insist on having everything go through them. We're never really sure what's going on inside and who is getting what. I worry that some of the *shawīsh* just keep all the aid for themselves."

As he and many others understood it, *shawīsh* camps were yet another example of Lebanon's highly dysfunctional approach to refugee governance. And he was certainly not alone in this perception: it was an opinion shared by not only most humanitarian workers I met but many Lebanese friends and colleagues in urban areas as well. Echoing long-standing discourses about Lebanon as an "absent" or "failed" state, *shawīsh* camps were often understood as spaces of abjection and illicit activity, a small-scale expression of the corruption that existed across Lebanon's political system and economy.[8]

Toward the end of the evening, Carlos asked me what I thought residents of *shawīsh* camps needed most. More cash aid was the obvious answer, but I tried to think of something that wasn't typically provided by humanitarian organizations.

"Gloves," I blurted out impulsively. "They need . . . better gloves." I realized that this sounded quite absurd, but it was the first thought that came to my mind, as members of Abu Sharif's camp had been complaining to me for weeks about the rising cost of gloves. Most of them, like Rawia, wore cheap, disposable rubber gloves while working in the fields, the kind that one uses for washing dishes. The rubber often wore out after just a few days of vigorous use, and the cost of replacing them frequently was no small expense for large families. I had lately gotten into the habit of bringing extra pairs of gloves with me to the camp. "I mean, for work," I added, trying in vain to make my point clear. "Because that's what they do all day. They work."

Carlos nodded but didn't probe much further. Despite his genuine interest in my perspective as an anthropologist, the rest of the conversation flowed very much like this: we continued speaking past each other despite our best efforts to find a shared language. Carlos' humanitarian understanding of crisis was necessarily wedded to the temporality of emergencies and the immediate reduction of suffering. His sense of disappointment in the Lebanese government was the flip side of humanitarian idealism—a hopeful faith in the capacities of refugee governance to improve. Compared to such lofty commitments, I could sense how my fixation on work gloves appeared too specific, pragmatic, and even a bit cynical.

The ways that Carlos and I spoke past each other revealed something important about the concept of crisis itself: it has many meanings that are located in different, often incommensurate, orientations to time. While the idea of crisis goes back to antiquity, coming from the Greek *krisis,* meaning to decide or make a judgment, it took on unique significance within Enlightenment philosophies of history, as the conditions of modernity furnished the possibility of conceiving the past and present in light of a secular redemptive future.[9] In the modern context, crises are conceived as moments of truth or turning points that demand action. One of the most vivid expressions of this modern, secular understanding of crisis is found in the postwar humanitarian regime, where the moral imperative to reduce suffering is tethered to the telos of emergency resolution.[10] Though varying across space and time, humanitarianism is, by definition, a "crisis response," where the central goal is "saving lives and moving on."[11]

The gloves' awkward significance in this conversation revealed how refugees' labor conditions were mostly illegible to the humanitarian imperative to alleviate suffering. And this is precisely because Syrian farmworkers' predicaments were historically complex and lacking clear or measurable solutions. The culpability for their crises could not be so easily attributed to one person, government, or agency—and the "solutions" to these crises remained elusive because they were deeply structural. Pinning these structural problems on the ambiguity, violence, and incoherence of Lebanese state responses to the Syrian refugee crisis was certainly intuitive, and there was no doubt that Lebanon's "policy of no policy" contributed to the growth of *shawīsh* camps throughout the war. Yet, it was clear that these camps represented far more than a poorly managed humanitarian crisis.

It was also telling that Carlos and other humanitarian personnel I met routinely referred to these *shawīsh* camps as "informal tented settlements." It implied that the residents of these camps were on the margins of economic life despite their centrality to Lebanon's agricultural system as its largest and lowest paid labor force. Steeped in the humanitarian temporalities, procedures, and practices of aid oriented around emergencies, many humanitarian workers struggled to grasp that most Syrian refugees were not sitting idly in camps, nor were their predicaments necessarily legible through the present tense of an "emergency." In many ways, this framing of "crisis" excluded the very possibility of *seeing* refugees as engaged in any kind of labor at all, let alone as I had come to see them: as farmworkers coping with indebtedness.

RATIONS AND MOUNEH: WHAT KIND OF CRISIS?

Situated deep in the Bekaa Valley plains, Abu Sharif's camp was barely noticeable from the main road, a diminutive white cluster surrounded by fields of wheat and potatoes. Located on a small tract of fallow land owned by a Lebanese absentee landlord, his camp consisted of thirty tarpaulin tents reinforced by wood frames, steel poles, and concrete floors, hosting three hundred people. From the outside, the tents appeared as one might expect of a refugee camp: white tarpaulins bearing the iconic blue UN High

FIGURE 5. **Red peppers drying in front of a tent.**

Commissioner for Refugees (UNHCR) logo. Each household had a corrugated-iron shack covering a pit toilet adjacent to their tents, running water from a spigot reserved for each tent, and a water tank, though water shortages were a constant challenge.

In contrast, the interiors were so meticulously decorated, spacious, colorful, and comfortably furnished that it was easy to forget that one was inside a tent during long evenings spent sipping tea and coffee, watching Turkish and Indian soap operas, and listening to *dabke* music. Each tent had a separate kitchen, a living room containing a diesel-burning stove (*ṣōbiyya*) to keep tents warm in winter, and at least one bedroom. Camp families took immense pride in decorating the interiors of their tents, furnishing each room with brightly colored textiles, hand-sewn quilts stuffed with raw wool, mattresses, and pillows in bold floral patterns. Laden with memories and aspirations, these lovingly ornamented homes felt like anything but temporary structures.[12]

It was precisely because these refugees were no longer temporary migrants that they invested such resources in their new tent-homes. Purchasing the materials and furnishings for a tent was, indeed, a costly endeavor for those lacking cash savings, easily reaching thousands of dollars. Due to these unforeseen costs, refugee newcomers and formerly seasonal migrants alike were attracted to Abu Sharif's camp, which offered space to pitch a tent and all the materials required to build a tent on credit with no interest charged. In exchange, Abu Sharif was responsible for securing agricultural jobs for camp residents, negotiating payment and working hours with Lebanese employers, and transporting the camp residents to their jobs in his flatbed truck. Segmented by household, workers' daily shifts were recorded and pooled as a "family wage" under the name of the eldest male family member residing in each tent. The unspoken rule was that male elders wielded primary decision-making power about requests for credit, while women and girls carried out the bulk of agricultural and household work.

The layout and decor of the tents closely replicated the traditional style of rural homes in their villages along the Euphrates River in eastern Syria.[13] Kitchens were stocked with shelves of *mouneh*[14]—seasonal preserves such as za'atar, pepper paste, spicy pickles stuffed in old soda bottles, and jarred dairy products—alongside bags of rice and cooking oil that they received through the UNHCR's monthly food rations. Silver coffee pots, glasses, and mugs sat on wooden shelves festooned with fake flowers and golden doilies in the living room, where guests were received. Floor mattresses were carefully stacked in the corner of the bedroom, a highly significant symbol of one's readiness to host guests in eastern Syrian rural culture, while all clothing was stored in a chest beneath the mattresses to keep the house looking neat. As I was often told, the more floor mattresses one had, the more generous one was reputed to be. And when the UNHCR donated massive aluminum foil panels to insulate their homes, women gathered the leftovers and cut them into decorative trim to adorn their shelving units.

In contrast to the stark uniformity of their tarpaulin exteriors, these tents' colorful interiors conjured the distinctive traces of farmworkers' homes back in Syria and the daily labor that went into maintaining them. They were also scenes of jarring juxtaposition: the *mouneh* that sat alongside the UN rations,

FIGURE 6. Blankets and mattresses gathered in a camp resident's tent.

the insulation panels cut into hearts, the blankets stacked against tarpaulin walls. In their dissonant coexistence, each was a powerful metaphor for the tensions underlying Syrian farmworkers' predicaments. The donated products bearing the UNHCR logo were internationally recognized symbols of refugees, while the *mouneh* and blankets were deeply cherished signs of hospitality within eastern Syrian culture.

These disjunctures between intimate household objects and humanitarian provisions signified more than the contrast between life before and after the war. They were the material manifestations of the protracted crises that Syrian farmworkers had long endured and were still enduring, including the often invisible labor of women to rebuild the comforts of a home in exile, however feeble and seemingly temporary their tarpaulin walls and wood beam structures appeared to be. Given that the vast majority of camp residents had migratory ties to Lebanon that predated the war, these interiors marked both the ruptures *and* continuities in their families' decades-long pursuits of rural stability. The unspoken but omnipresent material condition sustaining all of it was debt, the burdens of which were borne disproportionately by the work of mothers, wives, sisters, and daughters inside and outside of their homes.

For decades, migrant labor from Syria has underwritten entire industries in Lebanon, particularly those organized around low wages and seasonal employment. Essential to Lebanon's economy, yet structurally excluded from the benefits of citizenship, Syrians were once popularly described in a newspaper headline in 1972 as those who "melt away like sugar in tea."[15] The attraction of cash wages in Syrian cities, Lebanon, Türkiye, Jordan, and the Persian Gulf drew many rural men into seasonal labor migration to supplement household incomes in an increasingly cash-based economy, especially construction, tractor driving, and machinery operating. These early waves of mostly male migration came on the heels of Syria's experiment with state-led agrarian reform, which sought to redistribute land and build up a base of self-sufficient smallholder peasants throughout the 1960s and 1970s. But in practice, few farmers could survive on subsistence agriculture or pastoralism alone, and rural families were under enormous pressure to diversify their incomes and pursue waged work abroad.

Designated by their employers as "temporary" seasonal workers, Syrians were systematically paid wages below the living standards of Lebanese citizens and worked in precarious conditions without formalized benefits. For this reason, it was highly unusual for Syrian labor migrants to settle long term or raise their children in Lebanon until the war began in 2011. Instead, most farmworkers used to pack up their tents and return to their villages in

Syria throughout the winter season. In turn, the prohibitively high cost of living in Lebanon meant that it was virtually impossible for most rural Syrians to afford to settle there as long-term immigrants.

While earlier waves of Syrian labor migration to Lebanon were largely composed of single men, women began to migrate with greater frequency throughout the 1990s and 2000s. With the collapse of the Soviet Union, and particularly following the accession of Bashar al-Asad to the Syrian presidency in 2000, Syria's centrally planned economy progressively shifted away from the paradigm of state-led agriculture toward the globalized market economy.[16] One of the unintended outcomes of this process was a shift in rural household strategies for making ends meet, as unprecedented numbers of women and teenagers—particularly from the Jazīra region—entered seasonal waged work through teams coordinated by *shawīsh* to support family subsistence.

Across these multiple waves of migration and displacement, it was the underpaid and often unpaid work of women that sustained their kin, allowing some more prosperous families to build up savings and others to avoid a slide into indebtedness. Women remained primarily responsible for maintaining their families' village homes and small parcels of land back in Syria, including the work of cultivating, harvesting, and storing the ingredients of *mouneh*, raising livestock, and managing dairy production. Throughout the year, all members of these rural households subsisted on *mouneh* in its many forms: at home with their families during home migrations, carried in suitcases to Lebanon during the high harvest season, and sent in care packages across the border with a trusted friend or relative whenever needed. Subsisting on *mouneh* allowed labor migrants to minimize their everyday costs in Lebanon and maximize remittances to their families, which perhaps explains an often-cited stereotype among Lebanese that Syrians "only eat tomatoes."

Like many other *shawīsh*, Abu Sharif's life trajectory as a labor broker was a story of upward mobility rooted in this cross-border economy of seasonal waged work and subsistence agriculture. He first came to Lebanon as a child with his mother and siblings in 1978 from their village in the countryside of Aleppo. His family was part of a pioneering generation of tribal populations (*'ashā'ir*) from northeastern Syria who began seasonally migrating to Lebanon for the high harvest season in search of waged work to supplement household incomes. As he once told me, "We used to come to Lebanon as children with my mother for a particular season, like potato picking. And my father worked in many different jobs in the city. . . . We would bring goat-hair tents (*bayt shaʿr*) or plastic tarps from our villages, just a basic cover, since you do not need much in the warm, summer months."

After over a decade of saving, he finally built up the necessary capital to become a *shawīsh* in the early 1990s, which required three things: a pickup truck, money to rent a tract of land for a temporary farmworker camp, and connections to employers in Lebanon and seasonal workers in Syria. Abu Sharif's emphasis on the temporary nature of prewar housing arrangements for seasonal workers—"just a basic cover," as he put it—conveyed the fundamental transformation that took place as Lebanon became a site of long-term refuge for Syrians fleeing the war: a shift from highly mobile, seasonal tent structures to more permanent, year-round camps paved with concrete.

This history also illuminates the daily crises of social reproduction that Syrian farmworkers were facing as refugees in Lebanon after 2011: how to procure affordable food and shelter. Unable to return to Syria to cultivate their land (or land to which they claimed customary rights) throughout the war, many rural Syrians struggled with the higher costs of living in Lebanon year round. Relegated to purchasing rather than cultivating their food, they often went into debt to their more well-established Syrian compatriots—including *shawīsh* like Abu Sharif—to cover the costs of maintaining their households' basic needs.

Shadowing farmworkers from Abu Sharif's camp helped me see how the war's reverberating effects were inseparable from the longer-term rural dislocations that had long characterized many Syrians' lives, particularly their growing dependence on waged labor. In this sense, their struggles were emblematic of what feminist scholars have described as the "permanent reproduction crisis" that has driven unprecedented numbers of rural people, especially women, to migrate in search of work, internally and across borders since the 1990s.[17] Though rarely remarked upon directly, these histories of migration found expression in Syrian women's deeply embodied capacities to endure hard labor and rotate between tasks, from the field to the home, including the laborious tasks of cleaning, cooking, mending blankets, and preparing *mouneh*. More than "crisis" in the humanitarian sense, this embodied capacity for endurance was honed through the unrelenting pressure to meet rural families' reproductive needs in ever-more-difficult circumstances. This crisis did not originate with the Syrian conflict but was undoubtedly exacerbated by it.

But as Abu Sharif's trajectory suggests, the reverberating effects of the war were not borne the same way by everyone. Abu Sharif was among the small segment of well-established Syrian migrant workers who was in a position to capitalize on this crisis by scaling up his farmworker camp operations, while those who found refuge in these camps were often saddled with mounting debts. Syrians' mass displacement was, in turn, initially a boon to Lebanese contract farmers operating in a competitive and unregulated agricultural market, as hiring low-paid Syrian farmworkers helped drive down the costs of production.

Coming on the heels of a half-century of agrarian change on both sides of the Lebanese-Syrian border, these compounding crises were reflected in the pronounced divisions of labor among agriculturalists in the Bekaa Valley. While some of these inequalities were obvious—as that between the masculinized work of *shawīsh* and the feminized residents of their camps—Abu Sharif's own life trajectory from humble farmworker to labor broker suggested that the material conditions that gave rise to them were considerably layered and complex. This shifting nexus between displacement, debt, class differentiation, and reproduction was also significant for understanding what the "refugee crisis" meant for Syrians' Lebanese hosts.

CRISES BEFORE THE CRISIS: DISPLACING THE LEBANESE PEASANT

It was a chilly morning in late March 2019, but Ibtissam's face was flushed and sweaty after several hours standing under the sun. Ibtissam, her two sisters, and her brother had hired fifty-eight workers from Abu Sharif's camp that day to weed a field of onions by hand with hoes. She was one of the two dozen Lebanese contract farmers (*ḍammān*) who regularly hired Abu Sharif's workers on the Salam family's estate for seasonal work. She often described her relationship to Abu Sharif and his workers with genuine affection.

"We've known Abu Sharif for over twenty years. There is friendship between us [*fī ṣadāqa*]," she told me, as she lifted her wide-brimmed straw hat to adjust her hijab.

The workers were organized into small groups, proceeding side by side in rows so that Ibtissam and her siblings could assess their speed and accuracy. The workers remained in a hunched position as they deftly uprooted each weed with the edges of their hoes in one fell swoop, one by one. They worked in rapid bursts, occasionally standing up to relieve the pressure from their lower backs. Though weeding work in Lebanon is considered unskilled, it requires immense endurance and strength. It also requires precision, as workers must take care not to damage the delicate onion sprouts.

Ibtissam emphasized that she knew every one of the workers by name. "If one of them is missing, I notice." As she spoke, one of the workers from Abu Sharif's camp, Halima, was walking across the field with a nine-liter water bottle in one hand and the bottom half of a two-liter soda bottle in the other. She was using the latter as a makeshift cup for each worker to take a drink periodically.

"I've known Halima since she was a little girl," Ibtissam told me over the din of dull hoes hitting the ground, a rhythmic *thwak, thwak, thwak*. "I don't

FIGURE 7. Weeding an onion field in March.

like the idea of a formal hierarchy between us. I want to be able to shout and yell and joke with them." *Thwak, thwak, thwak.*

As was typical at that time of year, the morning work shift started between 6:00 and 7:00 a.m. and lasted five hours. At exactly noon, Ibtissam lined up all the workers and counted them to make sure everyone was present. She also instructed all the workers to place their tools in a pile and counted them to make sure none were missing. As I wrapped up my conversation with Ibtissam, three workers from Abu Sharif's camp—Halima, Rawia, Buchra—gathered nearby.

"Honestly, compared to what the Syrian workers do now, the work for Lebanese workers was more exhausting [*atʿab*]," Ibtissam told me. She was looking at me but was speaking loudly enough for Halima, Rawia, and Buchra to hear. They grinned wordlessly.

"I'm telling you from personal experience, work was harder back then," Ibtissam continued. "These girls are lucky! When I was their age, if we took a break, it was deducted from our earnings." She flashed a smile in their direction. "I pay them regardless of how well they work. . . . Even when they're lazy like Rawia!" she teased, smiling in their direction.

The three young women were wearing worn-out pink rubber gloves. Halima had the name of her boyfriend scrawled on the inner palm of her glove. I remembered how, a few days earlier, she had asked me to write his name on hers, to remind her of "happy things" while she worked. "Write it in English," she whispered, "So no one will know what it says!"

She yanked off the glove with a pop. I noticed that her palm was covered in raw blisters.

Later that evening, Rawia and I talked about Ibtissam's comments after eating dinner in her family's tent. "So, what do you think Ibtissam meant when she said the life of Lebanese farmers was harder back when she was your age?" I asked her.

Rawia scoffed. "Oh, you know how Lebanese love to make 'empty talk' [*kalām fāḍī*]. I have no clue what she was talking about," she said with a sigh. "All I know is that everyone in the camp is exhausted. And work on Ibtissam's land is the most exhausting [*atʿab shī*]."

It is telling that both women—Ibtissam and Rawia—used the term "exhaustion" to describe their predicaments, which showed how crises are often manifested in deeply felt, yet barely perceptible, experiences of bodily pain. For Ibtissam, claims about exhaustion were about marking the affinities that existed between her and the workers, and thus disavowing the obvious inequalities that existed between them. For Rawia, in contrast, exhaustion was something generalized, diffuse, and ongoing. Unlike Ibtissam, Rawia's exhaustion had no "end" to narrate.

Though their historical circumstances were quite distinct, Ibtissam's individualized narrative of self-making, overcoming adversity, and mobility shared a great deal in common with Abu Sharif's style of narrating his agrarian past. Both were deeply invested in portraying toil as something with which they were deeply familiar yet ultimately relegated to the past. Instead, for Rawia, like most other farmworkers from Abu Sharif's camp, exhaustion was stuck in the present, inserting itself into the contours of everyday life in their blisters and back pains. And despite their best efforts to protect their faces from the sun and wind, it was etched into their chapped, weathered skin that made even children appear uncannily like tiny adults.

Halima's glove, printed with her lover's name, was also significant. One of the great challenges Syrian farmworkers faced in exile was how to finance their marriages. The rising cost of bridewealth—which at the time of my research ranged from $2,500 to $4,000—was one of the primary reasons that many Syrian men began migrating to cities and abroad from the 1970s onward. Rising rates of indebtedness throughout the war made these life transitions exceedingly more complicated, as families juggled the costs of marrying their sons. In turn, unmarried women's labor was valued as a fraught trade-off between their long-term contribution to the household in the form of their agricultural wages and unremunerated labor and the substantial short-term infusion of cash their family could obtain from the value of their bridewealth upon marriage. As a divorced woman longing to find true love, Rawia gave expression to her difficult position within her indebted family through her deeply embodied concept of exhaustion, as her life plans were not entirely her own to make.

These different ways of reckoning with exhaustion subtly conveyed the fraught histories by which Ibtissam and Rawia were conscripted into very different positions within Lebanon's agricultural system—positions that could only truly make sense when viewed over a life course and across generations. Ibtissam and her siblings usually referred to themselves as *muzāriʿīn* (cultivators), but their seasonal contract with the Salam family designated them as *ḍammān* (guarantors). Ibtissam's work entailed taking on the risks of production and marketing as the profitability of agriculture in Lebanon was falling, yet agricultural rents—especially the fertile land of the Salam family—were rising. Despite her obvious affection for the workers, Ibtissam's livelihood thus depended on maximizing her workers' productivity and keeping their wages low. Rawia, in her own way, conveyed this point when she described working for Ibtissam as "the most exhausting."

A *ḍammān* like Ibtissam would seem, at first, an unexpected subject of Lebanon's refugee crisis. Yet it turned out that this work was central to Syrian refugees' everyday lives in the Bekaa, as *ḍammān* were Syrian farmworkers' main employers via the *shawīsh* labor recruitment system. In its contemporary form, *ḍammān* is akin to contract farming, a type of fixed-term agricultural agreement between cultivators and agricultural firms that has expanded significantly since the 1970s as a result of globalizing markets, the growth of food-processing industries, and the vertical integration of food commodity chains.[18] This work ensures a steady flow of rents to landlords (both small and large) and shifts the risks of cultivation and marketing onto farmers who can afford to hire workers.

The work of the *ḍammān* in Lebanon includes a diverse group of people.[19] Many, like Ibtissam and her siblings, are from relatively modest Lebanese families who built up their base of capital over time. Others come from members of tribal clans (especially the Bou Eid and the Hrook) with long-standing roots in the Bekaa Valley who acquired wealth from truck driving.[20] More recently, *shawīsh* like Abu Sharif also started engaging in this work to diversify their incomes and ensure liquidity within their accounts. Though the responsibilities of *ḍammān* vary widely depending on the size and quality of the land and the type of crop, their work on the Salam family's estate required managing virtually every aspect of the land's use, from planting to irrigation works, to overseeing labor hiring and payments. They purchased imported seeds, fertilizers, saplings, and machinery from a handful of regional Lebanese-owned agro-industrial export and food production companies.

The divisions of labor on the estate and many other properties of this scale—between *ḍammān* like Ibtissam, *shawīsh* like Abu Sharif, and the mostly female workers in his camp—are a product of several decades of agrarian transformations. The Salams' estate was divided in two parts: the foothills and the plains. They leased the plains to a dozen *ḍammān* in winter and two dozen *ḍammān* in summer, each of whom rented plots ranging from 100 to 300 *dūnam*[21] (10 to 30 hectares). The plots were not fenced off from each other but left open to allow for pastoral families who lived on the family's estate to graze their flocks freely. The family supplied land and a water source and the *ḍammān*'s responsibility was to pay a seasonal rent and cover the costs of all equipment and inputs (sprinkler systems, tractors, fertilizers, pesticides), labor, and marketing. *Ḍammān* usually cultivated one type of crop at a time and followed a strict seasonal rotation schedule between wheat, potatoes, and vegetables to reduce soil erosion and susceptibility to pests and pathogens. Because of the temporary contractual nature of their work, *ḍammān* did not usually cultivate the same plot for multiple seasons but rather continued moving from plot to plot. Fed by a natural spring and snowmelt from the nearby mountains, this land was especially fertile and valuable, and the rents the family charged were some of the highest in the region.[22]

Like many Lebanese cultivators, Ibtissam and her siblings' experiences as agriculturalists were marked by decades of displacements. They were originally from a border town in South Lebanon and were forced to flee in the 1970s due to Israeli military incursions against the Palestine Liberation Organization.[23] "During the time of the (Israeli) invasion [*waqt al-ijtiyāḥ*], we fled as small children with our parents to the Bekaa Valley," Ibtissam told me. They worked as a family unit on different farms across the Western Bekaa, paid as a family wage, including harvesting and planting potatoes and sugar beets. Though Ibtissam and her family were displaced by the growing violence at the Lebanese-Israeli border, their dependence on waged labor was symptomatic of a broader crisis of social reproduction taking place across Lebanon's countryside from the 1960s onward.

Ibtissam and her siblings became waged laborers on the heels of Lebanon's brief experiment with developmentalist policies under President Fuad Chihab in the 1960s, which led to state-sponsored extensions of electricity, piped water, roads, land reclamation, and irrigation, and introduction of new cash crops. Yet, this model of developmentalism left Lebanon's liberal emphasis on the banking sector intact, which incentivized landlords to rent out their estates and produce for the market directly or sell their land to financiers seeking to invest in capital-intensive farming.[24] It was in this period that a new agro-exporting class—composed of Lebanese traders from Tripoli, Sidon, Beirut, Zahle, and Tyre and wealthy emigres who amassed fortunes abroad—purchased or rented property from landed elites like the Salam family. This emerging class of agrarian capitalists monopolized imports of fertilizer and farming equipment, water for irrigation networks, agricultural banks and lending institutions, and distribution networks.[25] This shift to capitalist modes of agrarian production went hand in hand with agriculture's dwindling significance within Lebanon's economy as a whole: the share of agriculture in Lebanon's GDP decreased from 20 percent in 1948 to 12 percent in 1964 to less than 9 percent by 1974.[26]

Farmers like Ibtissam and her family were not passive in the face of these profound transformations. The 1950s through the early 1970s marked a period of mass mobilization and protest among Lebanese sharecroppers and smallholders in the Bekaa, including sugar beet plantations, vineyards, and potato farms, as well as daily protests by tobacco workers throughout South Lebanon.[27] Through their union activity, Lebanese workers successfully secured social security coverage and unionization for agricultural workers, and it was precisely at this time that a narrowing class of Lebanese landlords and contract farmers sought to circumvent the power of organized labor by hiring temporary Syrian workers.[28] In 1968, the Lebanese Communist Party held a large conference among agriculturalists, culminating in the publication of a widely circulated pamphlet in 1973 outlining a radical platform for labor and land reforms. Syrian workers make a brief appearance in the pamphlet:

> Tens of thousands of Syrian, Palestinian, and other laborers work in Lebanese agriculture. The presence of these workers has become permanent and necessary, and they have in fact become part of the Lebanese rural toilers [*al-kādiḥīn*]. They carry out the most difficult labor and are subject to the harshest forms of exploitation, as they receive the lowest wages without adherence to working hours in general, not to mention the deprivation of various guarantees. The conscious Lebanese agricultural workers resist attempts to explain this as the existence of "conflict"

> between them and the Arab workers. They realize that their legitimate demands and rights are never separate from the demands and rights of these people. . . . That is why the Lebanese rural toilers see these workers as class brothers who suffer from the same exploitation as them.[29]

These ambitious visions for Syrian-Palestinian-Lebanese class solidarity were fundamentally transformed, and ultimately cut short, by the Lebanese Civil War that began in 1975 and lasted until 1990.

Further, despite such radical activity in the countryside, the crushing reality was that most Lebanese agriculturalists were not becoming organized in unions but rather had exited agriculture under the pressures of indebtedness, a reflection of a deepening agrarian crisis.[30] As Lebanese agriculturalists pursued off-farm waged work, many began to rent, mortgage, or sell their land. By the eve of the Lebanese civil war, an estimated 40 percent of Lebanon's entire rural population had left their land.[31] Among agriculturalists from Shiʿa majority regions like Ibtissam's village, these numbers were even higher: 50 percent of rural populations in the Bekaa and 65 percent in South Lebanon left their villages, with three-quarters moving to Lebanon's cities and the remainder moving abroad to Africa, the Americas, Australia, and the Persian Gulf.[32] Those who remained in agriculture, like Ibtissam's family, were those that acquired the necessary capital to remain competitive.

Throughout the civil war, Lebanese agriculturalists became further stratified into unequal classes. At the top were a handful of firms that monopolized marketing, inputs, and agricultural credit and lending mechanisms.[33] Underneath these firms emerged a highly diverse class of Lebanese *ḍammān*, which included upwardly mobile waged workers like Ibtissam and her siblings, smallholders striving to remain in agriculture while supplementing their income with off-farm employment, and medium-sized landlords looking to further capitalize their properties. This trend toward contract farming deepened throughout the war as the Lebanese state broke down into territorialized statelets and militia entrepreneurs managed local infrastructures throughout Lebanon. Across small towns and villages, many official land registers were burned or destroyed, creating a fertile environment for land grabbing, as thousands of unregistered land transactions took place.[34]

Given its tendentiousness, this history was rarely mentioned at all in my conversations with agriculturalists, and when it was, only in vague, euphemistic terms. As Ibtissam put it, "each leader of the different political factions 'put his hand on the land' [*ḥaṭṭ īdu bil-arḍ*]" and began cultivating for their own purposes. Leaders of these warring factions benefited greatly from real estate sales, and the early 1980s saw a massive real-estate boom across the country, including high-rise luxury hotels, gated communities, seaside resorts, and shopping malls. Within the agricultural sector, militia-controlled checkpoints in Lebanon produced artificial shortages and inflated prices for particular goods through the imposition of customs duties. These factors, coupled with Lebanese out-migration and internal displacement, Syria's military intervention in Lebanon beginning in 1976, and Lebanon's weakened capacity to regulate its borders, drew an unprecedented number of Syrian workers into low-waged sectors facing labor shortages, including agriculture.[35]

When the war ended with the signing in 1989 of the Ta'if National Reconciliation Accord,[36] the Salam family reclaimed portions of their land that were appropriated or left fallow throughout the war. This period ushered in an unprecedented phase of Syrian military and political involvement in Lebanon that came to be known as "Pax Syriana."[37] Upwardly mobile emigree entrepreneurs who amassed fortunes abroad—including former Prime Minister Rafiq al-Hariri and Speaker of the Parliament Nabih Berri—stood at the helm of the reconstruction process, as huge sums of money and resources for postwar reconstruction flooded Lebanon's economy. As part of the postwar consensus, Lebanon became engaged in a path of aggressive trade liberalization, bolstered by the General Arab Free Trade Agreement. Though I was never able to ascertain exactly how Ibtissam and her siblings acquired their capital, they became *ḍammān* on the Salam estate in the late 1990s, initially cultivating sugar beets and switching to onions, cabbage, and other vegetables when the Lebanese state ended its subsidy for sugar beets in the early 2000s.[38] "I'm an engineer of experience [*muhandisa ʿal-khibra*]" is how Ibtissam described her mobility from humble worker to *ḍammān*.

Lebanese *ḍammān* usually narrated the postwar trajectory of agriculture in Lebanon in quite pessimistic terms, often woven with deep grievances toward the Lebanese state. "No one looks after the Lebanese," Ibtissam once told me. "The state doesn't care about us at all." Abu Charbel, another *ḍammān* with whom I worked closely throughout my fieldwork, often juxtaposed Lebanon's agrarian policies against Syria's price supports, which he viewed as a model of state protection for farmers. "In Syria, the state regulates the price. It's guaranteed [*maḍmūn*]. But here in Lebanon, it's a totally free market [*sū' ḥurr*]. There's no protection for the farmer [*mā fī ḥimāye lil-muzāriʿ*]. I'll give you an example, last winter, there was a huge frost that destroyed the apple market completely. And the farmers simply had to eat their losses. One bad frost can kill a whole season of work."

When I asked Ibtissam's sister, Fatima, how the war in Syria has affected their production, her response was impassioned but somewhat elliptical.

"Capitalism came [*ijit ar-ra'smālīye*]. This is what rules us now."

"What do you mean? Who are the capitalists?"

"There are opportunists [*al-intihāzīyyīn*] who are benefitting from the situation."

Realizing I was confused, she backpedaled slightly.

"I'm talking about Syrians. . . . Not these workers, of course. They are simple people [*nās basīṭa*]. I'm talking about capitalists. I'll give you an example. You know the vegetable market [*sū' al-khuḍra*] in Qab Elias?[39] On paper, it's only Lebanese who are allowed to have a stall in the market, but actually nearly all of them are Syrians who are registered under a Lebanese name. Two-thirds of the people are Syrian, maybe more. In the end, I blame the state for this. It's fraud [*iḥtiyāl*] and corruption [*fasād*] by the state. The state enables this."

"What do you think should be done? Is there a solution?" I asked her.

"The solution needs to come from the state. This corruption is from them. Instead of getting rid of corruption, they're fighting each other."

These different discourses about the state—Abu Charbel's claim about the Syrian state as a model of agrarian protections, Fatima's portrayal of the Lebanese state as corrupt, and Ibtissam's claim that the Lebanese state was uncaring—each expressed the sense of risk and constant uncertainty that marked the lives of Lebanese agriculturalists, even those who were prosperous enough to work as *ḍammān*. Except for landlords like the Salams who collected a steady stream of seasonal rents, agriculture for most cultivators was very risky business because it was almost completely unregulated.

Abu Charbel's use of the word "guaranteed" (*maḍmūn*) to describe the Syrian state's historically state-led approach to agriculture was important in this sense. It comes from the same root in Arabic as *ḍammān*. As he understood it, the state's obligations to provide "guarantees" were being shifted onto the Lebanese cultivator. This volatility and riskiness put pressure on the *ḍammān* to keep wages extremely low, and it is in this context that *shawīsh* camps grew in importance since the 1990s. These were small-scale expressions of the broader economic crisis that was engulfing the region, one that was certainly connected to the refugee crisis but ultimately a product of the much more protracted, interlinked histories of agrarian class struggle, displacement, war, and economic liberalization.

"GIRLS" ON TRUCKS: DISPLACEMENTS FROM SYRIA'S JAZĪRA REGION

Across the Bekaa Valley, I was often met with the same sentiment: without Syrians, there would be no agriculture in Lebanon. Lebanese agriculturalists in the Bekaa often made sense of this by claiming that Syrians had a "lower" standard of living and an extraordinary capacity for cost-cutting and constrained consumption.

"Everything in Syria is cheap," Abu Charbel once explained to me. "Their wage in Lebanon might be nothing here, but that money goes a long way in Syria. They come to Lebanon and live in tents. Or an apartment with a dozen guys [*shabāb*]. They bring all their food with them. Big suitcases full of *mouneh*, everything you can imagine, even cooking oil. How could any Lebanese afford to live like that?"

Like other *ḍammān*, Ibtissam and her siblings began heavily recruiting labor from *shawīsh* camps in the 1990s during Lebanon's postwar reconstruction period. When I asked her why she hires Syrian workers, her answer was simple: most Lebanese cannot afford farming.

"There aren't any Lebanese workers anymore," she said.

"Why is that?" I asked her.

"The cost of living."

As Ibtissam explained, "Until the 1990s, Lebanese were still being hired as farmworkers, mostly Shiʿa from villages in Nabatiya," pointing south. "But they were paid an even lower wage back then. How could any Lebanese survive on this?"

"Were there *shawīsh* back then?" I asked her.

"Very little. All of them were from the same tribe as Abu Sharif. Back then, it was just him and his siblings. And his mother!"

"Oh yeah, Imm Jaʿba!" Ibtissam's brother, Khaled, interjected with a giggle, holding his arms out to indicate that Abu Sharif's mother had a hefty bosom. "Jaʿba" literally means a cartridge pouch or arrow quiver used for hunting, but colloquially it can also mean having something up one's sleeve. It can refer to a town gossip, but in this case, I took it to mean her propensity to keep her valuables—and stealthily gleaned vegetables—stuffed in her chest.

Though the name Imm Jaʿba was a playful joke, it was not insignificant. When considered more closely, it symbolized the invisible yet vital processes by which rural Syrian women managed long periods of uncertain subsistence, especially as they migrated across borders. Indeed, when weeding throughout the early spring season, I noticed how women would often furtively stuff their chests and pockets with edible wild plants that grow among the weeds at that time of year, including mallow (*khubbayza*) and wild chard (*silaq akhḍar*) for making stew for their families. When weeding in vineyards, they did the same with grape leaves for making stuffed *waraq ʿinab*. I quickly caught onto this tacit practice of gleaning when I realized that everyone's bosoms and bellies magically doubled or tripled in size after some weeding shifts. Here, I was reminded of how crisis is, quite literally, embodied.

Such stealthy acts of provisioning were honed over lifetimes and generations, well before the war began. These daily practices exemplify what Lauren Berlant has memorably described as the "ordinariness" of crisis. Crisis, she states, "is not exceptional to history or consciousness" but, rather "a process embedded in the ordinary that unfolds in stories about navigating what's overwhelming."[40] What appears extraordinary—that which gets named as an event, turning point, or crisis—is always, in a certain sense, an amplification of more mundane processes of survival. Seen in this way, Imm Jaʿba's reputation for gleaning conveyed the often unspoken, yet vital, forms of survival that emerge when crisis is, as Diana Allan puts it, a "long turning"—continuous, chronic, and protracted.[41]

The roots of such practices among eastern Syrian women run deep, reflecting the ways that gendered divisions of labor were indirectly and directly institutionalized within Syria's state-led agrarian policies and their uneven aftermaths. Like other cases of land reform across the world that largely excluded women as direct beneficiaries, Syria's land reforms in the 1950s and 1960s did not directly aim to revolutionize the traditionally patriarchal structure of rural smallholder families.[42] For those who acquired land or became employees on state-owned farms, male household heads remained the primary decision-makers regarding divisions of family labor and the use of household income. In this context, women's share of agricultural work was treated as an extension of their unremunerated domestic duties within the family.[43] Among villagers from eastern Syria's Jazīra region, women's work in dairy production and husbandry served as a household savings account and cash reserve while men migrated abroad. Women could obtain cash for their families by selling milk, clarified butter (*samneh*), eggs, and yogurt to local merchants, while the purchase or sale of livestock maintained a baseline of liquidity.[44]

Paralleling Syria's liberalization period starting in the 1980s and especially from the 1990s onward, a new sight began to appear across the countryside of Lebanon and Syria: women and girls crowded on the backs of large flatbed trucks and auto-rickshaws. Women from the Jazīra began joining seasonal work teams coordinated by *shawīsh*, which were of two main types. The first was local, where *shawīsh* recruited women and their children as seasonal workers in or near their villages for labor-intensive tasks and crops, especially the high season of weeding in the spring, the summer lentil harvest, and the cotton harvest in the fall.

Work teams of the second type were coordinated by *shawīsh* with extensive migratory experience outside of their villages or abroad, like Abu Sharif. These "girl workshops," as they are locally called, recruited women and their children for seasons of migration away from their homes to Lebanon, Türkiye, or Jordan in particular crops, as well as greenhouse and citrus work on Syria's coast. Though *shawīsh* often recruited women from poor, landless families, it was not uncommon for women from better-off families with some land and livestock to join these teams for seasonal work as well in order to secure cash for themselves. When pooled as a family income, farmworkers' earnings helped cover the rising costs of bridewealth, daily expenses, and home renovations, while upwardly mobile *shawīsh* like Abu Sharif used their earnings to invest in pickup trucks, purchase land, or speculate in contract farming. The combined effects of drought and Syria's aggressive path of economic liberalization from 2000 onward reinforced this trend toward westward migrations among women from eastern Syria.[45]

According to one estimate, the reported share of women in Syria's agricultural production doubled from 1980 to 2010, from 31.7 percent to 60.7 percent just before the war began.[46] This marked shift to feminized migrant labor was not especially unique; it was a process that was taking place in different ways across the Global South. It reflected an emergent and deepening gendered division of globalized labor, where work in agriculture, assembly lines, sweatshops, and domestic spaces has been increasingly carried out by rural migrant women.[47]

I remember well that when I was first introduced to Abu Sharif, he told me in a beseeching tone that the members of his camp were surviving on "a day's sustenance [*al-qūt al-yawmī*]."[48] At first glance, it might have appeared that he was simply engaging in a stylized performance of suffering intended to elicit compassion, accustomed as he was to his newfound position brokering access to humanitarian aid and services for residents of his camp. Yet in a deeper sense, it was indeed an important claim about how Syrian farmworkers' sources of income and everyday household provisioning had been transformed by the war in Syria. For Syrian farmworkers long accustomed to seasonal mobility across the Lebanese-Syrian border, their protracted exile in Lebanon brought to light the poverty of their wages.

Their long-term displacement was also a crisis of gender and generational obligation. As female-majority work teams coordinated by *shawīsh* became increasingly common across the region in the decades preceding the war, the traditional stigma against women and girls working on others' land outside of the home also began to shift. Paradoxically, the growing *visibility* of women's agricultural work in Syria went hand-in-hand with the relative *invisibility* of men's labor abroad. Male labor migrants' back-breaking days toiling in Beirut's restaurants and nights crammed in small apartments with other men or delivering pizzas at odd hours thrived within an economy of gendered propriety and invisibility. There was a tacit understanding that these men could endure such exploitative labor conditions, in part, because they were never *seen* by their neighbors and female kin.[49] Working abroad

FIGURE 8. Harvesting peas at sunrise in June.

alleviated men from the everyday obligations toward hospitality, allowing them to self-exploit and defer their returns until they had the means to fulfill social obligations back home.

What changed throughout the war was that men and women alike could no longer migrate freely across the border, nor could they depend on the seasonal subsistence and sources of income they derived from their land and animal husbandry. Many middle-aged men in *shawīsh* camps opted to retire early rather than endure the indignity of working alongside their female kin and neighbors on another's land after years of seasonal autonomy from their families. The war thus laid bare a series of delicate gendered tensions and shifting inequalities that structured these intersecting cross-border economies of seasonal labor, remittances, moral obligation, and household subsistence for decades.

It was also a crisis that affected Syrian refugees differently depending on their origins in Syria and prewar migratory ties to Lebanon. My friend Abdullah had quite a poetic way of explaining the rise of *shawīsh* camps:

it was a struggle, in his words, between "girls' hands" (*ayādī banāt*) and "machines" (*ālāt*). Living with his adolescent children and wife in a modest rented apartment a few kilometers away from Abu Sharif's camp, Abdullah worked as a seasonal day laborer in tree pruning and grapevine tying, while taking day jobs in stonemasonry whenever possible. With a university degree in agricultural engineering and, though politically unaffiliated himself, connected by kin to the Syrian Communist Party, Abdullah was an organic intellectual with a knack for Marxist class analysis. As a "free worker" who was employed directly by Lebanese *ḍammān* without a middleman, Abdullah was keenly aware of how the shift to "girls' work" was linked to cutting labor costs.

"Those girls don't know anything about agriculture," he grumbled as we discussed his work in viticulture. "When you come to a vineyard, you always know when work has been done in the previous season by the *warash banāt* because the vines are tied to the wires in a shoddy way."

"So why do you think they hire them?" I asked him, as he poured me a cup of maté tea.[50]

"Lebanon as a society is driven by a capitalist mentality. If it means profit today, they'll think about today rather than the long term. Never mind that the work is of lower quality, and *ḥarām*, that it's exploitative," he replied with characteristic erudition, taking a sip of maté through a silver straw.

Abdullah's evocative portrayal of the struggle between "girls' hands" and "machines" ran against the more conventional culturalist explanations for eastern Syrian women's overrepresentation within agriculture. He understood very well that the shift to labor-intensive techniques was connected to a political economy of wage repression, where tasks such as weeding were lower paid because they were considered "women's work." Working within narrow profit margins, Lebanese employers turned to *shawīsh* camp workers for their flexibility, as they were expected to be highly compliant and adaptable to the varying duration, intensity, and nature of their work assignments. One of the ways that Lebanese employers worked to maximize their productivity was by alternating between a "*yawmiyya*" schedule (five-hour shifts) and a "*maqṭūʿa*" schedule (piece rate), depending on the job. *Maqṭūʿa* measures workers' output in terms of a set number of filled crates or a stipulated distance, which incentivizes the workers to labor much more quickly.

Abdullah's misgivings about "girls" also underscored the inequalities within Lebanon's labor markets that existed among Syrian refugees themselves, who were differentiated according to class, regional origin, and prewar migratory connections to Lebanon. Unlike the residents of *shawīsh* camps, Abdullah was from a comparatively prosperous village in the countryside of Damascus where most families worked in skilled trades such as stonemasonry, while subsistence agriculture was reserved for household consumption. As Abdullah himself acknowledged, hierarchies of skilled and unskilled work in Syrian agriculture were deeply embedded in long-standing inequalities within Syria that were only partially overcome by the land reforms. In contrast to the *iqṭāʿ* system that dominated eastern Syria, Abdullah's village in the countryside of Damascus was populated by the "orchard peasant" (*al-fallāḥ al-bustānī*), skilled cultivators of tree orchards who tend to reside in Syria's urban hinterlands.[51] Whereas eastern Syria's impoverished Jazīra region was completely revolutionized by the cotton boom in the 1950s and mass irrigation and electrification works in the 1970s, Abdullah's village in the countryside of Damascus was more gradually incorporated into the capitalist urban economy, as the Lebanese-Syrian borderlands became an entrepôt between Beirut and Damascus at the turn of the nineteenth century, and later benefited from the parcelization of land through reforms in the 1960s. For skilled workers like Abdullah, the war was a distinct experience of class demobility that brought his family closer to the long-standing tribulations of the comparatively poorer Jazīran farmworkers residing in *shawīsh* camps.

Abdullah's comments also conveyed another dynamic that deepened throughout the war: despite the notion that the agricultural labor market was sharply differentiated by gender and skill level, Syrian "free workers" and *shawīsh* camp workers were often in direct competition with each other, and gender (as well as citizenship) was a mechanism of normalizing wage repression. While free workers like Abdullah were known to perform higher quality work and were often better paid, they were also, in many ways, more precarious. They had few social guarantees compared to *shawīsh* camp residents: they secured their own housing, transportation to work, and access to humanitarian and state services, and worked directly with employers without help from a middleman. And as Syrian men's movements were being increasingly criminalized across the country, Abdullah also constantly worried about how he could get to work safely each day. Relegated to pursuing farm work accessible by motorcycle on the unpatrolled back roads of the Bekaa plains, he spent many periods unemployed between seasonal work and intermittent day jobs.

The conversation with Abdullah revealed the ways that Lebanon's refugee "crisis," while often invoked in the singular noun form, was better understood as a manifold, layered, and fractured tapestry of disparate yet interlinked experiences. These *multiple* crises came together in Syrians' lives in different ways depending on their class, gender, and regional origins. In turn, the disparities between Abdullah's life circumstances and that of *shawīsh* camp residents conveyed the limits not only of the humanitarian crisis concept but also of the very notion of "Syrian refugees" as a collectivity.

COMPOUNDING CRISES AT THE CARCERAL BORDER

As Abdullah's struggles made clear, 2018 and 2019 marked a new phase of economic and political uncertainty for Syrians in Lebanon. Bashar al-Asad was hastily trumpeting "victory" after a summer of recapturing most of Syria's embattled territories, active combat was abating in most regions, popular dissident movements were violently crushed, and a growing anti-Syrian movement in Lebanon was calling for their mass repatriation. Though the Lebanese state lacked the capacity and legal legitimacy to forcibly deport Syrians under the international principle of non-refoulement, its hobbling security apparatus was working to intimidate Syrians into returning through the sheer terror of unpredictability, including a wave of closures of Syrian-owned small businesses, crackdowns on restaurants employing Syrians throughout the country, and the imposition of nighttime curfews across urban neighborhoods and villages. When driving on the main roads, riding with a female relative (or me) up front, dressing in fancy clothes, and even going so far as to hang a crucifix on the rear-view mirror were among the many carefully cultivated forms of disguise that helped my Syrian male friends "pass" as Lebanese and safely reach their destinations. In short, Lebanon's "policy of no policy" was consolidating into a carceral regime policing Syrians' movements as never before. It was in this context of increasing criminalization that farmworkers' everyday talk about debt and mobility converged, a dynamic that became vividly apparent to me during a work shift with Imm Bassam, a resident of Abu Sharif's camp.

"Border checkpoints are getting really strict," Imm Bassam told me as we harvested green beans in early July 2019. "The Lebanese are putting pressure on us from every direction." She recounted to me how her sister's camp in the northern Bekaa town of Arsal had been recently raided by the Lebanese army. "They raided the camp three times and they're not letting anyone leave the camp." She was referring to the high-profile raids and evictions that captivated the attention of UN officials like Carlos.

We were on a piece rate, so Imm Bassam was working quickly with both hands, keeping her body bent over to maintain a steady rhythm, as she swiftly yet gently snapped each bean from the vine with her rubber-gloved fingers and dropped them into a plastic bucket. In the background, I could hear a dispute brewing regarding the piece rate between Abu Khaled, a Lebanese *ḍammān* who oversaw the harvest, and Abu Sharif. They had agreed to set the piece rate at six crates that day, but now Abu Khaled was raising it to seven and a half. Abu Khaled was working to maximize the workers' productivity while the market for green beans was momentarily profitable. Abu Sharif was, for his part, trying to negotiate a more modest piece rate to satisfy the workers, but he wasn't successful this time.

"Curse him" (*Allāh lā ywafaqu*), one of the workers next to us muttered under her breath, as she tossed beans into her bucket. I couldn't tell which of the men she was talking about.

Following the typical gendered division of labor for vegetable work, women, girls, and young boys were harvesting while their teenage and adult male relatives walked periodically between the rows to empty the buckets of green beans into plastic crates. The men's job was to stack and load the full crates onto Abu Khaled's cargo truck for transportation to the open-air agricultural market in Qab Elias. Given that local market prices could fluctuate from one hour to the next, Abu Khaled was calculating in real time the exact number of crates he would need to bring to the market to maximize his earnings.

Imm Bassam's teenage son passed behind us with a crate of beans perched on his right shoulder. "Ya Bassaaam! How much (have I) done [*shgad*

FIGURE 9. Harvesting green beans in July.

ṣārun]? How many [*cham waḥdeh*]?" Imm Bassam called out to him in her heavy northeastern Syrian dialect, without looking up from her work. "*Yalla*, China, go check for me." I walked over to Abu Khaled who was tallying each worker's output on a piece of cardboard. I peered over his shoulder to look at the list. Next to each worker's family name, he was making a tally mark for each crate filled. Many of the teenage women were nearly finished, while the middle-aged women like Imm Bassam were struggling to keep up.

"Yalla ya banāt!" (Come on, girls), Abu Khaled called out. "Qaṣṣarna!" (We're running out of time). Wearing a white cotton scarf wrapped over a baseball cap, Abu Khaled had a gruff, rugged appearance and tanned complexion that revealed a lifetime of hard work. For the past two decades, he had been recruiting workers from Abu Sharif's camp to harvest peas, green beans, onions, and a variety of other vegetables. He knew each worker by name, though he usually just addressed them as "girls" when speaking to them in the aggregate. "Yalla ya banāt!" he shouted again.

We had arrived at work at 1 p.m., and it was now 3:30 p.m. The workers knew that the faster everyone worked, the earlier they could all go back home to the camp. The mostly teenage girls who had finished their mandatory piece rate congregated around the truck, scrolling through TikTok or cracking jokes with the men. A few left to wash their hands in the nearby irrigation ditch or sneak a cigarette, safely hidden from view. The growing crowds of young women who had finished for the day put extra pressure on the stragglers, most of whom, like Imm Bassam, were their mothers.

I walked back to Imm Bassam and crouched down next to her. "You still have three crates to go," I told her apologetically.

"Come help me! I'm exhausted!" she exclaimed with a sigh, plopping her plastic bucket between us. We worked quietly at first, but after a while, we found a swift, meditative rhythm.

Imm Bassam started to tell me about her husband's plans to return to Syria—"but just for a short visit [*bass ziyāra*]." Their eldest son was planning to get married later that year. She and her husband, Abu Bassam, had recently taken out a $3,000 loan from a local NGO to help finance the costs of bridewealth. Abu Bassam was planning to pay a month-long visit to their village in the northeastern Syrian countryside to start building a home next to theirs for the newlyweds-to-be. This was the first time in years that he had contemplated such a trip. As she and other members of the camp explained, the regional economic situation finally seemed to be stabilizing under the Kurdish-led Autonomous Administration of North and East Syria after the Islamic State's caliphate in their village was defeated.

Returning to Syria for the long term, Imm Bassam insisted, was impossible for now. Imm Bassam and Abu Bassam did not consider themselves political dissidents and expressed their desire to return to Syria eventually, but they were not able to relocate their family back to Syria at that time. After all, they were still working off their debts to the NGO and to Abu Sharif. They were also nervous about how they would secure a long-term living as the Syrian pound had experienced a tenfold devaluation.[52] Going for a month-long visit seemed like the most reasonable alternative given that their sources of income and debt obligations remained in Lebanon. But they were concerned about how Abu Bassam would get there, and more importantly, how he would return. Under the Lebanese state's tightening regulations, refugees who entered Syria through the official checkpoint risked being considered to have voluntarily repatriated.

Imm Bassam, Abu Bassam, and their children debated these different options, each of which carried a set of risks, every evening for a week. There was the certainty of going deeper into debt to Abu Sharif to pay for a smuggler, and the less certain possibility of getting caught and deported. There was the certainty of being barred reentry, or at least paying a hefty fee, if he tried to cross in either direction through the official checkpoint. And there was the uncertainty of how long the period of stability in their village would last. In the end, Abu Bassam ended up taking the month-long trip by borrowing money from Abu Sharif to be smuggled in both directions. He borrowed this money very reluctantly, as he and his family were trying to reduce their debt burdens and eventually leave the camp.

Abu Bassam arrived back in Lebanon just in time for the first day of ʿEid al-Aḍḥā, the holy feast of sacrifice, wearing a crisp new *jalabīyya* robe, carrying bags full of medicine and clothes for the children, and something else unexpected: a collection of fake gold watches and plastic prayer beads, which he planned to sell in an open suitcase on the road next to the vegetable market for extra income. All these products were, of course, cheaper in Syria, but buying them put him deeper into debt. His hope was that his short-term investment would yield a profit and ultimately get the family closer to being debt-free.

The scene, taken as a whole, encapsulated the many threads of crisis—writ large and small—that transformed the lives of rural Syrians and Lebanese on both sides of the border for decades before the war began. At a larger scale, there were the histories of migration that brought multiple generations of eastern Syrians like Imm Bassam and her family to Lebanon. There was Abu Khaled's contradictory position as the *ḍammān*, squeezing the workers' time to make a profit, because his livelihood, like so many other Lebanese agriculturalists, depended on it. And there were Syrian farmworkers' proliferating debts to the *shawīsh*.

On a more minute scale, accumulated crises of agrarian life were present in bodily movements. They were apparent in the division of labor in the green bean harvest, as women engaged in the repetitive motion of picking and bending, while the more punctuated work of heavy lifting was left to the young men. They were also present in older men's absence from the scene, except in their names, written in Abu Khaled's handwriting on a piece of cardboard, tallying their female kin's output. Crises resided in the calluses and blisters on Imm Bassam's hands, and in the way she talked about border closures, raids of Syrian camps, and the cost of bridewealth in the same breath.

Crises are often conceived as moments of revelation or transition, and therefore with a capacity to galvanize some kind of unified political action. Yet what makes crises under capitalism so remarkable is precisely that they are born out of *recurrent* contradictions. Crisis, as Ruth Wilson Gilmore notes, "is not objectively bad or good; rather, it signals systemic change whose outcome is determined through struggle."[53] Who bears the burdens of these recurrent crises? How are they embodied and negotiated in daily life?

It is significant that these histories of rural displacement and class differentiation were rarely called "crises." Instead, they were expressed in the aspects of agrarian life that were often the most taken for granted, especially women's labor in the fields, in the home, and across the border that was honed over generations, often in response to the looming threat of indebtedness. The war in Syria brought these debts to light, but the labor that sustained them nevertheless remained mostly invisible. For their supporters and detractors alike, "refugees" seemed to stand for everything that was eventful, galvanizing, and spectacular about Lebanon's crisis, from the border closures to the police raids, to the home demolitions, to the camps that caught on fire. And beneath the clamor of statistics and humanitarian appeals, the Syrian "girls" in the landscape—their worn-out gloves, their chests stuffed with weeds, their bodily pains—seemed to quietly stand for all the struggles that came before, and those that endured.

Two

AGRARIAN AFTERLIVES

IT WAS AN UNUSUALLY HOT MAY AFTERNOON DURING THE HOLY fasting month of Ramadan. I was seated cross-legged next to Imm Hassan on one of the embroidered purple cushions that she had carefully arranged around the perimeter of her family's tent in Abu Sharif's camp. The Bekaa Valley's dusty summer heat had set in early that year, clinging to our sweat-drenched clothing, as an occasional breeze passing below the tent's tarpaulin walls cooled our backs.

Having spent the morning weeding a vineyard while fasting, Imm Hassan and her daughters were utterly exhausted, but we were gathered for a joyful occasion. Imm Hassan's younger brother, Abu Ibrahim, was visiting from Syria for the first time in several years. Unfortunately, as a Syrian national without refugee status, he had already overstayed his maximum three-day visitation rights in Lebanon. He had plans to return to Syria within the coming week, and he was in touch with several smugglers on WhatsApp about the going rate, which seemed to fluctuate daily. Lacking the usual distractions of sweet tea and cigarettes to busy our hands, and trying to forget our growing thirst from the fast, we passed the time by scrolling through old photographs and telling stories.

"Wherever you go, you have water all around you" (*wein ma timshī al-māy ḥawālich*), Imm Hassan told me, as she pulled out her phone to scroll through images of her village and its surroundings in the countryside of al-Raqqa. Many were stock photographs and video montages of the Euphrates Dam that regularly circulated on her TikTok network, some set to regional *dabke* music.

Abu Ibrahim was seated across from us, bearing a dimpled grin that was somewhere between smug and expectant. Dressed in a gray *jalabīyya* robe, he was leaning forward with his hands on his knees as though preparing to deliver a punchline or joke but barely cast a glance at her phone. It was clear that he'd seen these images many times before.

Imm Hassan held up her phone for me to see a stock image of Qalʿat Jaʿbar, a castle perched on a hill overlooking the Euphrates Valley. Though the castle's fortifications extend back to the eleventh century, she explained that it was surrounded by water only a few decades ago when the Euphrates Dam was constructed. It is now an island in an artificial lake named after Hafiz al-Asad—the former president of Syria and the late father of Bashar al-Asad.

"That's where our village used to be!" Abu Ibrahim exclaimed suddenly.

I looked at him, baffled.

"We are the *maghmūrīn*," he said with a smile, enunciating the word carefully. "Have you heard of us?"

"The drowned?" I asked.

"The drowned. That's what we're called. Our houses went away [*buyūtnā rāḥu*]. . . . Our village is under Lake Asad now." Abu Ibrahim was speaking with an air of pragmatism, even nonchalance, as though he were sharing something as banal as street directions. "If you ask anyone in Qamishli, 'Where is the *maghmūrīn* land?', they will know it and point it out to you."

As I learned over the course of many subsequent conversations, their father's village was one of dozens that were submerged by the raising of the Euphrates Dam in the early 1970s, just a few years after Hafiz al-Asad took power. The Syrian state relocated their family to a village further downstream and compensated them with five hundred *dūnam* (50 hectares) of rain-fed land in Qamishli, the Kurdish-majority region situated along Syria's northeast border with Türkiye. This land was then split among five sons, including Abu Ibrahim. In addition to the land they received in compensation, their father, and eventually his sons, became employees on a state-owned farm.

"Look at the floodgates!" Imm Hassan chimed in, as she turned her phone to reveal a video of water descending forcefully from the dam. This was the site of the flooded village of Tabqa that was renamed Medīnat al-Thawra (Revolution City) when the Euphrates Dam was completed. "See how powerful the water pressure is? It produces electricity," she said, grinning widely.

"But weren't people upset about being displaced?" I asked, somewhat taken aback by her enthusiasm.

"Ilāaaa," Imm Hassan replied, still smiling, using a common linguistic interjection from the *shāwi* Arabic dialect that usually means "Of course" or "Obviously," but here it carried a tone of weary acceptance, something closer to "Well, that's just how it is."

She continued scrolling through what looked to be dozens of images and videos of the dam collected from her social media networks, interspersed occasionally with other more recent photographs that she had taken herself or received from relatives over WhatsApp. Her face darkened as she lingered for a moment over a slightly blurry picture of her late husband, Abu Hassan, who had suddenly passed away from a stroke earlier that year. It was a photograph of a photograph, likely sent to her by her son who had remained in Syria and cared for the family's belongings throughout the war. In the picture, Abu Hassan was driving a tractor and wearing his signature *jimdāna* checkered scarf.[1]

I remembered how Imm Hassan had told me in a previous conversation, leaning over a hoe as she took a short break from weeding, that Abu Hassan had started migrating seasonally to Lebanon and Jordan to work as a tractor driver because he was from a landless family and needed the extra income. Though her own family, as descendants of the *maghmūrīn,* had received some land in compensation from the Syrian state, I gathered that Imm Hassan had effectively renounced any claim to this land when she got married to him, following patrilocal custom. And, as I learned later, even those families that had been compensated eventually depended on labor migration in the decades that followed the dam's construction.

"May God have mercy on him," she murmured, and moved on to the next photo.

Much as I described the meanings of "crisis" in the previous chapter, this conversation conveyed how certain forms of displacement, especially in their quotidian forms, reside subtly in the margins of more spectacular events. With extensive technical and financial support from the Soviet Union, the Euphrates Dam project became the central pillar and icon of the Baʿth Party's plans for rural development. As part of a broader wave of state-led redistributive land reform spreading across the decolonizing world, Syrian state planners envisioned the creation of a modern irrigation network and the extension of electricity throughout Syria's poorest provinces. Displaced by the flooding of the dam, the *maghmūrīn* were expected to be the vanguard of Syria's "Pilot Project," model agricultural communities forming the building blocks of Arab socialism.[2] By harnessing the hydropower of the Euphrates River, the dam promised to transform the downtrodden inhabitants of Syria's northeastern Jazīra region into revolutionary peasants on state farms, emancipating them from tribal bonds, servile labor, and the forces of "backwardness" (*al-takhalluf*).

Five decades removed from the heyday of land reform, the Euphrates region is better known today around the world as the former capital of the Islamic State and the heart of the Kurdish struggle for autonomy. Yet the contested legacies of this project retained enduring significance among the *maghmūrīn*'s descendants like Imm Hassan and Abu Ibrahim, which they routinely invoked in their everyday habits and ways of speaking about the past. In this chapter, I present a series of ethnographic encounters with these descendants of the *maghmūrīn* who became farmworkers in the Bekaa Valley. How, I ask, were the struggles, promises, and losses associated with this era of agrarian reform resurrected under contemporary conditions of wartime displacement, particularly by those who stood to gain, or lose, the most from it?

This chapter builds on this book's larger aim to fundamentally rethink the politics of displacement through the lens of agrarian life. As I argued in the previous chapter, the modern refugee is typically understood as a figure of catastrophic events and crises. "Refugee" is a powerful political and legal category that is often deployed in contrast to other forms of displacement, particularly labor migration. The humanitarian designation of a refugee crisis, as such, often obscures the diverse historical factors that govern mobility and narrows the frame of what is deemed properly political or worthy of redress—including, as in the case of Syrian farmworkers, the inherited legacies of state-led development.

From the submersion of their villages to the decades of seasonal out-migration that followed it, rural eastern Syrians like Imm Hassan were not only uprooted by war but had experienced waves of direct and indirect displacement in the wake of land reform. Displaced yet again in 2011 by the Syrian conflict, their experiences as refugees were continuously refracted through attachments to those layered and seemingly more distant agrarian pasts.

It is telling that the word for displacement in Arabic, *nuzūḥ*, has an etymological tie to the drying up of water in a well.[3] *Ba'th*, in turn, means resurrection. These are more than linguistic affinities; they gesture to a haunting past and ideal future that deeply structured how rural eastern Syrians like Imm Hassan and Abu Ibrahim were conscripted as rural subjects within the Syrian state and subsequently forged their aspirations. Exchanged against the backdrop of war, their narratives about the dam served as a claim to past injuries and future guarantees that the state would rectify the *maghmūrīn*'s sacrifices through the fruits of rural development. Such expectations of improvement, however, sat in tension with their ongoing and inherited material predicaments, including a history of out-migration and labor exploitation spanning generations. Some, like Imm Hassan's father, were given small tracts of land in compensation and became employees of state-owned farms. Others never received compensation.

And despite the promise of stability, most of the *maghmūrīn* were unable to derive a secure livelihood from state-led farming alone. Throughout the decades that followed the dam's construction, the *maghmūrīn* supplemented household incomes through seasonal migration abroad and squeezing women's unremunerated labor in subsistence agriculture and animal husbandry. Out-migration continued as these state-owned farms were eventually privatized and distributed in small parcels to their former employees in the early 2000s during Syria's liberalized transition to the "social market economy" under Bashar al-Asad.[4] When the Syrian uprising began in 2011, many of the first protests took place in rural and peri-urban areas coping with economic dislocation. As this popular uprising devolved into a brutal conflict, it was the rural poor of Syria who bore the brunt of the devastation. Many of the *maghmūrīn* and their descendants, like Imm Hassan, sought long-term refuge in *shawīsh* camps in Lebanon, while others, like Abu Ibrahim and Imm Hassan's two eldest sons, made the difficult decision to stay behind.

Emblematic of what critical agrarian scholars refer to as the "migration-development nexus,"[5] the *maghmūrīn*'s intergenerational struggles ultimately reveal an aspect of displacement that is often overlooked in studies of refugees: the decades-long interconnections between agrarian change, the making and unmaking of land reform, and rural displacement across the world.[6] By approaching the *maghmūrīn*'s displacements as an ongoing afterlife of agrarian developmentalism embedded within their everyday lives as refugee farmworkers, this chapter thus brings a critical agrarian perspective to a diverse body of scholarship on the mediation of memory[7] and the shifting afterlives of modern political imaginaries in the wake of crisis, conflict, and revolution.[8] Inherited as debts to an unresolved past and attachment to a yet-unfulfilled promise of a stable future, what emerges from these farmworkers' accounts is a picture of wartime exile not only as a rupture but also as an ongoing process, defined by decades of cyclical economic instability, unraveling guarantees, and recursive loss, where the "end" of displacement remained in a state of continuous deferral.

RESURRECTING THE DEVELOPMENTALIST STATE: THE INHERITANCE OF DISPLACEMENT

I was first introduced to Imm Hassan's family just a few weeks before her husband, Abu Hassan, passed away. A boisterous middle-aged woman with bright blue eyes, she was considered one of the "original" (*aṣli*) members of Abu Sharif's camp—that is, the families who began migrating seasonally to his camp before the Syrian uprising began in 2011. As one of the central matriarchal figures within the neighborly life of the camp, she had the unique virtue of being both a consummate host and a gracious guest and was one of the few women in the camp who could comfortably sit among a group of men and command their attention. Even while in mourning, she exuded a magnetic warmth that brought levity to even the heaviest conversations. Shrouded in a black hijab and black abaya since the day he passed away, she relished sharing stories about Abu Hassan, particularly memories of him from before the war. Storytelling, I sensed, not only buoyed her in this time of immense grief but also was a constant reminder to herself and those around her that life once was, and therefore *could be,* more secure.

Among the many significant moments from my fieldwork, I often come back to that Ramadan afternoon when I learned that Imm Hassan and her brother were descendants of the *maghmūrīn*. Above all, I remember the jarring contrast between the intimate picture-of-a-picture of Abu Hassan and the stock images of the Euphrates Dam she had culled from her social media networks. Taken in the 1990s when Abu Hassan started migrating abroad to work as a tractor driver to supplement the family's income, the image hung in silent abeyance, somehow painfully inscrutable in the flow of celebratory conversation about the dam's achievements.

The photograph of Abu Hassan, and the ways that it interrupted the flow of iconic dam images, carried dual significance. It revealed a history of out-migration from eastern Syria that stubbornly contradicted the economic security that land reform was, in principle, meant to guarantee for Syria's poorest agriculturalists. And it was a brief, poignant reminder of Imm Hassan's longing to return to Syria. She had been lately receiving nightly dream visitations from Abu Hassan's ghost beseeching her to come back to Syria now that his soul was properly laid to rest. However, as she lamented to me time and again, she and her children were thousands of dollars in debt to Abu Sharif, the *shawīsh* who served as the moneylender, patron, and labor broker of the camp where they were living, effectively preventing their return.

Like many other agriculturalists from the Jazīra, Imm Hassan and her brother remained deeply attached to narrating eastern Syria's agrarian history—and their place within it—in terms of the officially state-sanctioned history of Baʿthist development and progress. In Abu Ibrahim's words, "The dam brought development [*al-taṭawwir*]. . . . Before the dam, all our houses were made of mud and straw [*tīn u tibn*]. Raqqa was nothing before the dam came. Everyone stole in order to live [*kānat al-ʿālam tasruq u taʿīsh*]."

"And now we have houses made of concrete [*bāṭūn*] with multiple floors [*ṭawābiq*]," Imm Hassan added. "We cultivate everything where we're from. Cotton, wheat, vegetables, chickpeas, olives, melon . . . flowers as far as you can see [*ʿala mud nazrich tshūfī wurūd*]."

Abu Ibrahim's highly stylized emphasis on the transition from "mud" to "concrete" exemplified how official Baʿthist slogans of progress shaped their ways of talking about the past, as state-mediated ideals of rural development provided the metanarrative framework through which they emplotted their family history. This was clear not only from their references to material transformations in the built environment and the electrification of eastern Syria but also in their enthusiasm about cultivating "everything," an implicit reference to the shift from rain-fed agriculture to irrigated agriculture that the dam promised to enable. Notably, Imm Hassan's effusiveness about the dam's power was matched by a seemingly dispassionate attitude toward what it cost her family, as she calmly refused to perform pathos or dwell in tragedy when I pressed her in our conversation.

Despite these promises of stability, Imm Hassan and Abu Hassan—like many eastern Syrians—had become accustomed to long periods of precarity and familial separation well before the war began. Characteristic of how translocal agrarian households depend on "invisible economies of care"[9] across the world, their family was sustained by a delicate balance between seasonal flows of remittances from Abu Hassan's work as a tractor driver alongside Imm Hassan's work in subsistence agriculture and livestock in their home village. They also kept their household costs low by taking advantage of Syria's low-cost and free public services, including schooling for their children and healthcare, which are privatized and comparatively costly in Lebanon. As Imm Hassan put it to me, "Everything [in Syria] was cheap [*kul shi balāsh*]."

Eventually, Abu Hassan's remittances were no longer sufficient to sustain them. In 2006, Imm Hassan and her children joined scores of other eastern Syrians who began migrating westward to seek waged labor opportunities in the face of compounding ecological and economic pressures. Working in a variety of summer crops, they were initially recruited by a *shawīsh* in Baalbek and were later connected to Abu Sharif.

As the 2011 uprising in Syria gave way to militarization, state repression, and popular strife, their village became engulfed in a series of battles and offensives known as the Raqqa Campaign (2012–13), culminating in the Battle of Raqqa and takeover by the Islamic State (2014–17).[10] Throughout this period, Imm Hassan and Abu Hassan joined the legions of seasonal labor migrants who sought long-term refuge in *shawīsh* camps, as the second Raqqa Campaign raged on from 2016 to 2017, culminating in the tenuous victory of the Kurdish-led Syrian Democratic Forces in October 2017 and the proclaimed "defeat" of the caliphate in March 2019.[11]

Though registered as refugees, they rarely, if ever, used this word to describe themselves. It was during those long Ramadan hours spent with Imm Hassan's family that I came to understand why that might have been the case. For the *maghmūrīn* and many other eastern Syrians who had migrated to Lebanon for years or even decades before the war, displacement was a layered inheritance of land reform whose afterlives were deeply embodied in their everyday labor and long-standing dependence on seasonal migration across borders. Inheritance, as such, meant coming to terms with a debt that was "never at one with itself" insofar as their wartime uprooting carried continuities to multiple, unresolved displacements from the past.[12] Inheritance implied that they remained in debt to the struggles that came before them, whether this debt was acknowledged, unconscious, or disavowed. Unlike the idea of a "refugee crisis" as an acute emergency, these inherited laboring conditions were generalized, protracted, and familiar to the point of being unremarkable. As a member of Imm Hassan's camp put it to me with resigned simplicity: "From bed to work, that's our life" (*min al-farshe lil-warshe, ḥayātnā haich*).

This is a predicament that Imm Hassan shared in common with many rural labor migrants across the world. As high-modern ideals of development have given way to austerity and widening economic inequalities regionally and globally, the promises of statist developmentalism remain tension ridden, contradictory, and deeply present in everyday agrarian life. David Scott famously described this as the transition from "anticolonial utopias" to "postcolonial nightmares."[13] For many of the world's poorest agriculturalists—the landless and the land-poor—this is experienced as a growing gap between a state-led promise of stability and a reality of their deepening dependence on labor migration.

Imm Hassan's handling of the different photographs conveyed this sense of fractured inheritance. While Imm Hassan and Abu Ibrahim recited narratives about rural development with almost script-like jubilation as they beheld iconic images of the dam, other histories of displacement—decades of labor migration abroad, everyday struggles with a loss of seasonal mobility, Abu Ibrahim's dependence on a smuggler, and Imm Hassan's mounting debts—remained hauntingly latent in the margins. If the submersion of their villages and their forcible relocation were somehow intelligible as the price paid for "progress," this state-led metanarrative appeared to reach its limit when confronted with their ongoing material predicament as displaced seasonal labor migrants.

Their orientation to the Ba'thist state spoke to the massive social and economic disparities that were brought into tension by the war. Within the fractured terrain of competing Syrian nationalist imaginaries, Imm Hassan, Abu Ibrahim, and their ancestors are sometimes called "Arabs" (as opposed to Kurds) or more specifically *shawāya*. Generally referring to pastoralists from northeastern Syria and western Iraq, the term has an ambiguous etymology. Among Syrian urbanites, the word *shawāya* has pejorative connotations, meaning something akin to "country bumpkin." It was nevertheless a very common and even proud self-designation among residents of Abu Sharif's camp, who claimed that it comes from the verb *shāwi* (to grill), a mark of their reputation for generosity as "those who grill meat."[14] Distinct from camel-herding Bedouin who trace their origins to the Najd in the Arabian Peninsula, *shawāya* were historically sheep and goat herders.[15] While the term likely derives from *shāa* (a less commonly used word for sheep), others have linked it to the word *shway*, meaning "people of little consequence."[16]

The polysemy of the term was revealing in itself and representative of the class anxieties that were often projected onto Syrian labor migrants long before the war began, particularly those from the Euphrates region. Rural eastern Syrian villagers became a familiar sight across Syria's urban peripheries and Lebanon's countryside over the past several decades, as unprecedented numbers of men from this region, and later women, migrated for work. Some, like Abu Sharif and those wealthier than him, bought up property in Aleppo and started entering skilled trades and brokerage, much to the dismay of the "real" urbanites.[17] But most were precarized agriculturalists migrating in pursuit of cash wages to support their families and prevent a slide into indebtedness, including many of the *maghmūrīn* and their descendants. Against this backdrop, rural eastern Syrians like Abu Hassan found themselves caught between an old Ba'thist discourse that positioned them as the "backward" subjects of rural uplift, on the one hand, and an increasingly entrenched urban middle-class and elite discourse that constantly belittled them, on the other.

That these conversations took place against the wartime backdrop of Baʿthism's twilight, and creeping retrenchment, was also significant. Circulated widely among Imm Hassan's networks of friends and family as representations of prewar stability, iconic images of the dam's achievements demanded commentary precisely because they were in an ongoing state of destruction and withdrawal. This particular conversation with Imm Hassan and Abu Ibrahim took place in mid-2019, after the Syrian Democratic Forces had declared victory over the Islamic State's caliphate and were consolidating their Autonomous Administration in the Euphrates region. At the time, the Syrian Democratic Forces were receiving extensive US military backing, and Imm Hassan's second-eldest son was working as a non-Kurdish Arab auxiliary member. Though Imm Hassan did not seem especially committed to either the Kurdish political project or US military involvement in Syria, she was proud that her son was making, according to her estimate, around $200 per month. That this wage was paid in US dollars was significant in Syria's sanctioned and cash-strapped economy.

Vacillating between celebratory slogans and oblique acknowledgements of what they lost, talk of the Euphrates Dam and Syria's agrarian reforms stood in for a broader attachment to a prewar life that was, as they so often put it, *maḍmūn* (guaranteed). "We wish we could return, but there is no source of livelihood in Syria right now" was a sentiment I encountered frequently, often accompanied by impassioned, rose-colored references to prewar economic security and comfort, evidenced by expressions such as "We were all comfortable before the war" and "No one was in need except a few." Even among those who quietly acknowledged the hardships of prewar Syria, many described that time as one of "poverty with dignity" and "stability" (*istiqrār*). Embedded in this notion of dignity was a longing for the social entitlements once guaranteed by the Syrian welfare state, encapsulated in the familiar populist refrain: "Syria was the mother of the poor [*umm al-faqīr*]."

This sense of optimistic investment in the prewar Syrian state—and more specifically Hafiz-era developmentalism—stood in obvious contrast to the perspectives of my middle-class Syrian friends in Lebanon and the diaspora, especially those who were explicitly supportive of the 2011 uprising. Imm Hassan's and Abu Ibrahim's insistence on maintaining continuity to Syria's socialist past also sat at odds with the new generation of urban, upwardly mobile Syrians who had embraced the market-oriented promises of Syria's neoliberal transition.[18] And although Imm Hassan never shared with me her views on the 2011 uprising itself, I sensed that there was little space for her perspective within the contested terrain of Syrian opposition movements that either ignored the *shawāya* or readily dismissed them as simple-minded apparatchiks of the regime.[19] What this suggested was that, although every Syrian was touched by the 2011 uprising-turned-war and its aftermaths, they did not experience its losses equally, evenly, nor equivalently. In a significant sense, this unevenness reflected how rural-urban disparities (both imagined and material) mapped onto Syrians' concepts of their past and present and expectations for the future. It also signaled how rural eastern Syrians were uniquely interpellated within the Ba'thist state through the promises of agrarian reform.

As a commentary about the past, the idioms of "stability" and "guarantee" indexed both an idealized relationship to the Syrian state, on the one hand, and the material pursuit of a sufficient livelihood as agriculturalists, on the other.[20] The latter spoke to the basic precepts of a "subsistence ethic," understood in the broadest sense as a historically contingent tendency among subsistence-oriented farmers to seek out conditions that ensure the stability of their incomes.[21] The former, in turn, conveyed how the Ba'thist state—as in other cases of agrarian reform—conscripted rural masses into the nationalist project by positioning itself as the preeminent guarantor of that stability. As Lisa Wedeen notes in her research on Syria, ideals of order were part of a decades-old nationalist repertoire that was taken up in incommensurate ways by different segments of the Syrian public as its economy liberalized. While many urban Syrians fused an attachment to order with a vision of market-oriented prosperity, Jazīrans like Imm Hassan represented the contingent of Syrians who never fully abandoned a sense of entitlement and moral attachment to the welfare state, even as the state progressively retreated from this role long before the war began.[22]

This attachment to prewar stability was also a claim about the wartime *present*: namely, their struggles to survive the cost of living in Lebanon year-round as refugees. Imm Hassan and her neighbors often juxtaposed the Syrian welfare state (or what they selectively remembered it to be) against a life that was *muḍayaqa* (stifling) in Lebanon, where the cost of living was comparatively high. Relegated to Lebanon's patchwork of privatized social services and limited streams of humanitarian aid, camp residents constantly lamented the loss of free healthcare, schooling, and subsidized goods they used to enjoy during return migrations. Instead of geopolitics, day-to-day talk about the war in Abu Sharif's camp revolved around economic matters, such as the devaluation of the Lebanese lira and the Syrian pound, growing remittance obligations, the loss of income from their land in Syria, the costs of rehabilitating their homes, and, most importantly, their proliferating debts to the *shawīsh*. "Here in Lebanon, work is eating us up," Imm Hassan's son once lamented to me, exhausted from spending his days working intermittently with his mother and sisters in agriculture and his evenings DJing at weddings across Lebanon. "There's nothing and no one to catch you if you fall. If you don't work, you starve."

It was against this backdrop of wartime economic precarity that Syria's heyday of agrarian developmentalism took on newfound significance as a mirror and counterpoint to their everyday lives as precarized refugees. More than a nostalgic yearning for the past, these were scenes of optimistic attachment to the promise of state-backed stability that, as Berlant puts it, "makes life bearable as it presents itself ambivalently, unevenly, incoherently."[23] Here, this unevenness was most acutely evident in the ways that the *maghmūrīn* and their descendants selectively countenanced their experiences with displacement. While the submersion of Imm Hassan's grandfather's village was a singular, final, and irreversibly tragic event that was *legible*, nonetheless, through a broader state-mediated narrative about agrarian progress, the conditions of her family's wartime displacement were multiple, structurally invisible to state narratives, and could not be encapsulated by the retelling of one event. The inscrutability of these latter forms of displacement resonated with other postsocialist contexts, where communities long accustomed to the socialist state experienced the end of the Cold War as a collapse of signification and an acute state of uncertainty.[24] Yet, Imm Hassan's dilemma was distinct in that it was not only an aftermath of the Cold War but also a proliferation of aftermaths: an uneven state-led agrarian transformation, the postsocialist unmaking of this promise, a crushed popular uprising, and a seemingly endless war. Born out of the shifting imperatives of agrarian survival spanning three generations, these afterlives were the material form through which different arcs of life histories could be remarked upon, silenced, or mourned.

THE TIME OF "BACKWARDNESS": SPECTERS OF THE *SHAYKH*

A few weeks after my conversation with Abu Ibrahim and Imm Hassan, I met Ahmad, another descendant of the *maghmūrīn*, during the spring cherry harvest with a group of "free workers" (*shaghīl ḥurr*). I had been invited to join the harvest by Abu Charbel, the Lebanese contract farmer I introduced in the previous chapter, who seasonally recruited Syrian farmworkers for harvests throughout Lebanon's May to November high season. Though most of these workers were registered as refugees, some had been migrating seasonally to Lebanon for decades. I had gotten to know many of these women and men quite well over the past year as Abu Charbel had allowed me to shadow his work team during the autumn grape harvest six months earlier. Ahmad was a newcomer who had joined the cherry harvest that day to supplement his usual day-job as a *ballāṭ* (tiler).

Tall and lanky, sprightly but soft spoken, Ahmad was seated above me on the crook of a cherry tree, his legs straddling a thick branch on which his bucket of cherries hung before him. Khadija, one of the other workers who knew me from previous harvest work, was seated on the ground, separating the underripe cherries from the juicy ones, as they would command different prices on the local market. Ahmad gently pulled the leaves aside to peer down at me as Khadija introduced my project to him in her own words. "She's doing a sociological research project [*baḥth ijtimāʿī*] about the struggles of Syrian workers," she shouted up to him. "You know, how our life was before, how it turned out. . . . Right?" A broad smile spread across Ahmad's face as Khadija spoke; he told me that he was relieved that I was not a humanitarian worker, as he was tired of their, in his words, "empty promises." I shared more about my research and asked him if he could tell me about his work history and how he ended up in Lebanon, and he obliged. The three of us carried on harvesting as we talked.

Over the course of our conversation, I learned that Ahmad was from the flooded village of Tabqa, which was renamed "Revolution City" when it became the site of the Euphrates Dam. Ahmad used to work in a state-owned yogurt factory while saving up for bridewealth and land on which to build a house in his village. To supplement his income, he began seasonally migrating to Lebanon in the early 2000s, where he could secure a higher wage for work in construction and agriculture. At the time we met, it had been more than five years since he had returned to Syria because he was *maṭlūb lil-jaysh*—that is, he was avoiding army conscription amid Syria's ongoing conflict, a strange paradox given his professed support for the regime.

"The state gave my grandfather an option," he told me, when I asked if his grandfather was compensated for the flooding of their village. "He could choose between an urban dwelling [*manzil*] in Damascus or agricultural land in Qamishli."

He paused and cracked a smile. "Well, *unfortunately*, my grandfather picked the agricultural land! And now I'm stuck with a few useless *dūnam* of rain-fed land all the way in Qamishli!"

Like Imm Hassan and Abu Ibrahim, Ahmad countenanced his family's displacement throughout our conversation in terms of the dam's broader achievements for the region as a whole—the spread of electricity, irrigated agriculture, mass schooling, growing literacy, roads and infrastructure, and state employment opportunities—in contrast to a "backward" past marked by poverty and inequality.

"Before the dam, we had *iqṭāʿiyya*," he explained, referring to the Ottoman institution of large landed estates that predated the spread of capitalism in the region. "There were powerful tribal *shaykhs* with vast lands. Everyone worked for them as sharecroppers. Including my relatives." Here, Ahmad was rehearsing the Baʿth Party's official rhetoric about Syria's Jazīra region as "held back" by *iqṭāʿiyya*. Though his discourse implied that this condition of agrarian servility was long standing, he was likely referring to an ascendant class of sheep and goat herding tribal clan leaders who were enriched by the development of mechanized capitalist agriculture in the Jazīra region through the expansion of cotton cultivation in the 1950s, known as "cotton *shaykhs*."[25]

"And what changed after the dam?" I asked him.

"We became employees [*muwaẓẓafīn*] of the state, and they killed *iqṭāʿiyya*," he replied matter-of-factly.

"Who killed *iqṭāʿiyya*?"

"The state killed *iqṭāʿiyya* completely," he told me, and then switched to the present tense, as though speaking of an enduring, ongoing condition. "What I mean is that from that point onward, you no longer have any relation to anyone [*mā ilik ay ʿalāqa bi-shakhs*]. You're now under the care of the state [*riʿāyat al-dawla*]."

Ahmad's personification of the state as the force that "killed" *iqṭāʿiyya* and superseded personalistic, servile forms of labor conveyed the particular centrality of Syria's Jazīra region to the Baʿth Party's developmentalist imaginary, and, in turn, the ways that Jazīrans like him were interpellated as subjects of agrarian reform. Yet, until today, the Jazīra is racked by poverty and inequality, with some of the highest rates of illiteracy and out-migration in the country. Indeed, as Ahmad explained his own labor history over the course of our conversation in more depth, this neat division between an exploitative, servile past and a comfortable, equitable present began to break down, as it became clear that the land and employment they received in compensation was insufficient to cover a rising cost of living. It was also evident in Ahmad's darkly humorous reference to the uselessness of the tiny, rain-fed tract of land that the state bequeathed to his grandfather, partitioned into smaller bits with each passing generation. Further, for all the talk of overcoming "backwardness," Ahmad, Imm Hassan, Abu Ibrahim, and the other eastern Syrians I met remained deeply attached to their tribal clans as a form of collective self-identification, as the figure of the "tribal *shaykh*" hung like a specter over seeming breaks with the past.

The Baʿth Party's rise to power in 1963 was, above all, a rural rebellion against the inequalities of Syria's traditional agrarian structure, a culmination of two decades of political tumult following Syria's independence from the French colonial mandate. As part of a broader global historical conjuncture of developmentalist planning and Cold War political alignments from the 1950s to the 1970s, land reform was at the heart of decolonizing states' plans for food self-sufficiency and emancipation from colonial land tenure systems. The stakes of this struggle were high in Syria; according to one estimate, around the time of independence, the wealthiest 10 percent of Syria's population claimed 87 percent of land as private property, two-thirds of whom were absentees, and irrigated land was even more unequally distributed.[26]

In this context, eastern Syria's Jazīra region figured centrally within a nascent agrarian developmentalist imaginary about the problem of *iqṭāʿiyya*, an Ottoman mode of tenure that expanded in the region as the Levant became increasingly integrated into the world economy around the turn of the twentieth century. Opposition to *iqṭāʿiyya* was linked to a broader ideological indictment against "traditional" bonds, as tribalism, sectarianism, ethnonationalism, and regionalism were considered "dangerous social diseases" that needed to be overcome so that the unifying force of "Arabism" could prevail.[27]

Yet, in practice, tribalism could not be so easily assimilated to a bygone era, as it was intimately tied up in processes of agrarian capital accumulation in the region. *Iqṭāʿ* land tenure consolidated during the interwar period of French and British mandatory rule, as colonial authorities registered formal land titles to various tribal chiefs across eastern Syria and western Iraq.[28] Under the French Mandate in Syria and Lebanon, colonial officials distinguished between the "real Bedouin," in whose name they registered land titles, and the *shawāya*, agro-pastoral clans of a lower status.

The ancestors of Ahmad, Imm Hassan, and Abu Ibrahim, as members of al-Walda clan,[29] were considered *shawāya*. "Our lineage is named after the color of the goat's milk," Abu Ibrahim once told me, laughing self-deprecatingly as he motioned with his hands the movements of milking a goat. As mentioned earlier, the term refers to pastoralists who herd goats and sheep as their main source of livelihood, therefore of a lower status than camel herders. In contrast to the "pure" Bedouin, administrators of tribal affairs for the French High Commissioner of the Levant characterized the *shawāya* as "semisedentary tribes" or "degenerate Bedouin" who had lost their noble virtues and were stereotypically associated with lying, theft, and impropriety.[30]

During the cotton boom of the 1950s, eastern Syria witnessed the emergence of "cotton *shaykhs*," an upwardly mobile class of enterprising *shawāya* who capitalized on the introduction of mechanized production to the Jazīra region. The land along the banks of the Euphrates was filled with overgrown brush and thistle, and *shāwi* chiefs took it upon themselves to clear it when urban traders from Aleppo began renting land in the Jazīra region to cultivate cotton.[31] These tribal leaders hired labor, often from their own clans, to clear the land and install diesel-powered irrigation pumps, thereby claiming this land as private property through a customary practice known as *waḍʿ al-yad*.[32] As the Korean War generated worldwide demand for cotton and global prices soared, cotton quickly became the most important cash crop in eastern Syria, and this new class of cotton *shaykhs* consolidated. In the mid-1950s, the Syrian government abolished the French Mandate–era tribal law that had granted Bedouin tribes autonomous status, and its unintended effect was that it further formalized cotton *shaykhs*' claims to land.

Given their mediating role in the expansion of capitalist agriculture in the Euphrates region, the figure of the *shaykh* was central to many Syrians' narratives about everyday life in the Jazīra before the advent of the dam. In keeping with the Baʿthist narrative, the *shaykh* sometimes stood for an exploitative landlord. As evidenced in Ahmad's earlier references to "*shaykhs*" and "sharecroppers," the majority of *shawāya* who lacked land titles became wage laborers or sharecroppers (*murabbāʿin*) on the land of their fellow kinsmen, which contributed to their increasing sedentarization along the Euphrates, while they maintained sheep raising and dry-land farming in the steppe.[33] Yet in other accounts, the *shaykh* appeared as a figure of caregiving, protection, and simpler times.

Abu Ibrahim's narratives moved seamlessly between two figurations: *shaykhs* as caregivers and exploiters. "In the olden days [*awali*], there were *shaykhs* with lots of sheep," he once told me. "So our forefathers [*ajdādnā*] would sneak into the herd and steal some milk. Or . . . they would break into the *shaykh*'s goat-hair tent [*bayt shaʿr*] and steal his gold jewelry." As he repeated to me on several occasions with great sincerity, his grandfather had no choice but to "steal for a living" before the dam came. The trope of stealing, which came up frequently in my friends' narratives about eastern Syria, appeared to be their vernacular version of the Baʿth Party's rhetoric about the region's "backward" past. However, when speaking about the specific history of the Walda clan or other tribal clans in the region, Abu Ibrahim spoke wistfully of the pre-dam era as the *ayyām al-baraka*—"the days of blessings"—a time of greater simplicity, social cohesion, and tribal solidarity.

Imm Hassan's narratives, for her part, tended to collapse the *shaykh* into a singular composite figure of what came "before" the dam. "In the olden days before my brother and I were born, there were *shaykhs* and slaves [*bī shuyūkh u ʿabīd*]," Imm Hassan once told me as I helped her remove the carpets and floor pillows of her tent to prepare for a deep spring cleaning.

"What did slaves do?" I asked her, as Imm Hassan dumped a bucket of soapy water onto the concrete floor, spreading the water around the perimeter of the tent with the rubber blade of a large squeegee. The water quickly turned gray from particles of soil and gravel that, despite Imm Hassan's best efforts, inevitably made their way inside past the flimsy tarpaulin.

"They would milk sheep, gather wood, and transport water. They'd go, gather, unload, return. And repeat. All day long," Imm Hassan huffed, as she flicked the dirty water out of the tent onto the surrounding gravel with her squeegee in swift bursts. She paused to take a breath. "They needed to work after all, no?" (*muḥtājīn li-shughl, mū*).

"Were . . . your relatives considered slaves?" I stammered, grasping for the appropriate way to ask.

"Noooooo," she retorted emphatically, tsking her tongue. "Slaves were . . . how shall I put it? The needy [*miskīn*]. People who had no one." By this, she meant those who fit within the category of "needy" within Islamic jurisprudence, especially those without a male breadwinner, such as orphans and widows, as well as the sick and the disabled.[34]

In the eastern Syrian context, *ʿabd* ("slave") referred to a person bound in servitude to a tribal *shaykh*, though the ways eastern Syrians themselves recalled and described this relationship were distinctly gendered. In her research among self-identified descendants of *ʿabīd* in Qamishli, for example, Noriko Sato found that women described bondage primarily in terms of deprivation and hunger, emphasizing that they could not even afford wheat bread.[35] Their recollections often centered on domestic obligations within the *shaykh*'s household—washing, cooking, cleaning—and on the sense of being beholden to his wives and children. Men, in contrast, tended to describe their dependence in political rather than domestic terms, focusing on their client-like attachment to the *shaykh* himself and the obligations and connections this entailed, often using the phrase "attached to the shaykh" (*tābiʿ ilā al-shaykh*).

Other research on eastern Syrians has also linked this dualistic register to a distinctly gendered politics of narrative. In her path-breaking research with descendants of the *maghmūrīn*, Katharina Lange found a divergence between, on the one hand, "official" regional histories of tribal deeds and heroic battles over which male elders claimed authoritative knowledge, and, on the other, various forms of "submerged" histories, mostly shared by women, that often obliquely addressed histories of social and economic loss, including the consequences of the Euphrates Dam, while avoiding explicitly critical commentary on Baʿthist modernization.[36] Words exchanged *through* processes of seasonal labor—weeding or harvesting together, stuffing a comforter with raw wool, or making vegetable preserves—often became conversations *about* labor: wage rates, the nature of the work in which we were engaged, feelings of exhaustion, frustration with their household workload relative to male members, and more. As in Imm Hassan's case, these more visceral, embodied ways of speaking about the past often revolved around the touching or handling of objects such as photographs, working tools, or food items.[37]

In this context, Imm Hassan's dogged insistence about what came "before" the dam was a significant claim about her family's history: her ancestors were *never* slaves and slavery was *in the past*. Her attachment to the "pastness" of slavery revealed its enduring power precisely in the ways that it furnished the grounds for making her sense of living "after" it imaginable. It was as much a commentary on land reform's emancipatory promises as it was a more tacit expression of how eastern Syrians like her—particularly women—were living in the wake of its partial successes, unintended consequences, and uneven effects.

That Imm Hassan was now a widow herself, toiling in exile to work off her family's mounting debts, was a heavy subtext to the conversation, though it remained unspoken. Indeed, the shifting figure of the eastern Syrian *shaykh*—exploiter, overlord, protector—haunted camp residents' ambivalent attachments to Abu Sharif, the *shawīsh* of the refugee-labor camp where they lived and to whom most camp residents remained indebted.

The parallel to *shaykhs* was not only metaphorical; Abu Sharif claimed *shaykh* origins and organized the camp around the trappings of *shaykh*ly distinction. This included a *maḍāfa* (guesthouse), where the *shawīsh* received his honored guests: representatives of humanitarian organizations, occasional journalists, other *shawīsh*, Lebanese landlords and other employers, members of his tribal clan, Lebanese municipal officials, male heads of household in the camp, and apparently an anthropologist like me.[38]

Constructed from tarpaulin sheets bearing the UN High Commissioner for Refugees logo, the exterior of Abu Sharif's guesthouse appeared like any other tent in the camp, yet the interior was adorned with all the paraphernalia of *shaykh* hospitality: fancy embroidered floor cushions, traditional coffee pots, ornate serving trays, and an honorific portrait of his father hanging on the wall. While he appeared to speak a regional dialect of Arabic nearly identical to that of the camp residents, he and his family made a point of vigorously denying that they were *shawāya* through constant reference to their *shaykh*ly status.

As a narrative construct, tribally mediated servile agriculture was securely located in the past for Imm Hassan. Yet, as a concrete social relation, it continued to haunt the wartime present, embodied in her ongoing

FIGURE 10. Ramadan iftar at Abu Sharif's house.

daily labors, proliferating debts, and hierarchical obligations to the *shawīsh*. Most immediately, this disjuncture revealed the fiction of anteriority: the idea that time necessarily works in a linear way or that the past is transparently available to us in the present.[39] From an agrarian perspective, this disjuncture would, thus, seem to confirm the now-familiar postcolonial critique of Marxist historical stageism, namely, the notion that there is a singular "transition" to capitalism wherein uneven development is merely evidence of postcolonial lack or failure.[40]

At the same time, this did not appear to be a case of noncapitalist forms "interrupting" capital,[41] nor of lingering remnants of precapitalism intermingling with capitalist ones.[42] In other words, tribal forms of redistribution, moral authority, and social cohesion were not simply other-than-capitalist ways of being that eluded or constrained capital's reach, as it were. Far from mere holdovers of the past, kin-based communal solidarities of sect, tribe, and ethnonationalism were and continue to be, as Arab Marxist scholars have long recognized, dynamic relations mediated by labor, landed property, and state power.[43] As the previous chapter showed, the growing possibilities of a class-based worker- and peasant-led movement among Lebanese citizens, Syrian migrant workers, and Palestinian refugees were reconfigured and ultimately cut short by the Lebanese Civil War, just as the uneven outcomes of Syria's land reforms were becoming ever more apparent. Communal solidarities continue to serve as key forces of social reproduction that have kept the region's working masses alive, where class-based organizing did not, or could not.

This specter of the *shaykh*, thus, expressed a fundamental contradiction at the heart of the agrarian question in eastern Syria's Euphrates basin: the tension between the Syrian state's official rhetoric about overcoming communal bonds, and the ways that these forms of belonging continually mediated agrarian transformations from the 1950s onward. Where "cotton shaykhs" helped facilitate the Jazīra region's incorporation into capitalist agricultural production through the expansion of pump irrigation and land clearing, this process was reconfigured by the Baʿth Party's 1963 coup, followed by the victory of a left-wing faction of the party in 1966. It was in this period that large-scale state-led plans for the Euphrates Dam took shape, after the USSR granted Syria a $100 million loan for the construction of the dam.[44] This new phase of land reform led to the formation of expropriation committees and peasant unions that divested landlords, for the first time, of the right to choose which lands they would give up.[45]

Yet in practice, many land-poor and landless Syrians objected that it was wealthy peasants who primarily benefited from land distributions. Delayed distributions of credit and inputs left many peasants dependent upon traditional clientage obligations to landlords and merchants or utterly destitute when expropriated landlords suddenly withdrew their pumps from irrigated lands.[46] To maintain incomes on smaller holdings, landlords began investing in advanced irrigation technology, sprinklers, improved seeds, and mechanized harvesters. In effect, the land reforms facilitated the replacement of underutilized *iqṭāʿ* estates with smaller, capital-intensive tracts of land.[47] In the Euphrates region, tribal *shaykhs* and urban merchants monopolized access to chemicals, fertilizers, agricultural machinery, and motorized irrigation pumps. The families of Ahmad, Abu Ibrahim, and Imm Hassan were among the majority of smallholders in the region who depended instead on undercapitalized rain-fed crops, eking out a partial income by marketing wheat and barley to the state through price-fixing arrangements, while pursuing off-farm employment and labor migration abroad.[48]

This uneven process of land reform was exacerbated by yet another coup in 1970 led by Hafiz al-Asad, which consolidated Syria's evolution away from any meaningful model of socialism. Setting out to broaden the base of the Baʿth Party while consolidating his cadre's hold on power, Asad's "corrective movement" curried favor with some segments of Syria's wealthy classes by reversing some of the land reforms of the late 1960s. A massive influx of petrodollars following the oil crisis of 1973 contributed to the further rightward shift of Asad's regime, as Syria bolstered security cooperation with Saudi Arabia and Egypt in the name of fighting Israeli military encroachment. Seen in this light, by the time construction of the Euphrates Dam began in earnest, it was already taking place in a socialist aftermath—or, in Reinhart Koselleck's words, a "future past."[49]

This rightward drift applied not only to Syria but also to a range of decolonizing states that often fell short of their revolutionary promises for complex historical reasons. Eqbal Ahmad evocatively characterized Hafiz al-Asad's Syria as a "radical-nationalist" type of postcolonial rule.[50]

While such postcolonial states sought to pursue a nominally socialist path to self-reliance under charismatic leadership, their revolutionary promises began to ring hollow as they harshly repressed popular demands and political opposition. Placing Asad's Syria in the same league as Saddam's Iraq, Boumediene's Algeria, and Nasser's Egypt, Samir Amin argued that these states shared a self-styled commitment to socialism yet in practice were closer to state capitalism, marked by an overestimated faith in the Soviet-aided model of "catching up" through industrialization, in contrast to more autarkic models of independent socialist development.[51] Insofar as it selectively adopted socialist principles of welfare and agrarian development, Hafiz al-Asad's regime was effectively a "military-mercantile complex" that relied on clientelist networks and heavy military and political recruitment from rural areas.[52] State allocation of resources to different provinces of Syria was steeped in "communal corporatism," wherein sectarian and tribal leaders were strategically incorporated into the state as mediators between their regional constituencies and the central state.[53] By forging nodal connections between the state and certain disadvantaged sectors of the population on a sectarian, ethnic, tribal, or geographical basis, this strategy had the effect of undermining a sense of class solidarity and national unity.[54]

For the diverse rural inhabitants of eastern Syria, this legacy of state-led communal corporatism has manifested in the enduring struggles over the dam's significance: how it began, who benefited, who lost, for what reasons, and why this matters today. For example, among eastern Syria's Kurdish population, the resettlement of the *maghmūrīn* in Qamishli is unequivocally remembered as the "Arab belt" (*al-ḥizām al-ʿarabī*),[55] though I never heard Abu Ibrahim or Imm Hassan refer to it this way. In its most radical form, the Arab Belt plan envisaged a forcible demographic reengineering of the region through dispersion of the Kurdish population and their gradual replacement by resettled tribal Arabs along the border with Türkiye. For many Kurdish activists, historiographers, and inhabitants of eastern Syria, the Euphrates Dam is, thus, inextricably bound up in this history of institutionalized discrimination and oppression.

This intertwined history ethnonationalist division and land tenure hung like a specter over my conversations with the *maghmūrīn*, particularly in the ways that some Syrian farmworkers described the establishment of Kurdish rule in their villages throughout the Syrian conflict. The following conversation I had with Ahmad and Khadija was an especially haunting expression of this. As we were finishing up our shift harvesting cherries, I asked Ahmad what he planned to do with the small tract of rain-fed land he inherited from his father in the Kurdish-majority region of Qamishli.

"It's gone. It belongs to the Kurds now" (*rāḥit, ṣārat lil-Akrād*), he replied tersely. "Hasn't Qamishli become part of a different state?" (*mū ṣārit Qāmishlī dawla tāniya*).

"Ahh, right, the Syrian Democratic Forces [*al-Dīmuqrāṭiyya*]," Khadija muttered.

"They took your land?" I asked.

"Yeah, they said, 'That's ours, you took it before, and we want to take back our rights [*bidnā nirjaʿ ḥaqqnā*].' So they took their rights [*u rajaʿū ḥaqqun*]."

"And look how the right is lost [*al-ḥaqq yiḍīʿ*]!" Khadija sighed.

"Perhaps the regime will come back and return Syria to the way it was [*tirjaʿ Sūriyā mitl mā kānat*] and restore our land to us [*tirjaʿ arāḍīnā ʿalaynā ilnā*]," Ahmad said under his breath, in a way that seemed directed at no one. He was speaking quietly but clearly, with measured exactitude. It was as though, lacking the proper words, he was reaching for slogans or promises he had heard before.

DEVELOPMENTALIST FUTURES-PAST: THE DROWNED AND THE DISPLACED

The dam was formally inaugurated in July 1973, a culminating achievement of the twelve thousand Syrians and nine hundred Soviet technicians who built it. Aspiring to double the total area of irrigated land in Syria, it was at once a symbol of the promise of agrarian development, the modern capacity of human-made infrastructures to harness nature, and the state's power to meet the welfare needs of its inhabitants. Young cadres of different political stripes ranging from communist to nationalist flocked from all over Syria to work for the nascent General Administration for the Development of the Euphrates Basin as engineers, technicians, and agronomists. Many were filled with optimism that they were participating in a project that would uplift eastern Syria's destitute inhabitants, serving as a model of postcolonial food self-sufficiency and rural electrification on the world stage.

Sixty-six villages were submerged by the flooding of the dam, displacing over sixty thousand people.[56] *Shawāya*, especially of the Walda clan, were overwhelmingly affected by the construction of the Euphrates Dam: around 40 percent of their clan became *maghmūrīn*.[57] A minority of the *maghmūrīn* were relocated onto fifteen state farms originally conceived as "model communities" for a "new society" free from the "archaisms" of the past.[58] Some of the *maghmūrīn*—especially those who could prove private property claims to land that had been submerged—were given land in compensation along the Turkish border as part of the Arab Belt plan. The majority, however, did not leave the area, but attempted to continue sheep rearing and dry farming by migrating further inland into the steppe away from the dam.[59] Abu Ibrahim and Imm Hassan's family were among those who enjoyed compensation, both in the form of rain-fed land in Qamishli and through employment on state farms. Abu Ibrahim narrated this transition evocatively to me as a moment when the state gave them "everything."

"At the beginning, the state gave us everything, everything was on their dime, all the machines," Abu Ibrahim explained to me, as we took respite from the heat in Imm Hassan's tent. He was referring to the Syrian state's monopoly in "strategic crops" (*al-maḥāṣīl al-istrātījiyya*), including wheat, barley, dry fodder, cotton, sugar beets, and tobacco. Cultivators of these crops sold their harvest to the state at fixed prices, and the state took responsibility for marketing them locally.

"They gave us free housing. The whole family lived on the state farm. They subsidized the harvest. Life was good [*zayn*]!" Abu Ibrahim continued. After reciting all the names of the state-owned farms that he could recall from memory, he pivoted to the present tense.

"And then all the land from the western side of Raqqa city to the dam was distributed," he declared. "The state gave the land to the farmers. Everyone who worked in the state-owned farms received thirty *dūnam* (three hectares). We cultivate everything now: watermelons, flowers, wheat, cotton, vegetables for our *mouneh*. But now the state doesn't give us inputs. It's all on the farmer's dime [*ʿa ḥisāb al-muzāriʿ*]."

What he was referring to as "distribution" was actually privatization of state-owned land, which took place in the early 2000s during Syria's liberalization period when the state farms were dismantled and redistributed in parcels to their former employees under the banner of "land to the tiller." Abu Ibrahim summed up the process pithily: "We were employees [*muwaẓẓafīn*], and then we became owners [*mālikīn*]."

I asked if he felt that these "distributions" were ultimately beneficial to the farmers. "Yes, of course! [*Ilā!*] Our production used to have a fixed price set by the state. Like I told you, there were state-owned factories, like the cotton factory of Raqqa and the sugar beet factory. Now, the whole harvest belongs to us. We're free to sell as we like."

He paused for a moment.

"And then, what happened?" he asked me rhetorically. "Daʿesh [the Islamic State] came and stole it all. And now the Kurds are in power. Now all the traders are ruling over us [*yījū tujjār yaḥkumū bīna*]."

This short exchange, in its own way, summed up the tumultuous fifty-year arc of Syria's uneven postsocialist transition, which arguably began with Hafiz al-Asad's "corrective movement" in the 1970s, shifted toward austerity under 1980s sanctions, deepened after the collapse of the Soviet Union, formalized under Bashar al-Asad's leadership after 2000, and took unexpected turns in the long and painful aftermath of Syria's 2011 revolution-turned-war. Tellingly, Abu Ibrahim never explicitly described the breakup of state-owned farms in 2000 as privatization but rather adopted the euphemistic language of "distribution" (*tawzīʿ*) found within official state proclamations as it pursued liberalizing reforms of "opening" (*infitāḥ*). From his perspective, it seemed, the state was merely "distributing" to cultivators their rightful share of the state's wealth. I could see that tension at work in the way that Abu Ibrahim was celebratory about life on state farms and, at the same time, seemed equally supportive of their dismantling.

Abu Ibrahim's discourse of distribution left intact an idealized vision of the state as a benevolent provider, which sat in tension with a basic material reality: it was precisely throughout this long, uneven postsocialist transition that many rural Syrians, including members of his own family, were compelled to seasonally migrate to Lebanon, Jordan, and the Persian Gulf to supplement their incomes. Yet I rarely heard anyone claim that the Syrian state bore responsibility for these slow, unspectacular processes of displacement. Resurrected like a "magical state"[60] as though liberalization never happened, the heyday of Syria's developmentalist promises remained vividly present in their narratives, eliding four decades of rural out-migration that intervened between the construction of the dam and the start of the 2011 uprising.

It was also significant that Abu Ibrahim described the privatization of the farms as a shift from his position as an "employee" to an "owner." It reflected the structural reality of the state farms: they were not truly collectivized. Rather, they were akin to state-owned company towns populated by employees receiving a wage to cultivate crops at fixed prices set by the state. Unlike the Soviet model, the Syrian state did not extract surplus from peasants but confined its role to providing price supports. State-farm workers like Abu Ibrahim thus viewed the farms not as a site of revolutionary food self-sufficiency or even collective decision-making, but rather more pragmatically as a steady wage in a region where access to hard cash was becoming increasingly necessary for household reproduction.

This was symptomatic of a more general dynamic: while Baʿthist ideology glorified the peasant-smallholder as the base of development and progress, the figure of the "peasant" (*fellāḥ*) was a fraught self-designation for many eastern Syrians, even at the zenith of the Euphrates project. One researcher writing in the early 1980s found that workers living on the farms were "in no way committed to the ideology of state farming."[61] This researcher also noted that local villagers perceived the *fellāḥīn* as weak and subjugated, as compared to the noble Bedouin pastoral ideal.[62] Reminiscent of Abu Ibrahim's portrayal of the state as a benevolent provider, Euphrates villagers referred to themselves as *fellāḥīn* only to assert what the "powerful state" *owed* to a "powerless peasantry," such as inputs, irrigation, and land.[63] As the *maghmūrīn* endured the weight of past and ongoing displacements in wartime, such lingering attachments to an ethics of distribution were ultimately a means of grappling with the stalled, unfulfilled, or only partially realized promises of agrarian development.

Coming to fruition under Hafiz al-Asad's corrective movement, which sought to build alliances in the private sector, state farms immediately fell short of any socialist ideal. Only about 10 percent of the employees of the farms were descendants of the *maghmūrīn*, while the rest were from nearby villages.[64] The farms struggled to yield returns on state investments even ten years after their implementation, as Syria's agricultural sector chronically lacked sufficient capital to remain productive or finance development.

Syrian agricultural production also remained highly dependent on foreign aid and loans from the Soviet Union, which contradicted the party's vision of food self-sufficiency.[65] Of course, there were also macrostructural reasons for Syria's ailing agricultural sector. An acute economic crisis began when the US government deemed Syria a "state sponsor of terrorism" in 1979 and placed the country under harsh sanctions. As Soviet aid began to dwindle and Syria drained its resources fighting a proxy war with Israel in war-ridden Lebanon, the crisis reached its peak in 1979–1982, followed by a series of austerity measures.[66]

It was against this backdrop of Cold War twilight that the agrarian developmentalist vision for eastern Syria began to unravel rapidly. Many Syrian agriculturalists, including members of families employed on state-owned farms, began to migrate abroad in search of higher wages in that period, as Syria's rural inhabitants were becoming dependent on cash remittances to survive rising costs of living. Young men like Ahmad were especially motivated to migrate seasonally in order to get married, as flows of remittances and Gulf capital were driving up the cost of bridewealth.[67] In short, many rural Syrians were facing a massive crisis of household reproduction throughout Syria's long postsocialist transition, which was especially acute in eastern Syria. According to one estimate, about half of all workers from the state farms left between 1976 and 1986.[68]

These circuits of predominantly male seasonal labor migration were also predicated on the squeezing of women's labor in subsistence farming and animal husbandry. Imm Hassan's mother and sisters were not considered formal employees of the state-owned farms like their father and brothers. This stemmed from the particular division of labor on the state farms, where the male head of household received a wage, some young men migrated to cities or abroad, and women and children supplied their unremunerated labor during peak harvest seasons. In the case of Imm Hassan and Abu Ibrahim's family, they supplemented the family income by selling raw wool and dairy products, especially *samneh* (clarified butter), to a door-to-door milkman. In some families, teenage girls and adult women helped supplement the family's income with seasonal cotton picking in nearby villages, which in eastern Syria is considered "women's work" paid at a piece rate. When pooled together, a family's earnings could sometimes be significant enough to purchase land or make home renovations, especially when at least one of the young men of the household was sending remittances from abroad. The fact that most state farm workers maintained a side job in steppe agriculture and dairy production had the unintended effect of strengthening tribal clan affiliations—despite the promise that land reform would overcome them.[69]

When Lebanon's fifteen-year civil war ended in 1990, labor out-migration from Syria increased considerably, as new jobs related to the reconstruction economy emerged in day labor, harvesting, construction, machine operation, services, metalwork, and garment making.[70] This trend continued after Bashar al-Asad succeeded his father in 2000, ushering in Syria's formal neoliberal transition, which included opening a stock market and forming private banks in Syria for the first time, slashing state-subsidized goods, and subjecting previously state-mandated food prices to a competitive market dominated by regional traders and agro-processing capital.[71]

It was in this period of accelerated liberalization that Syria's state-owned farms were privatized and distributed in parcels to their former employees, between 2000 and 2002.[72] From the outset, the parceling of land was fraught with confusion and ambiguity regarding *who* was entitled to land and on what terms.[73] There were those, for example, who claimed rights to restitution based on kinship and others who claimed their entitlement through labor. Thus, when Abu Ibrahim remained attached to the idea of the state as a benevolent "distributor" of goods, he was not merely rehearsing Ba'thist rhetoric but also coming to terms with a changing field of values in which both persons and land had been positioned. The fact that so many state farm employees were dependent on off-farm labor migration added to the confusion, leading to intense struggles regarding the status and rights of former employees who had left the state farms or who happened to have been away for seasonal work at the time that the decree to disband the farms was announced.[74] Here, too, tribal bonds mediated Syria's agrarian transition despite land reform's promise to eliminate them; by the late 2000s, many state farm employees-turned-owners had reverted to tribal alliances in order to gain access to irrigation, as many contiguous plots were distributed to members of the same clan who collectively managed hydraulic works.[75]

According to some estimates, between 2002 and 2008, Syria lost 40 percent of its agricultural workforce.[76] The devastating effects of these economic reforms on Syria's poorest populations were exacerbated by a series of recurrent droughts from 2006 to 2011, leading to mass migrations of destitute rural populations in search of waged work to Syria's cities and further west to Lebanon.[77] Imm Hassan, Abu Hassan, and their children were part of this wave of migration of displaced sharecroppers, pastoralists, and subsistence farmers from eastern Syria.

Throughout this period, the specter of the *shaykh* returned once again, this time in the figure of the *shawīsh*, as a segment of upwardly mobile labor migrants invested in pickup truck driving across the Syrian-Lebanese border.[78] As Abu Sharif once explained to me, many former pastoralists built up the necessary capital to become *shawīsh* in Lebanon by working as pickup drivers, which became especially lucrative in the 1980s as a vast cross-border smuggling network emerged during the Lebanese civil war. With enormous sums of money for postwar reconstruction flooding Lebanon's economy, *shawīsh* like Abu Sharif were well positioned to broker access to expanding waged work opportunities for seasonal migrants from Syria, including Imm Hassan's family. Abu Sharif's family consistently narrated this transition from pastoralism to pickup truck driving as a story of economic and social mobility. "Practically all of us tribal people were poor until recently," Abu Sharif's son told me over tea in his tent. "When we started driving trucks, we became blessed. Before that, if one didn't steal, he didn't survive."

THE TIME OF GHOSTLY RETURNS: OUR HOMES ARE OUR GRAVES

Throughout 2019, speculation about when and how to return to Syria became an increasingly frequent staple of conversation in the camp amid the growing backlash across Lebanon calling for Syrians' repatriation. Many camp families were also buoyed by the Kurdish-led defeat of the Islamic State's caliphate earlier that year, particularly as US military backing was infusing dollars into their cash-starved villages, however controversial and ephemeral this support proved to be. While a few families entertained the idea of returning for good once their debts were paid off, others were more reluctant to relinquish their refugee status, as they were concerned about the long-term viability of their livelihoods amid Syria's unfolding economic crisis.[79] Imm Hassan, for her part, had deeply personal motivations to consider returning to Syria: the ghost of her late husband, Abu Hassan, was begging her to come home. I first heard Imm Hassan express her intention to return to Syria during a visit from an elderly friend, Abu Ayman, who lived in a nearby camp.

"I swear to God, this life makes my heart swell" (*Wallāh warmat galbī hal-ḥayāt*), she exclaimed, clutching her chest. "Ever since Abu Hassan died, may his soul rest in peace, I feel my heart will burst. I swear, sometimes I go to work and I feel as if I want to explode. . . . Abu Hassan came to me again last night. He was wearing his *jalabīyya* robe and his *jimdāna*."

"What did he tell you, *ḥajjeh*?" Abu Ayman asked her.

"He told me it's time to go home. I swear, if he were still alive, he would curse Abu Sharif. God does not bless the arrogant. I cried from my whole heart [*bakayt min kul qalby*] when I saw Abu Hassan. May God have mercy on his soul."

The conversation digressed in many directions for the next hour, from camp gossip to complaints about Abu Sharif, to talk about the cost of fuel and the devaluation of the Syrian pound. "The *shawīsh* wants to plunder the world [*yanhab al-dunyā*]," Abu Ayman declared, as if preparing to give a speech or recite an epic. "People talk, people fight, people loot others, the workers toil for nothing [*yshtaghal al-ʿummāl bi-balāsh*]. There is no fear of God, no fear! See what the world has become? . . . Imm Hassan, are you with me?" Imm Hassan looked up and nodded, half-listening, while she scrolled through her phone.

Abu Ayman continued. "In the beginning, we had *iqṭāʿiyya*, right? Before the Baʿth Party. I remember in the 1950s and 1960s, in the time of *iqṭāʿiyya*, the *shaykh* had a guy [*zalame*] who was untouchable [*mā ḥada yaqdar yaḥkī*]."

By "guy," he seemed to be referring to a strongman or mediator of sorts. He repeated, "He was untouchable," literally meaning in Arabic "No one could talk to him." He then switched to the present tense, which gave me the sense that he was describing a more universal, or continuous, condition that did not necessarily pertain to a particular person. "The guy watches over the peasant [*al-fellaḥ*]. The peasant stays all year working until the end of the season. And then the peasant turns up broke [*yṭlaʿ maksūr*]. For all the toil of the peasant and his family, what does the *shaykh* give? The peasant gets 20 percent, and the other 80 percent goes to the *shaykh*. And then the Party [*al-ḥizb*] came in the 1970s and the peasant starts getting 40 percent!"

Abu Ayman had a penchant for allegorical digressions and flowery non sequiturs, so Imm Hassan was, by that point, barely paying attention. She gave a perfunctory response and then resumed her earlier litany of complaints about the cost of chicken.

But the allegory stuck with me. The "40 percent" seemed a powerful metaphor for the sense of longing—and disappointment—that the Euphrates Dam and the broader agrarian developmentalist promises of the Baʿth Party evoked. That Abu Ayman subtly likened the *shawīsh* to a pre-Baʿth era of tribal strongmen who oversaw laborers on behalf of wealthy landed *shaykhs* spoke to manifold temporal afterlives of agrarian developmentalism, where the presence of seemingly dead pasts continuously haunted the living. As many Syrians made a point of emphasizing to me when I started working with them on family-owned farms, Lebanon never underwent land reform and thus, large *iqṭāʿī* estates were never broken up. Servile forms of agriculture were alive and well in Lebanon, mobilized in new ways through the *shawīsh* labor recruitment system. That Imm Hassan and her fellow camp residents now found themselves working for poverty wages as an on-call labor force on an *iqṭāʿī* estate powerfully recalled the words of the Syrian Peasants' Union, which once lamented that the *iqṭāʿiyyīn* "who left through the door" had managed to "return through the window."[80]

As a dream-apparition, Abu Hassan's soul was also a direct participant in an ongoing process of reckoning with displacement and its layered temporal significance. The souls of the departed have a central place in peasant history and literature, often communicating that which is unspeakable, overabundant, unresolved, or enduring about a past filled with extraordinary loss.[81] The cruel paradox, in this case, was that it was the *shawīsh* himself who ensured that Abu Hassan's body made it across the border to be properly buried in his village, a basic dignity afforded only to those few Syrian refugees with money or connections. Abu Sharif happened to be well connected to a Lebanese border guard through his years of cross-border experience in pickup truck driving and labor recruitment.

As I listened to Imm Hassan recount her dream, I was reminded of the service that Abu Sharif had arranged in Abu Hassan's memory for the camp residents earlier that year. Before I proceeded to Imm Hassan's tent to offer my condolences that day, Abu Sharif ushered me into his *shaykh*ly guesthouse to sit among his honored guests. Two dozen men were seated cross-legged on plush red cushions around the perimeter of the tent, except for one person: the Lebanese border guard. He sat on a plastic chair slightly elevated above the rest of the group, as Abu Sharif served *qahwa murra,* a traditional bitter coffee left unsweetened on such somber occasions. Presiding over the room as Abu Sharif's most esteemed guest, the guard had ensured that Abu Hassan's body was transported across the border and properly laid to rest despite the ongoing war. At that time, I had not yet learned about the *maghmūrīn,* nor the full extent of Imm Hassan's family history. Looking back upon this tragic day in retrospect, I am still haunted by the words of those who refused to be relocated when the Euphrates Dam was first constructed: "*Buyūtnā qubūrnā.*" Our homes are our graves.

Toward the end of my fieldwork, I came upon *The Drowned,* a novel written in 1979 by ʿAbd al-Salām Ojeilī, one of Raqqa's most prolific writers. In pained prose, he opens the novel with a dedication to the *maghmūrīn*, "those who, upon their submerged heads in the Euphrates Dam, glories were built and fortunes flourished."[82] Describing the Jazīra's villagers as mere "screws" and "scraps" within the state's machinery, it captures the tragedy of the moment in which it was written. Though the novel was written in a pastoral genre, Ojeilī was far from nostalgic; even before the dam came, the peasants of the Euphrates Valley were already being sacrificed to a slow death by "the sun, the well, thirst, and the desert."[83]

With its focus on peasant rootedness and belonging to the land, Ojeilī's novel was nevertheless criticized by some of his leftist contemporaries in the Syrian literary world as hackneyed and retrograde.[84] They lamented its emphasis on individualism rather than class consciousness, and that it valorized the small-scale ties of traditional village belonging rather than class struggle.[85] Ultimately, in their words, he proffered a vision "against progress" (*ḍudd al-taqaddum*)[86] conjuring "a narrative world in the *iqṭāʿī* camp."[87] These allegations, toeing in various ways the official Baʿthist line of developmentalist promise and a Marxian understanding of class antagonisms, speak to the stakes of this vision for the transformation of eastern Syria at that time.

Of course, the issues that plagued the making and unmaking of Syria's experiment with state farms, and broader ideals of agrarian developmentalism they represented, were not confined to Syria alone. While the specter of Marxism haunted zealous neoconservative pronouncements about the triumph of liberal democracy and the supposed "end of history" in the immediate aftermath of the Cold War, the ghosts of Soviet collectivization's internal critics seemed to haunt the left.[88] For example, in his evocative essay on the "treble death" of Soviet agronomist Alexander Chayanov, Teodor Shanin recounts the uneven legacies of Stalin's collectivization in ways that echo eastern Syria's enduring predicaments: ecological decline, mass out-migration from rural villages, stagnating agricultural production, and authoritarian retrenchment.[89]

While there is no doubt that land reform, as part of the great tide of postcolonial liberation, was marked by real gains across the Global South, these advances were often uneven, unequal, and incomplete. Decades removed from this heyday of progressivist state-led development, agriculturalists are now contending with the complex aftermaths of these projects across the world: the post–Cold War unmaking of statist redistributive land tenure, a global wave of neoliberal land titling projects, and new frontiers of accumulation through speculation in land rents.[90] One of the most urgent manifestations of these contradictory legacies of uneven development is staggering rates of mass migration within and across borders. Though often obfuscated by the economistic language of "choice," where "voluntary" economic migrants and "involuntary" refugees are differentiated by virtue of the presence or absence of political coercion, the predicaments of the *maghmūrīn* vividly exemplify how these displacements structurally intersect.

For Imm Hassan, Ahmad, and many other descendants of the *maghmūrīn* who eventually sought refuge in Lebanon, Hafiz-era developmentalist ideals supplied frameworks of intelligibility that made certain forms of displacement narratable or eventful, where others receded into the background of people's daily acts of survival. Narrated through war and its wake, a history of agrarian dispossession, ethnonational division, and literal submersion at the hands of Ba'thism ran up against enduring attachments to the dam as an icon of the prewar Syria that was lost. Seemingly banished to the past by agrarian reform, the strange specter of serfdom continually haunted Syrian farmworkers in exile, in the figure of the *shawīsh* and through their daily labor in the Bekaa Valley.

Alongside these specters stood another: that of the Syrian developmentalist state that may have been—or perhaps never was—but for which they nevertheless seemed to yearn as they prepared for an uncertain return. With the foreseeable end of displacement locked in a continuous deferral due to their mounting debts in Lebanon, these developmentalist hopes and losses were resurrected precisely at a moment when the *pastness* of this particular vision of agrarian futurity seemed most apparent. As the tragic centrality of electricity, food, jobs, and water to Syria's war attested, the specters of unfulfilled socialist futures—and the pasts that refused to be submerged—seemed to weigh heaviest upon the displaced.

Three

DEBTS OF DISPLACEMENT

"I'M LIKE A FATHER TO THEM. I GIVE THEM EVERYTHING. I SHELTER them, find them jobs, and transport them to work. I take them to the hospital when they're sick. I give them money when they need it," Abu Sharif declared with characteristic swagger, his gravelly voice slightly muffled by the whirr of the pickup truck's engine and the sound of Qur'anic recitation blaring from the radio. "I even ensure the proper burial of their dead," he added emphatically, taking his eyes off the road for a moment to look over at me jotting down notes in the passenger's seat. Speaking in his distinctly Aleppan countryside dialect, Abu Sharif was referring to his responsibilities as a *shawīsh* in the Bekaa Valley, where he ran a refugee camp for twenty-six displaced Syrian families.

We were returning from the morning shift on a local vineyard, where Abu Sharif's workers had just spent five hours weeding. Peals of women's laughter and lively conversation resounded from the back of the truck as he turned onto a dirt path flanked on either side by fields of wheat and potatoes. The snow-capped mountain range that forms the border between Lebanon and Syria was visible in the distance, an arid light brown illuminated by the late morning sun. As we drove farther, a cluster of tarpaulin tents appeared to our left. My view was partly obscured by a massive white decal reading *Allāhu Akbar* emblazoned across Abu Sharif's windshield, worn at the edges from countless daily journeys to different farms. True to Abu Sharif's penchant for extravagant self-distinction, his seats and dashboard were upholstered with bright red faux fur and pleather, a strangely garish contrast to the bucolic spring landscape.

As he took a drag from his cigarette and braced his other hand against the steering wheel, I noticed that his face still bore the trace of a jagged scar that ran from his right cheek to the tip of his nose. Two months earlier, he'd had an altercation with Taha, one of the farmworkers living in his camp, who claimed that Abu Sharif had spoken disrespectfully to his father. Overcome with anger and frustration over his family's conditions, Taha slashed Abu Sharif's face with a kitchen knife, as the other members of the camp looked on in horror. Taha and his family were immediately expelled from their tent on the night of the fight.

News of the incident spread instantly across the various WhatsApp networks of *shawīsh* who run refugee camps in the Bekaa. "We destroyed their house and kicked them out," Abu Sharif's nineteen-year-old son, Sharif, recounted proudly as we drank coffee in his tent the next day. He meant "destroyed" proverbially; he was implying that there was an unspoken rule that other camps had an obligation not to provide refuge to Taha after he violently attacked a *shawīsh*. After all, Abu Sharif's tribal clan from the Aleppo countryside was one of the most prominent groups running refugee camps in the region, and his network of relatives would ensure that this obligation was honored.

From Sharif's boastful talk of retribution, I surmised that such threats of violence were what kept farmworkers loyal to Abu Sharif. But another event a few weeks later revealed a more complicated picture. As I learned from the other camp residents, Taha and his family eventually received a cash transfer from Abu Sharif via Western Union. According to Abu Sharif's ledger, Taha's family had earned more in credit-wages for their agricultural work than they had borrowed from Abu Sharif to cover their daily expenses over the past season. Despite the tensions that now ran between these two men, Abu Sharif had honored their mutual credit-debt obligations.

In many ways, this incident epitomized the mundane yet increasingly pervasive power of debt in the lives of displaced Syrians, particularly those residing in *shawīsh* camps. Several aspects of the fight between Taha and

Abu Sharif were significant to understanding what gave these debts their binding force. One was how debt regulated the mobility and value of farmworkers' labor in this context. Though refugee camps are often presumed to be on the margins of economic life, *shawīsh* camps were, in fact, central to Lebanon's highly liberalized market in low-waged agricultural labor. Abu Sharif brokered work opportunities for Syrian farmworkers like Taha in exchange for a commission on their wages, which he used to invest in and expand his camp operations. As profit-oriented ventures, *shawīsh* camps were a specific instance of a more general trend toward debt-based labor brokerage and capitalization across the agrarian world, where debt functions as a disciplinary mechanism compelling worker-borrowers to intensify their labor until their debts are paid off.[1] By ensuring the recruitment and reproduction of a low-waged, flexible migrant labor force, debt in *shawīsh* camps was a pernicious form of "self-managed" exploitation that has contributed to the precarization of agricultural work and wage repression, thereby undermining the material basis of farmworkers' organizational power.[2]

It was nevertheless telling that Taha's major grievance revolved around matters of respectability—that is, how Abu Sharif spoke to his father—rather than his low wages, precarious labor conditions, or constraints on his mobility. Taha was not alone in this moral orientation; residents of the camp most often framed their expectations of Abu Sharif through ideals of good treatment (*muʿāmla*) that honored workers' dignity (*karāma*), while more traditional labor demands concerning wages and the length of the working day were less commonly invoked, and efforts at collective bargaining were virtually unheard of.

This helped explain another significant aspect of the incident: Taha and his family had *already* worked off their debt obligations but were still living in the camp at the time of the fight. And Abu Sharif, in turn, made sure to pay back Taha even after he had violently attacked him. Taha was not the only one in this situation: there were several other families residing in Abu Sharif's camp who had already worked off their debts. Some were there to wait out the economic and political crisis in Syria and build up their savings, while others simply could not afford living elsewhere or were unwilling to take on the risk of finding work and shelter in Lebanon without the help of a patron. The fight and its aftermath, thus, brought into relief a multiplicity of factors that bound farmworkers and *shawīsh* together in a context of long-term displacement, and the often contradictory set of aspirations, needs, and desires that suffused these credit-debt relations. It ultimately laid bare the tensions within debt itself as a lived set of moral obligations: debt is, on the one hand, one of the oldest instruments of class rule and, on the other, a time-honored practice of mutual aid through which poor communities across the world have managed hardship and redistributed resources.[3]

Through a multidimensional exploration of debt's binding power, this chapter traces how *shawīsh* came to be regarded as essential patron figures and service providers for farmworkers struggling with the costs of living in Lebanon year-round as refugees. While this camp system was obviously steeped in inequalities, many Syrians turned to *shawīsh* camps as they coped with the loss of social benefits provided by the Syrian state and the income they derived from their land in Syria, both of which were predicated on seasonal cross-border movements that became more difficult, and in many cases impossible, throughout the war. Existing on a tense continuum between coercion and interdependency, these camps offered displaced Syrians the possibility of making distributive claims upon others in conditions of extraordinary unpredictability, providing not only a source of affordable housing, reliable income, and services but also a sense of community and baseline security.[4]

The *shawīsh* debt system was also powerful because it was highly personal. Abu Sharif was, quite literally, the face of credit in the camp, as he was the only member of the camp with a bank account and access to hard cash. By exploring Abu Sharif's rags-to-riches story, this chapter recounts how he built up his camp through cross-border networks of trust over the course of decades, which were predicated on maintaining a reputation for generosity in his workers' home villages as a father-like patron and pious Muslim. Two multivalent practices—*ma'rifa* (know-how, connections) and *amāna* (trusteeship, protection, care)—served as key moral frameworks through which Abu Sharif recruited labor, located jobs, and bolstered his reputation. The embodied, personalistic nature of this role sustained, and was sustained by, everyday moral expectations among camp residents for high-quality services, generous credit flows, and ceremonial gifts. Camp residents were themselves aware of Abu Sharif's paradoxical role as both an exploiter and provider, which formed the moral grounds on which they made claims upon him and negotiated his authority.

Yet this reputation for generosity was attenuated by the need to keep his camp profitable within Lebanon's increasingly competitive market in cheap labor. As Abu Sharif faced growing pressure to constrain his lending throughout Lebanon's mounting financial crisis in 2019, this debt system placed him in an increasingly contradictory position, where the moral obligation to give abundantly existed in tension with the economic imperative to maintain liquidity in the camp's bank account and maximize profit. The coming pages will trace how these tensions materialized by following a family's decision to move from Abu Sharif's camp to a "free" camp, where they were relieved from mandatory labor, yet became utterly vulnerable to eviction and joblessness in the absence of their patron. Taken together, this chapter probes the complex meanings of freedom and unfreedom for Syrian refugee-farmworkers, for whom debt was not only highly constraining and exploitative but also a vital source of belonging and sustenance in radically uncertain wartime conditions.

THE AGRARIAN ROOTS OF THE *SHAWĪSH* CAMP SYSTEM

Known for maintaining side jobs in smuggling and speculative real-estate ventures alongside labor brokerage, the *shawīsh* seemed to encompass virtually every caricature of the unsavory middleman. When presented as the overlord in a system of "modern-day slavery," as these camps were often described in humanitarian and media reports, the *shawīsh* appeared as the radical antithesis of the stereotypically feminized image of refugee suffering.[5] Yet Abu Sharif, too, was a registered Syrian refugee: one with long-standing migratory experience in Lebanon predating the war whose camp has supplied workers to a variety of small family farms and estates since the late 1990s.

Lebanese landlords I met in the Bekaa Valley were often at pains to portray *shawīsh* as brazen opportunists who were seeking to turn a profit from Syrians' long-term displacement. As a wealthy landlord once quipped when introducing me to the *shawīsh* who brought workers to his land, "Don't be fooled by his cheap clothes. That guy is a millionaire and he's making a killing from the crisis." Such sentiments were as much a claim about the exploitative nature of the *shawīsh*'s work as they were an exercise in delineating fraught class distinctions. Evident from the honorific portraits of landed elites bannered across the Bekaa, landlords in Lebanon were invested with enormous moral authority among villagers, in clear opposition to the stereotypically parasitic *shawīsh*.[6]

Landlords' anxiety about *shawīsh* entrepreneurialism was also a commentary on the latter's newfound and still-liminal class status: though *shawīsh* had accumulated the capital necessary to broker jobs and lend credit, many were of humble farmworker origins from tribal backgrounds. At a moment of rising anti-Syrian sentiment in Lebanon, the fact that most *shawīsh* were Syrian nationals only added to the disdain routinely directed at them. But a narrow focus on *shawīsh*'s opportunism obscured their embeddedness in the larger economy of market-led agricultural production that stood to benefit from their brokerage work—not least the role of Lebanese landlords and contract farmers in employing them under the competitive drive to keep labor costs low.

I was first introduced to Abu Sharif in 2018 by his employer, Jamil, the Lebanese engineer featured at the beginning of this book. Upon learning of my interest in the conditions of Syrians who worked as day laborers on the estate he managed, Jamil had arranged for me to interview Abu Sharif. But he seemed anxious to make sure that I didn't take Abu Sharif at his word.

"Be careful, he's a liar," Jamil murmured quietly as we approached his office. "He's going to tell you that he has no money. He has eighteen kids and two wives! And he's looking for a third." Jamil lowered his voice to a barely audible whisper as we reached the door. "He'll try to get your sympathy. The truth is that they are benefiting at the expense of us Lebanese. Especially men. They collect aid from the United Nations and sit at home in their tents while their women work."

A round-faced, boyish-looking man in his late forties was seated next to Jamil's desk when we entered. He was wearing a baseball cap and a black leather jacket over black slacks, a black dress shirt, and black leather loafers caked with dust. All-black ensembles, I learned later, were the unofficial uniform of *shawīsh*, in contrast to the brightly colored dresses of their mostly female workers.

"This is the researcher who wants to talk to you," Jamil said as he pulled up a chair for me to face Abu Sharif. "From the US Embassy," he added jokingly.

"Really?" Abu Sharif asked with wide eyes, sitting up on the edge of his seat.

"No, no, she's just a student from America. But her father is Iranian."

"*Aiwaaa,* a Muslima! . . . Does the girl speak Arabic?" he asked Jamil, not yet addressing me directly.

"Yes, and if you lie to her, I'll lock you in that room over there!" Jamil retorted with playful aggression, the first of a long chain of competitive ripostes that were, at once, friendly and agonistic.

Jamil's secretary placed a tray of tea in glass cups in front of us. Abu Sharif spooned sugar into his cup until it was almost as thick as cough syrup.

"*Aanisa* [miss], it's an honor to meet you," he addressed me with exaggerated respect. He then switched to a register of reportage, deepening his voice and furrowing his eyebrows, "Let me tell you about the situation in the camp. It's desperate. Women and children living on a day's sustenance alone. Their wages barely cover the cost of bread."

"Tell her how many *dūnam* of land you have in Syria, *ya shaykh,*" Jamil interjected sarcastically.

"I swear to God, I lost everything in the war."

"May God cut your life short, what a liar!" (*yaqṭaʿ ʿumrak shū kazzāb*), Jamil groaned.

"I worked my entire life in Lebanon," Abu Sharif replied, careful not to raise his voice to his superior, "only to have my house in Aleppo, my life savings, destroyed on Asad's dime." He was referring to a neighborhood of southeast Aleppo that was reduced to rubble by fighting between the Syrian regime, the Free Syrian Army, and various other opposition movements.

"Give me a break!" Jamil huffed. "Tell her how much commission you take from each girl, man! Tell her how you pack them like sardines in the back of your truck."

"What, do you expect me to work for nothing?" (*shū, bshtighil bi-balāsh*), Abu Sharif exclaimed, visibly flustered. "I have bills to pay, children that have to go to the doctor, girls that need new clothes."

We spent the next hour discussing Abu Sharif's extensive responsibilities as a *shawīsh,* which he framed as a vital paternal duty to serve the poor.

Though I sensed that Jamil was right about Abu Sharif's proclivity for embellishing and self-aggrandizement, there was a bitter irony to Jamil's portrayal of him as an exploiter. After all, it was Jamil who was employing Abu Sharif's camp to work on the estate: it was he who was ultimately setting their wages.

Abu Sharif was a highly contradictory figure who defied simple characterization. As an enterprising leader and paternalistic caregiver, his self-presentation was that of a classic patron or "big man."[7] In practical terms, his work also bore parallels to different types of brokers found across the world who contract out workers through cash advances, including the various mediators in migrant communities who channel resources to their more precarious compatriots by capitalizing on their well-connectedness.[8]

As these resonances to other contexts suggest, the growing prominence of *shawīsh* like Abu Sharif was ultimately a product of multiple historical, structural, and relational factors that far exceeded his particular position. Among these were the long-standing demand for cheap labor within Lebanon's food system and prewar patterns of labor migration that had drawn rural Syrians into transnational circuits of waged work. Compounded by the liberalization of trade and agricultural labor regulations on both sides of the border in the 1990s and 2000s, this was a fate the Bekaa Valley shared with many other borderlands elsewhere under the weight of globalization, including the US-Mexico border following the signing of the North American Free Trade Agreement in 1994.[9]

The war in Syria exacerbated these inequalities, as input costs skyrocketed and export through overland routes across Syria became more unpredictable and costly from 2012 onward. On a macro level, this precipitous increase in the costs of production and export exacerbated Lebanon's trade deficit and public debt crisis. Within its ailing agricultural sector, an already pronounced dualistic structure deepened, defined by a small and highly unregulated domestic consumption market for all varieties of vegetables and fruits, on the one hand, and import dependency for most manufactured food products, on the other. A narrow stratum of Lebanese agriculturalists with significant capital shifted to export by sea or air, while the majority were relegated to producing for volatile domestic markets.

Facing declining profitability, Lebanese landlords and contract farmers sought to reduce production costs by driving down wages and relying on labor-intensive cultivation techniques. Within this liberalized agricultural system, employers like Jamil were attracted to the flexibility of *shawīsh* camps, as they could cancel, shorten, or reduce labor assignments depending on local and regional market fluctuations—or as it was colloquially called, "on demand" (*'al-ṭalabiyya*)—in contrast to formalized labor recruitment systems in which compensation and benefits are contractually bound and state mandated.

As the 2011 Syrian uprising devolved into a protracted armed conflict, Lebanon's crumbling infrastructure could hardly accommodate the million-and-a-half Syrians seeking long-term refuge across the country. In the absence of a coordinated approach, what emerged instead was a patchwork of humanitarian services and privatized arrangements built upon prewar labor migrant networks, including the *shawīsh* system. Eventually, Abu Sharif's camp, like many other *shawīsh* camps, was registered with the United Nations as a refugee camp, but these camps are still locally known by their prewar name, "girl workshops."

THE FACE OF CREDIT: THE POLITICAL ECONOMY OF ABU SHARIF'S CAMP

"About eight Ramadans ago, Abu Sharif started giving out receipts. . . . It wasn't like that before," Imm Hassan once told me, seated on a plastic chair in front of her tent. As part of his responsibilities as a *shawīsh*, Abu Sharif had passed by earlier that evening to give her a pay stub. The pay stub was printed in letterhead that read in Arabic "The workshop of Abu Sharif" in bold script at the top, followed by her husband's family name, the number of people from her household who had worked in the fields that day, an accounting of their total wages, and the date. Distributed every night after sunset prayer, these receipts would be tabulated at the end of the season in November as assets against her household's debts.

Abu Sharif lived alongside the other camp residents in a modest white tent, along with his two wives and eighteen children. His elderly parents, younger sisters, younger brother, and their children lived in tents next to his. The rest of the camp residents lived in tents virtually indistinguishable from his. Despite the apparent uniformity of the camp infrastructure, he occupied a unique position as the camp moneylender. In addition to serving as a focal point for work opportunities and humanitarian aid, his central role in the camp was to lend cash and offer a variety of services on credit, which he recorded in a thick, leather-bound ledger.

At the time of my research in 2019, he paid an annual rent of $16,667 for the entire camp, which he divided among each tent, amounting to $500 to $700 per tent-household. His accounting system was measured in year-long seasonal commitments for each tent, which commenced every November when he renewed his camp's rental contract with the absentee landlord who owned the tract of land on which the camp was located. Those who remained indebted—usually the majority—were obliged to stay in the camp and continue working for the upcoming year. Those who had worked off their debt had the option to leave the camp, work in a different camp, or return to Syria. Residents were permitted to leave the camp midseason only in instances of extreme illness—or, as in the case of Taha, conflict with the *shawīsh*. Regardless, they were obliged to continue sending payments until they had worked off their debt.

As one of the most well-known *shawīsh* in the Bekaa Valley, Abu Sharif maintained a wide network of contacts with Lebanese landlords and employers. He was chiefly responsible for mediating with Lebanese employers like Jamil, who made informal work agreements at the beginning of each season, subject to shifts depending on labor needs on a given day. Lebanese

FIGURE 11. Heading to work in November.

employers paid Abu Sharif 8,000 Lebanese lira for each worker per shift, from which he took a 2,000-lira commission, meaning workers' take-home wage was 6,000 lira per shift, which was equivalent to $4 at that time. Called *yawmiyya* in Arabic, a typical shift lasted five hours. Corresponding roughly to Islamic prayer schedules, the first shift started after sunrise prayer and the second shift began from noon or afternoon prayer until sunset. Camp residents, in turn, depended critically upon Abu Sharif for daily transportation to work. He owned two flatbed trucks that could each fit up to forty workers if they stood shoulder-to-shoulder while riding in the bed of the truck.

The camp was located an hour's walk away from the nearest town center, which meant that residents had very few reasons or opportunities to leave the camp outside of their work obligations, though they were technically free to enter and exit as they pleased. Most camp residents purchased their daily food items from the camp bodega (*dukkāneh*), which was housed inside the camp and run by Rawia's mother, Imm Brahim, one of the few female camp residents with a high level of literacy, who was also my adoptive "mother" in

FIGURE 12. The camp grocery store.

the camp. She dutifully recorded all *dukkāneh* expenses in a notebook, for which Abu Sharif paid her the equivalent of one agricultural shift per day. At the end of every month, she tallied each household's *dukkāneh* purchases and sent her calculations to Abu Sharif, who deducted these expenses from workers' monthly earnings in his ledger.

Given that the camp economy was based on credit, the residents' wages were not paid in cash. Rather, Abu Sharif documented daily earnings through paper pay stubs recording the number of shifts performed by each member of a tent-household and a numerical calculation of each day's earnings. Every evening after sunset prayer, he walked from door to door throughout the camp to provide each household with an accounting of their daily wages and a summary of their labor obligations for the next day. He insisted upon the importance of conducting this process, referred to as *farz* (sorting), face-to-face. Doing so allowed camp residents to voice their disagreements or renegotiate their work assignment if a member of the household could not go to work the next day. Throughout the high summer season from April to November, work was abundant in the camp. During the frigid winter season from December to March, work opportunities were rare, and it was in these protracted slack periods that their debts to Abu Sharif proliferated.

This debt system was also deeply gendered, an issue I explore further in the next chapter. Members of every tent-household pooled their incomes as a "family wage" under the name of the eldest male in each family, even as women, teenagers, and young adolescent boys and girls performed the majority of agricultural work. When I asked various employers why women and children were relegated to the lowest paid and most tedious tasks, their responses were remarkably consistent: "That's their culture," they often said. As many saw it, eastern Syrian tribal women were culturally, socially, and economically predisposed to accept lower wages and worse labor conditions, given that many of them had a low level of literacy, were considered "unskilled," and could not expect to find work elsewhere. But as the previous chapters showed, Jazīran women's participation in low-waged agricultural work was a historically contingent process that expanded as Syria's state-led economy liberalized. Far from a static attribute of eastern Syrian "culture," their precarious labor conditions resonated with those of undocumented migrants in other contexts wherein gender, class, age, lack of citizenship, and racialized characteristics have become symbolic markers of exploitability that bolster justifications for lower wages and loosening labor protections.[10]

The reverberating effects of war dramatically expanded the scale and scope of this recruitment system, as Syrians were no longer temporary workers but refugees attempting to build a longer-term future in the face of multiple constraints. In this context, it was not only the disciplinary power of debt that made the *shawīsh* system such a tenacious system of labor recruitment, but also the attractiveness of credit as both a vital means of social reproduction and site of aspirational investment.[11] For families reeling from the uncertainties and traumas of long-term dislocation, credit helped them rebuild the material comforts, everyday routines, and simple pleasures of "a secure ordinariness" that they associated with their prewar life.[12]

The relative flexibility and social thickness of the *shawīsh* system played a key role in sustaining these needs and aspirations. Despite charging a hefty commission on workers' wages, Abu Sharif did not collect interest on loans and residents were under no strict obligation to make regular payments or to work off their debt within a certain period. His camp also maintained an unofficial system of unpaid maternity leave, where nursing and pregnant women were permitted not to go to work in the fields—and, thus, go deeper into debt—if they requested to do so. This meant that there were households that had accumulated several seasons' worth of debts. Households that lacked a sufficient number of workers relative to the number of dependents—small children, pregnant or nursing women, the elderly, the disabled, underemployed men—were often so deeply in debt to the *shawīsh* that they could barely envisage returning to Syria, but simply carried on collecting their meager daily salaries, assured that they would not be evicted as long as they continued working.

Here, the paradoxical binds of this system were clear: if they were to try to find housing within a conventional rental market or take a bank loan to pay their rent, they would not find the type of flexibility in repayment that the *shawīsh* offered to camp residents. In this way, debt's literal embodiment in Abu Sharif was a more intimate version of bank credit, which seemingly diminished the abstraction of monetary transactions because it was directly linked to concepts of trustworthiness. With few other options at their disposal, many residents found recourse in the social flexibility and stability of the *shawīsh* camp community, even as it locked them into long-term labor obligations. Much as James Ferguson described "declarations of dependence," they recognized that the alternative was to be utterly unbound, exposed to the impersonal forces of a "free" labor market that offered fewer social guarantees and protections.[13]

"I KNOW PEOPLE": BETWEEN GENEROSITY AND ACCUMULATION

The *shawīsh* system was also powerful due to its social depth and longevity, in contrast to other more nascent camp networks that emerged throughout the war. Before 2011, most *shawīsh* camps consisted of extended patrilocal family units from a particular village or clan in eastern Syria, a dynamic that continued after the war but expanded to accommodate newcomers as well. Hailing from a handful of villages along the Euphrates River, most residents of Abu Sharif's camp were *shawāya* who identified strongly with their lineage. The layout of the camp reflected these origins, with families living side by side in rows or clusters corresponding to their village and clan. In fact, the camp residents often referred to *shawīsh* camps as *ʿarab*, literally meaning "Arab," a northeastern Syrian colloquial term for an encampment of people, usually from the same village or clan.

Abu Sharif was well known to Lebanese employers in terms of his rags-to-riches story; he started migrating to Lebanon in 1978 as a child. His narration of the origins of the *shawīsh* system was entwined with his own trajectory of upward mobility, in which the concept of *maʿrifa*—an idiom meaning knowledge gained through experience—played a key role:

> I was just a kid when I started coming to Lebanon with my mother and siblings. Every year, we came to Lebanon from our village in the southern countryside of Aleppo from April to November, and then we would go back to Syria in the winter. When I was eighteen, I did my army service in Syria, and some of the guys serving with me were from the countryside of Raqqa. They introduced me to workers whom I could bring to Lebanon. After my army service, I started to gather up money to invest in a pickup truck and then in a *warsha* [camp]. I had experience and knowledge [*maʿrifa*] from all those years working in Lebanon. I became a *shawīsh* in 1992. I went to different villages in Raqqa. I told the people looking for money and jobs, "I know people [*ilī maʿrifa*] in Lebanon." So let's say there

> was a family, a man and woman with four or five kids. I'd lend him whatever he needs in exchange for a seasonal commitment to work in Lebanon in my *warsha*. I gathered all the furniture for them if they didn't have it, and then I would transport them and all their belongings to Lebanon in my truck. I have built a good reputation among the workers who come from Raqqa and employers here in Lebanon. Lebanese landlords like to work with me because they all know me [*biyaʿrifūnī*]. Every agricultural employer in the Bekaa knows me or has heard of me.

Marking the dual valence of "knowing people" and "experience," *maʿrifa* was a powerful form of social capital that sustained his paternalistic authority in the camp while making his work as a *shawīsh* materially possible within the Lebanese agricultural labor market. While Abu Sharif glossed the work of *shawīsh* with an aura of ease and sociability, his labor was constitutive of an entire cross-border economy of agricultural work.

As was typically the case within *shawīsh* camps, new families were recruited through a chain-referral system based on their degree of social connection to existing camp residents, which was a means of vouching for their reputation. Given the importance of trust and honor within these communities, this chain-referral system created a durable circuit of accountability between the *shawīsh* and camp residents. Because Abu Sharif had *maʿrifa*—that is, he knew how to reach every family's kin in their home villages—I never heard of a case where a family fled the camp or reneged on their debt obligations. In turn, this chain-referral system also put pressure on Abu Sharif to be relatively generous with requests for credit and fastidiously document workers' earnings; if he acquired a reputation for being too exploitative or stingy, he risked losing his authority in the villages where he had cultivated a reliable flow of workers.

Through his long-standing network of connections and range of skills, Abu Sharif also extended *maʿrifa* to his male kin through a guild-like structure of apprenticeship. At the time of my fieldwork, his two eldest teenage sons were apprenticing to become *shawīsh,* which involved taking over responsibility for driving the camp residents to work and acting as overseers during shifts. Abu Sharif had also trained his two eldest nephews through the process of establishing their own *shawīsh* camps in nearby villages. Constructed just a few years after the war began, his nephews' camps were still fledgling enterprises, with each hosting around three dozen people. As they navigated Lebanon's competitive market in cheap agricultural labor, they lacked the numbers and leverage to flexibly meet employers' needs during peak weeding and harvest seasons. To keep his nephews' small camps afloat, Abu Sharif often negotiated work assignments on their behalf or combined their workers with his for larger jobs.

Maʿrifa also played a crucial role in determining how and where *shawīsh* secured land to establish, expand, or relocate their camps. Many Lebanese landlords, especially absentees and those with very small holdings or fallow properties, opted to host camps on their land to secure a steady source of rental income. *Shawīsh* like Abu Sharif were central figures in this process of scaling up existing camps or establishing new camps, as they relied on their prewar connections to build trust with landlords and negotiate rental agreements. In turn, *maʿrifa* formed the basis of Abu Sharif's moral appeals to his superiors in key moments of need or unexpected emergencies. This proved significant when Abu Sharif's nephew, Mahmood, was obliged to relocate his camp suddenly after they were evicted from the junkyard where they had set up a small camp several years earlier. Mahmood called a wealthy Lebanese landlord whom he had known since childhood through Abu Sharif. Though the landlord did not normally rent out his land to refugees, he allowed Mahmood to set up a small camp on his property.[14]

Abu Sharif's reliance upon *maʿrifa* vividly underscored what it meant for credit to have a face: a carefully cultivated and near-constant performance of competency, reputation, and well-connectedness. Abu Sharif often went to great lengths to "prove" to me not only the breadth of this connectedness but also its apparent depth, especially among former workers. For example, he once called a former camp resident on WhatsApp as we rode in his truck together. She had returned to Syria in the previous year. Putting her on speakerphone, he addressed her with the warmth and familiarity of an uncle or brother. She responded in kind, as they exchanged updates about every family in the camp: who got married, who passed away, and who had left the camp or returned to Syria. As the call came to a close, she lamented that the economic situation in Syria was so dire that she was considering coming back to Lebanon. "I'll see if I can get my guy to take you," he replied, presumably referring to a smuggler or border guard. Though conveyed with an air of paternalistic confidence, the vagueness of his promise gestured to the grim reality of the regional situation. At the time, Lebanese security forces were criminalizing Syrians' internal and cross-border mobility, and the illicit movements of Syrians across the Lebanese-Syrian border were becoming riskier and more costly, even for experienced *shawīsh* like Abu Sharif.

The call, in a condensed form, revealed how the war in Syria transformed the *shawīsh* system, marked by a loss of cross-border mobility and increasing state surveillance. Like all other *shawīsh,* he was seeking to turn a profit through his work. This was not only for the sake of capital accumulation; it also was motivated by a desire to rebuild the personal retirement savings he lost in Syria. According to Abu Sharif's estimates, establishing a camp for three hundred people cost him around $30,000 in initial capital outlays. This was a paltry sum for most of Lebanon's elites, but a lifetime of accumulated savings and social connections for Abu Sharif. Indeed, in contrast to Jamil's caricatured idea of *shawīsh* as landed shaykhs, Abu Sharif had relatively little wealth to speak of. He had inherited thirteen hectares of nonarable desert land in Syria's steppe. Alongside his ventures as a *shawīsh,* he had put most of life savings into purchasing an apartment in the southeast suburbs of Aleppo in 1998. The entire neighborhood, including the home he had finished renovating just a few years before the popular uprising broke out in 2011, was decimated in the war.

In accounting for the ways that their obligations shifted after 2011, Abu Sharif and other *shawīsh* often made a point of distinguishing their camp operations from the sprawling camps for "free" workers (*shaghīl hurr*) that expanded throughout the war. "Free" camps were distinct from *shawīsh* camps in that they usually had no formal leader or middleman and were not as tightly organized around village chain migration networks. Free camps were also more transient and improvised, located in junkyards or adjacent to industrial properties, and often hosted a random mix of families from diverse areas of Syria. Unlike *shawīsh* camps, residents of these camps were obliged to find work and services on their own and thus were more vulnerable to eviction and joblessness.

When I asked Abu Sharif about the difference between free camps and *shawīsh* camps, he framed the contrast in terms of *amāna,* a polysemous term that can refer to trust, protection, or security. "Al-warsha killā bi-amāntī," he said, meaning that the entire camp is under his trusteeship or protection. Through the lens of *amāna*, he juxtaposed the free camp, as a site of anomie and crime, against the *shawīsh* camp, protected by a paternal figure who guarantees order, sociality, and moral propriety:

> The landlord in free camps is primarily concerned with collecting money. If the camp catches on fire, it doesn't matter to him [*mā ilu maṣlaḥa*]. Instead, I take care of people. By the way, the *mukhābarāt* [Lebanese central intelligence] don't like those free camps. There is no *shawīsh* in charge to keep things in order, so those camps have problems with drugs, weapons, and ISIS. Look, if there is no *shawīsh*, it's a disaster [*mṣība*]. It becomes a neighborhood of "every man for himself" [*kil min īdu ilu*]. Drunkards come to live there, cars roll through, everyone comes and goes, and no one cares [lit: no one asks of another; *al-ʿālam mū sāʾil ḥada*]. As the *shawīsh*, I want to know who is coming in and who is going. I am responsible for girls [lit: girls are on my neck; *fī banāt ʿala raqabtī*]. The entire camp is "on my neck" and I have to take care of their safety.

Employing idioms of thick sociality and security, he portrayed the *shawīsh* camp as a village-like, feminized space of harmonious social belonging. The evocative phrase "girls on my neck" (*banāt ʿala raqabtī*) underscored the paternalistic nature of his responsibility, implying that the camp conferred not just shelter but also a means by which people were brought into a community structure, albeit in a deeply hierarchical relationship to the *shawīsh*.

The contrast between "free" camps and *shawīsh* camps was obviously overwrought, filtered as it was through his masculine performance of competence and self-importance—not to mention his labor position as a broker. Still, his claim about the camp as a space of *amāna* revealed something important about the camp's moral economy. As an ethical framework that connotes protection, security, care, and paternalism all at the same time, *amāna* indexed the dual face of debt as a binding force in these camps. It was coercive and patriarchal, and at the same time, it offered vital moral and material guarantees.

It is also telling that he described the landlords of free camps as lacking *maṣlaḥa*. In everyday vernacular speech, *maṣlaḥa* can mean "benefit," "responsibility," "public good," or "interest."[15] Yet it can also carry pejorative connotations when used to describe economic transactions; my Syrian friends routinely invoked *maṣlaḥa* to characterize the ill manners of those they regarded as self-interested, calculating, or profit oriented.[16] Interestingly, however, Abu Sharif was here referring to *maṣlaḥa* in its more neutral sense of "interest," in order to denounce what he saw as landlords' lack of concern for the well being of refugees living on their land. As a commentary on class relations, his invocation of *maṣlaḥa* was also notable for the way it inverted the conventional moral opposition through which Lebanese landlords often distinguished themselves from *shawīsh*. Whereas landlords tended to cast *shawīsh* as opportunistic and unscrupulous middlemen, Abu Sharif emphasized the moral value of his own patronage work in contrast to what he perceived as the callous disinterest of landlords as mere rent collectors.

His proprietary reference to the *mukhābarāt* also spoke to the changing wartime function of *shawīsh* camps. Though never articulated in any direct way, I gathered that there was an implicit agreement between some *shawīsh* and the Lebanese central intelligence that a certain amount of illicit activity, such as smuggling workers from Syria, would be covertly permitted by the state in exchange for security cooperation. *Shawīsh* were required to register all residents in their camps and report if anyone appeared to be sympathetic to ISIS or other militant Islamist groups. Another *shawīsh* once explained the chain of command as follows: "Every time a new person arrives in my camp, I have to tell the *mukhābarāt* [central intelligence], then *amn al-dawla* [state security], then *amn al-ʿām* [general security], and finally the *baladiyya* [local municipality], in that order. And if someone wants to move out of the camp, same thing."

Alongside these security obligations, Abu Sharif understood very well that maintaining a benevolent, authoritative reputation among camp residents hinged on his capacity to provide consistent work opportunities. As scholars of agrarian debt have long noted, the cultivation of reputation is particularly important in casual work environments lacking formal legal protections, where thick social bonds form the basis of trust that another will honor her obligations.[17] "The most important thing is that I keep my workers employed," he once told me on a ride back from a shift. "If I don't make a profit, I at least need to break even. If the workers stay "sitting" (unemployed), it would be a disaster [*al- ʿummāl iza bārikīn, mṣība*]. Everything is on my dime [*ʿa ḥisābī*]." Abu Sharif was indeed not immune to the disciplinary effects of indebtedness, which generated a baseline need to keep wages low to ensure that Lebanese employers continued to hire his workers and, at the same time, keep the camp bank account solvent while managing distributive obligations to camp residents.

Though camp residents' capacities to transform or contest their working conditions were quite limited within this system, they were highly conscious of their power to make distributive claims upon Abu Sharif. In particular, they frequently demanded that his cash loans flow more "easily." Most of the time, they used these loans to cover everyday household expenses and major life-transition events, but they also borrowed from Abu Sharif to send remittances to relatives in their home villages who were coping with the devaluation of the Syrian pound. In turn, some who had already worked off their debts were deferring their return to Syria in order to save up for the costs of rebuilding or renovating their homes.

FIGURE 13. Making mansaf for a camp resident's wedding.

In addition to lending cash, members of the camp expected Abu Sharif to provide a certain amount of favors, especially on ceremonial occasions and major Islamic holidays. The most frequent grievance I encountered was when Abu Sharif refused to lend the amount of money a camp resident asked to borrow on a given day or failed to provide expected services. Though there were many explanations as to why he might grant, refuse, or downgrade requests for cash loans, his informal accounting and cash flow projections usually shaped his decision. Depending on their agreement, employers sent a check to Abu Sharif at the end of a given season, or in monthly or biweekly installments. Thus, for the duration of each season, he was obliged to carefully manage flows of payment from employers in relation to flows of credit to workers.

Tacking between the moral obligation to give generously and the drive to keep his camp profitable, his shifting position as a broker, patron, and moneylender spoke to the instability of his class status and the prospects of "sliding down" back to a mere worker if his camp ceased to be profitable.[18] As an entrepreneur, he was caught in a bind faced by many fledgling capitalists, compelled by the forces of market competition to seek out profits or else risk being pushed out of business. As Karl Marx states: "The capitalist who produces surplus value . . . is by no means the ultimate proprietor. He has to share it afterwards with capitalists who fulfill other functions in social reproduction taken as a whole, with the owner of the land, and with yet other people."[19] In other words, although those who hire labor for the explicit purposes of accumulating a surplus are often thought to be in a privileged position to maximize profits, they are always at the risk of becoming debtors or ceasing being capitalists after all other claims have been satisfied.[20]

This imperative was often in tension with the vital reproductive nature of his work as a patron, given that the farmworkers living in his camp were navigating the costs of long-term displacement. In this sense, the *shawīsh* camp system was deeply tied up with what feminists refer to as "crises of reproduction" or "crises of care."[21] In short: camp residents were forced by a lack of independent means to sell their labor-power for a wage, and Abu Sharif was compelled by the forces of competition to keep their wages low. This, in turn, shifted the burden of care back onto *shawīsh* in the form of credit lending, given that workers' wages were insufficient to cover their costs of living.

Tasked with fulfilling state-like functions for a displaced population lacking state support, Abu Sharif became like a Janus-faced state whose work was, at once, disciplinary and caregiving.[22] Because work assignments were structured around an on-call labor-reserve system, Abu Sharif's bank account was vulnerable to fluctuations and liquidity problems, especially in the winter low season. If he were to lend too much, the camp as a whole would be in debt, and he would be unable to pay the annual ground-rent and reimburse workers whose earnings exceeded their debts at the end of the season. This rendered his daily work into an ongoing performance of often incommensurate roles, as he sought to balance profitability against residents' ever-expanding needs for credit and services. It was also, as the examples of *maʿrifa, amāna,* and *maṣlaḥa* suggest, a daily practice of moral self-cultivation formed in and through his relations with others. Ultimately, it was the *moral* stakes of this work that formed the grounds on which workers staged their claims upon him, as the next section will show.

DEBT'S MORAL BINDS: THE PARADOXES OF PATRONAGE

Incidents of outwardly violent contention were a rare occurrence in the camp. Like many other migrant workers across the world, residents of Abu Sharif's camp enjoyed neither state protections nor union membership from which to collectively bargain to improve their labor conditions.[23] Instead, they made claims upon Abu Sharif through subtle repertoires of contention that appealed to his moral obligations as a Muslim and a father-like figure. These were not necessarily acts of *resistance* to authority; they were affirmative moral claims that *sustained and reproduced* his authority. Vacillating between joking, gentle rebuke, and measured deference, camp residents' repertoires were nevertheless always clear on one point: they refused to be pitied. While reproducing the hierarchies that existed between them, these interactional repertoires were a constant reminder that they expected to be treated with dignity.

This was made vividly apparent to me one evening when I was visiting Abu Sharif in his guesthouse after he had finished tabulating each family's earnings for the day. Abu Sharif, his son, another *shawīsh* from a nearby camp named Abu Muhammad, and I were playing cards together, while Abu

Sharif smoked an *arghile* water pipe. One of the camp residents, Zeinab, appeared at the door of the guesthouse. She hovered at the entrance quietly.

"What do you need, Zeinab?" Abu Sharif asked her disinterestedly, blowing smoke out of the edge of his mouth.

"There's a mistake!" (*fī ghalaṭ*), she shouted, waving her pay stub at him with a mix of indignation and sisterly admonition. Like many members of the camp, Zeinab could barely read, but she had mastered the art of calculating her family's daily wages and knew how to spot mistakes.

"Come in," the other *shawīsh* Abu Muhammad told her, and she marched confidently forward. She remained standing while everyone else was seated on the floor, which elevated the drama of the moment.

She smiled girlishly but spoke confidently. "Look, Abu Sharif, you made a mistake," she repeated as she passed the receipt to him. Abu Sharif glanced up for a moment to take the receipt, but his attention remained fixed on his cards.

"Calm down, sister, don't get angry!" Abu Muhammad exclaimed mockingly.

"Let's leave this for tomorrow" (*khallīnā li bacher*), Abu Sharif replied in a business-like way, though the words carried the colloquial warmth of the rural eastern Syrian dialect. "I'm in the middle of something."

Zeinab sighed, placing her hand on her hips and tapping her foot impatiently, indicating that she was not going to budge. She was still smiling, which gave me the sense that she was confident that she would get her way.

Abu Muhammad chuckled and put his cards down. Citing the Qur'anic injunction against arrogance and greed, he turned to Abu Sharif with a grin. "Shame on you" (*ḥarām*), he teased. "It's wrong to 'eat' orphans, the needy, and the poor" (*yutāmy wal-masākīn wal-fuqarā', ḥarām ta'kulhum*).[24] By "eating," he meant withholding wages.[25]

"Thank God, we're not orphans," Zeinab retorted flatly. Here, her response indexed two things. She understood that Abu Muhammad was poking fun at her and Abu Sharif. And she was refusing to be reduced to a beggar or object of pity.

"Well then," Abu Muhammad replied, turning to Abu Sharif, half-seriously this time. "Your actions are seen by God."

"Listen, Zeinab, your brother hasn't come to work in weeks," Abu Sharif pushed back, referencing the fact that her younger brother was away in Beirut, trying to supplement the family's income with intermittent restaurant work.

"He'll be back next week," Zeinab replied deferentially, understanding that Abu Sharif was asserting his leverage over her.

"Fine, let's talk tomorrow. I'll verify it in my notebook," Abu Sharif concluded.

"Tomorrow? Okay, tomorrow," Zeinab said, apparently satisfied that it would be resolved, and she turned toward the door.

The exchange between Zeinab and Abu Sharif revealed the complex tensions between debt's coercive power and the construction of moral authority. Agrarian scholars have long argued that credit-debt relations carry a deceptive social thickness; these relations are powerful because they produce a specific kind of morality, one intimately bound up in the dull compulsion of economic forces and characterized by "the relentless drive to calculate, trade, work, intensify and grow."[26] Indeed, the concept of guilt (*Schuld*) is historically related to debts (*Schulden*): debt's power lies in its capacity to produce guilty subjects who are self-disciplining.[27] It is precisely for this reason that the credit-debt relation is, in Marx's words, "all the more infamous and extreme" because it mediates "man's moral existence, man's social existence, the inmost depths of his heart."[28] To a significant degree, this account captured the nature of Abu Sharif's position: his work as a broker was indisputably capitalist, in that his power derived from his ability to command labor and he was seeking to turn a profit.

Yet the moral dimension of Abu Sharif's role could not be so easily assimilated to a capitalist logic of calculation and profit seeking, as Zeinab's appeals to Abu Sharif's piety were central to their interaction. Though Abu Muhammad's exhortations were steeped in playful banter, it was clear that Abu Sharif was striving to become a better Muslim, as he was performing his obligatory prayers and constantly listening to Qur'anic recitation in his truck. Through their explicit and oblique invocations of Islamic principles, Zeinab and Abu Muhammad were drawing upon the vast and ever-evolving discursive tradition to which all Muslims orient themselves through their daily practices, relations with others, and modes of ethical self-cultivation.[29]

Anchored within their shared orientation as Muslims toward divine authority, this interaction between Abu Sharif and Zeinab was based on mutual recognition of their differential social capabilities and political powers.[30] This was evident in how Abu Sharif signaled that he was aware that Zeinab's brother was not fulfilling his labor obligations but had allowed this to slide for weeks without mentioning it. It was only when Zeinab used her limited leverage to point out an accounting error that Abu Sharif invoked her family's more amorphous and ultimately incalculable debts to him due to his flexibility.

As an affirmation of hierarchy, this personalistic mode of patronage undoubtedly diffused the possibility of worker solidarity and other more collective forms of struggle in the camp. It did not, however, foreclose the importance of struggle itself, here understood in the theological sense of striving to cultivate virtue in the face of tribulations.[31] Both poverty and wealth, understood as such, are divine trials unique to each person—wealth may confer the possibility of enjoining good, or it may be a curse that leads a believer astray, depending on how one uses this divine endowment.[32] This encompasses the principle of *al-amr bi-l-maʿrūf*, which implies mutual responsibility among Muslims, rich or poor, to care for one another's souls—including through critique and persuasion—in the struggle to live virtuously.[33] Unlike a Protestant Christian understanding of morals based on belief or faith, this is a process of ethical cultivation oriented to *action*.

Zeinab's refusal to be seen as an object of charitable almsgiving was significant in this sense, though implicit. Orphans, widows, disabled people, debtors, and the very poor are considered unique categories of people deserving of alms within Islam, and their divine obligation is to accept gifts from their benefactors, who are tasked with justly distributing God's divine sustenance (*rizq*).[34] The Islamic scholar and leader of the Muslim Brotherhood Sayyid Qutb described this as "the right of the poor" (*haqq al-faqīr*), understood as the poor's "due share" of God's providence.[35] Once a gift has been given, the receiver cannot refuse, for the giving and acceptance of alms is an act of pious conviction.[36]

Camp residents were keenly aware of the famous hadith by the Prophet Muhammad that the "upper" hand of the giver is held in higher moral esteem than the "lower" hand of the receiver within Islam. For this reason, their appeals to Abu Sharif's faith remained a subtext that was rarely articulated explicitly, lest they be seen as beggars. Instead, the outward terrain of negotiation between them worked at two levels: they insisted on Abu Sharif's professional obligation, as an employer, to respect their dignity as workers by properly accounting their wages and, second, they appealed to his kin-like obligation to them as a patron to offer a certain amount of flexibility regarding work obligations and to keep credit flowing. Still, the exchange between Zeinab and Abu Sharif also showed how this slippage worked in Abu Sharif's favor. Though Abu Sharif fastidiously documented the camp residents' debts, the ambiguity of the kinship bond often overshadowed the need for transparency. In other words, his "flexibility," couched in terms of *amāna* (protection) and *ma'rifa* (know-how), created ambiguous pretexts for occasionally withholding, postponing, or reneging on wage payments.

This highlighted the importance of the material forms through which Abu Sharif accounted camp residents' debts—the ledger, receipts, and quality of language itself. Where Zeinab's labor was rendered as an abstract, calculable unit of labor-power in the receipt (and therefore a commodity to be bought and sold on the labor market), their mutual obligations to each other as Muslims both reinforced and exceeded that logic of calculability. As an economic exchange shot through with moral sentiments, the conversation between Abu Sharif and Zeinab was, thus, neither a socially thick "outside" of capitalism nor a frictionless, impersonal transaction, but rather an expression of debt's social plasticity and complex moral affordances. It therefore pointed to the powerful sociability of debt: that is, the ways that debt is not only a state of lacking or owing but can be a productive mode of affirming, redefining, or denying the moral value of one's relationships across different domains of social life, including in the realm of waged labor.[37]

"A PERSON WITH A FULL STOMACH DOESN'T KNOW ANYONE": *SHAWĪSH* CAMPS IN CRISIS

The pressure on all *shawīsh* camps to maintain liquidity deepened throughout Lebanon's economic crisis that accelerated dramatically throughout 2019. For the first time in years, many *shawīsh* were starting to face a labor shortage, a product of several converging factors. First, parts of Syria were stabilizing, and some refugees were preparing to return home. Second, increasing securitization of the Lebanese-Syrian border was making smuggling new workers from Syria more costly and difficult. And third, growing numbers of camp residents were becoming acquainted with Lebanon's labor market and realizing that they could move to a different *shawīsh* camp with a better reputation or a "free" camp after working off their debts. As scholars of debt peonage in Latin America have long observed, debt relations do not always imply worker subordination.[38] In situations of labor scarcity, workers are in a greater position to leave, strike, or negotiate repayment.

Against this backdrop, I noticed over the course of my fieldwork a tightening in Abu Sharif's credit lending. In order to save face and maintain a strong reputation, Abu Sharif did not directly convey to camp residents that he was constrained by the need to maintain a certain amount of liquidity in the camp bank account. From their perspective, his growing reluctance to lend cash was simply a sign of stinginess, as many became convinced that the money and prestige he had accumulated over the years were starting to corrupt his morals. This came to a head on the holiday of ʿEid when he failed to uphold his annual practice of slaughtering several sheep to distribute to the camp residents. In keeping with Islamic ideals of almsgiving, camp residents understood this failure as a violation of his divinely mandated obligation to share his wealth with the poor. Imm Hassan was particularly incensed.

"I can't bear it anymore!" (*mā ʿād aṭīq*) Imm Hassan exclaimed to Abu Ayman, the family friend we met in the last chapter, who was visiting her for ʿEid.

"Sister, mankind cannot be broken except by hunger" (*bani ādam mā yaksar ʿaynu ila al-jūʿ*), Abu Ayman averred with an air of stoic wisdom. "Sure, he's rich [*zangīl*]. It's money he doesn't need. A person with a full stomach doesn't know anyone [*al-baṭan lama taltaqī mā raḥ btʿaraf ʿala ḥada*]. But a person who has been wronged cannot fight back with an empty stomach [*bas iza fāḍī waḥad yaghlat ʿalayh, mā yaqdar ykāwan*]."

"That money is the dirtiness of the world [*wasakh al-dunyā*]," Imm Hassan sighed.

"He who does not fear God" (*illi ma yekhāf min Allah*) . . .

"One should fear him" (*khāf minu*), Imm Hassan chimed in, completing Abu Ayman's invocation of the famous Arabic proverb "He who does not fear God is the one you must fear."

"He's so stingy that he gives beat-up potatoes to his family" (*bakhil zād, jaʿd ya'khudh al-baṭāṭā al-mafshaqa lil bayt*), Imm Hassan went on, implying that Abu Sharif shamefully relegated his family to gleaning leftover potatoes from the fields surrounding the camps, a practice usually reserved for the extremely poor. "Bruised, broken, mashed up, no matter, he takes them home. No dignity!"

As the conversation continued, Imm Hassan expressed her intention to return to Syria and avoid going into any further debt. "If you're no longer borrowing from him, you'll be done with him [*takhlaṣūn minnu*]," Abu Ayman replied reassuringly.

Abu Ayman's final response to Imm Hassan underscored how Abu Sharif's efficacy as a provider and farmworkers' attachment to him were predicated on the continuous circulation of credit-debt bonds. The notion that Imm Hassan could be "done" with her obligations toward Abu Sharif when she ceased borrowing pointed to the mutuality of these bonds, despite their highly unequal structure. The strength and durability of these bonds were not only economic but also imbued with affective ties of fictive kinship, as well as concepts of honor, care, generosity, and reputation. By suggesting that a "full stomach" foreclosed the possibility of "knowing someone," Abu Ayman poetically referred to the diabolical and antisocial connotations of wealth accumulation.[39] Abu Ayman's invocations of the stomach also had theological implications; the Qur'an and hadith are replete with references to the risks of overindulgence beyond one's basic satiation. Emphasizing Abu Sharif's apparent stinginess with even his own family, Imm Hassan implied that it was not only the fictive kinship bonds within the camp that were breaking down, but the very meaning of kinship itself.

Abu Ayman's insistence that a person with an empty stomach "cannot fight back" was equally important. One of the ways that Imm Hassan sought to progressively emancipate her family from their debts to Abu Sharif was by squeezing her household's expenditures to a bare minimum, including by growing vegetables next to her tent, gleaning secretly at work, and cutting expensive foods like meat out of their diet. Well aware of eastern Syrian women's extraordinary power to self-exploit in times of dearth, Abu Ayman was cautioning Imm Hassan against unduly subjecting herself and her family to hardship, as working off her debts would require extended periods of endurance and foresight.

At the same time, camp residents' attachments to the *shawīsh* did not operate along a linear plane. After a summer spent listening to camp residents' simmering resentments against Abu Sharif, I witnessed a vivid instance in which his role was suddenly threatened to be taken away. As part of an escalating wave of criminalization of Syrian workers and arbitrary arrests by Lebanese security services throughout 2019, Abu Sharif was unexpectedly imprisoned under the charge of using a forged work permit.

For the two weeks that he languished in jail, the entire affective orientation among camp residents momentarily transformed, from one of growing frustration with him to one of overwhelming affection. During this time, the responsibility for assigning labor opportunities and fulfilling camp residents' credit loan requests fell upon Abu Sharif's nephews and teenage sons. There was palpably less work than usual, which the residents associated with Abu Sharif's absence. "He is the one with connections [*maʿrifa*], so he is the one who can find work for us," Imm Hassan lamented, a stunning reversal of her mounting grievances against him.

Throughout this uncertain period of Abu Sharif's imprisonment, even the most disgruntled camp residents spoke wistfully of his effectiveness in procuring work opportunities. "Without Abu Sharif, the camp is worthless" (*al-mukhayyam balā Abu Sharif mā byiswa*), was a refrain I heard several times throughout the camp. I was reminded of June Nash's classic study of Bolivian tin miners, where she describes the workers' attachments to their patron as follows: "Without the job, there would be no life."[40] In a similar way, it was the vital reproductive nature of Abu Sharif's work—that he literally guaranteed "life"—that made his absence so profound. Like an infrastructural channel whose value becomes apparent only when it breaks down, Abu Sharif's value to the camp residents became fully palpable when his caretaker-patron role was suddenly in jeopardy. That their seemingly all-powerful patron was not immune to the wave of discriminatory measures against Syrian nationals in Lebanon created a momentary reprieve from the obvious inequalities that existed between them.

Yet, as soon as Abu Sharif was back in the camp, the litany of complaints and resentments resumed as before, from Imm Hassan especially. This seemingly ambivalent orientation was a vivid example of what economic anthropologists refer to as "the elasticity of obligation," meaning the ways that patronage channels are reworked in response to shifting moral and political exigencies.[41] Abu Sharif's distributive role as patron, far from stable or pregiven, was a precarious achievement mediated by workers' shifting claims upon him and perceptions of his moral stature. Attending to the nuances of this type of hierarchical dependence suggests that, more than a mere absence of rights or form of false consciousness, *shawīsh* patronage was a dynamic and powerful relational orientation to wealth distribution.[42] Workers' dependence on him, in other words, was not a static or passive condition, but an ongoing affirmation of moral accountability.

DOUBLE BIND, DOUBLE FREEDOM

Abu Sharif's constrained lending brought to light a basic tension within the camp's debt regime: the trade-off between the security and predictability offered by *shawīsh* camps, on the one hand, and camp residents' longing for more autonomy and control over their labor time, on the other. While a few residents like Imm Hassan were making plans to return to Syria, others began contemplating moving to "free" camps, including Imm Bassam and Abu Bassam, the married couple introduced at the end of chapter 1. Frustrated by the camp's remote location and limited work opportunities outside of agriculture, Abu Bassam invoked the need for self-help. "No one will benefit you, not your mother, not your brother," he told me. "The clever one knows how to get by [lit: unshackle himself; *al-shāṭer yfukk ḥālu*]. Everyone races to live [*al-ʿālam yerkuḍ mnshān al-ʿaysha*]."

Resolving to leave the camp at the end of the season at any cost, they did their best to avoid borrowing from Abu Sharif throughout the high summer season. Eventually, they took out a $3,000 interest-bearing loan from an NGO to help cancel out their remaining debts. Beaming with pride as he showed me the Western Union receipt for monthly repayment ($102), Abu Bassam explained that he chose not to take a loan from Abu Sharif because they wanted to move to a free camp. "With free work, the conditions are much better," Imm Bassam chimed in. "There is no *shawīsh* telling you to work. . . . I get to decide when and where I go. With Abu Sharif, we're forced to work [*majbūrīn*]."

As a mother of six, including three small children, Imm Bassam's desire for more control over her labor was, in large part, related to the problem of childcare. Within the gendered divisions of labor that defined the family wage system in Abu Sharif's camp, she and her eldest teenage son were obliged to work in the fields, often for multiple shifts during the high season. This meant that she relied upon her adolescent daughters and husband to look after the smaller children throughout the day while she was at work. In their own way, Imm Bassam and Abu Bassam made clear to me what freedom meant to them in this context: more flexibility to determine the distribution and flow of labor obligations in their household in the day-to-day, whether that labor was waged or not.

When the new season began and accounts were settled in November, they fulfilled their plans to relocate to a free camp, where they paid rent directly to the Lebanese landlord with no middleman. I visited them on several occasions. What immediately struck me about their new life in the "free" camp was the unpredictability of each day, compared to the relatively structured work rhythms of Abu Sharif's camp. During one of my visits, Imm Bassam and I spent the better part of two days trying to locate the closest and cheapest dental clinic, as she had lately been suffering from a toothache. In Abu Sharif's camp, by contrast, residents benefited from his connections to a well-respected local dentist who made a point of serving Syrian clients at a discounted rate.

Throughout each of my visits, members of the family were constantly shuffling in and out of the house, moving from one job to another throughout the day. Their young adolescent son sold gum on the street, their teenage son worked in a restaurant, and Abu Bassam peddled prayer beads and watches in an open suitcase at the nearest taxi stand. Their adolescent daughters rotated between going to school and helping Imm Bassam look after her small children and do housework, while Imm Bassam intermittently took day jobs in agricultural work. Their goal was to save up for their eldest son's wedding expenses, including the bridewealth payment and the cost of building a house for the newlyweds on their small parcel of land back in Syria. But it was clear from how they were cutting household costs and pooling their incomes that these aspirations for the future remained subordinate to the weight of their debt repayments to the NGO and their nonnegotiable monthly rent.

Whereas Abu Sharif had earlier portrayed free camps as crime ridden and atomistic, Abu Bassam expressed a sense of relief that his family was no longer bound to mandatory labor in the *shawīsh* camp. "No one forces anyone to work here. You just pay rent to the landlord. He has no relationship to you [*mā ilu ʿalāqa fīkī*]," Abu Bassam explained, as he arranged prayer beads neatly in a suitcase to display for sale on the street. "With the *shawīsh*, what comes from you belongs to him [*minnik ilu*]."

But in all the talk about "free" labor, I couldn't help but be reminded of how Abu Sharif had described the difference between free camps and *shawīsh* camps: the latter was under his trusteeship (*amāna*) and it was his responsibility (*maṣlaḥa*) to care for the residents. Though Abu Bassam and Imm Bassam were enthusiastic about leaving Abu Sharif's camp, they quietly conceded to me during one of my visits that it was his camp that had temporarily given them refuge when they had needed it most. They had originally moved to his camp in the previous season after being evicted from a free camp due to their inability to pay monthly rent. For them and countless others, *shawīsh* camps functioned as a contingency housing market for families threatened with homelessness due to a lack of gainful employment.

The vagaries of navigating between these two distinct arrangements—the *shawīsh* camp and the free camp—suggested that more than a simple binary between freedom and unfreedom was at work. If life in the *shawīsh* camp existed on a tense continuum between care and coercion, life in the free camp seemed to reside precariously between autonomy and destitution. In other words, though they were finally emancipated from the grip of obligatory labor in the *shawīsh* camp, Imm Bassam and her family now seemed to be truly "free" in the cruel double sense that Marx described: free to dispose of their labor-power yet lacking the means necessary for the realization of that labor-power.[43]

A "GUARANTEED" WAGE: THE HIERARCHIES OF INTERDEPENDENCY

"Do you have your notebook with you?" Abu Sharif asked me out of the blue one day as we were driving back to the camp after buying medicine for one of the residents. "We're going to the supermarket now," he explained with an air of didacticism. "When you see the owner, I need you to tell him that you work for the United Nations. Also, you need to pretend that you don't speak Arabic, otherwise it won't be believable. I need you to act like a foreigner."

I was confused. "Okay. But why?" I asked.

Abu Sharif's half-grin was somewhere between playful and serious, which only confused me further. "Tell him that the UN is doing a study of the businesses that sell to Syrian refugees," he said, "Tell him that you are giving him an award for having the best prices in the whole neighborhood." I suspected Abu Sharif was playing a practical joke, but I decided to go along with it.

As we exited the car and ascended the stairs leading to the small supermarket, I noticed two large, white signs prominently posted on the window, bearing the blue logo of the World Food Program, which indicated that they accepted UN aid as payment. The owner was sitting at the checkout counter and greeted us with a warm "Ahlan!" when we entered.

"Assalamu ʿalaykum," Abu Sharif said politely, "This is my colleague. She's from the United Nations."

I smiled, feeling at a loss for words. "You . . . have a very nice store," I stammered in English, looking at Abu Sharif for a cue about what to do next.

Abu Sharif didn't skip a beat. "My colleague is doing a survey of businesses on behalf of the UN. I told her this store has the best prices in the Bekaa, so they want to give you a prize."

The owner looked a bit baffled but also happy.

"Congratulations!" I uttered sheepishly.

Looking over at me with a twinkle in his eyes, Abu Sharif guided me along, "Okay, write down the name of the owner and the store. Now, take a picture of him."

I clumsily pulled out my phone and took a few pictures. Abu Sharif could see that I was still confused and about to blow his cover, so he wrapped up our visit with a perfunctory goodbye and shuttled me out the door. "Okay, thank you for your time! We'll see you soon!"

When we returned to Abu Sharif's truck, I asked him why he had asked me to pretend that I work for the United Nations. "Because everyone in the camp buys food from him," he replied, "The owner keeps prices low and accepts payment through UN cash aid. I want him to stay 'afraid' of the UN.

That way, he'll continue taking care of everyone [*dīr bāl al-ʿālam*] and won't raise the prices on us."

"It seems like everyone knows you in this town," I remarked, suddenly realizing that this detour was not only to procure affordable goods but also a strategic performance of his social networks, in which I was also conscripted.

"Every Lebanese person here knows that I don't go into debt [*mā bdayyan*]," he replied with a confident grin, by which he meant that he carries the debts of his camp residents but does not let himself become indebted to Lebanese employers, businesses, or service providers. "And *everyone* borrows through me" (*kil al-ʿālam bidayyan ʿanī*).

As we drove back to the camp together, I recalled Jamil's initial introduction to Abu Sharif as a "liar." I could see that the grocery store performance was a vivid instance of Abu Sharif's *maʿrifa* in action, but it was certainly more than a self-serving gesture. His performance of well-connectedness was a means of ensuring that he could continue to meet the needs of the camp residents. Bringing together a foreign researcher, a grocery store owner, and the United Nations, this performance was also a testament to the many obligations that his position as a patron, moneylender, broker, and refugee held in tension. Indeed, despite his constant efforts to appear unburdened by these countervailing roles, I came to understand in such moments that he was treading an ever-more-difficult tightrope between maintaining profitability and protecting his workers' well being.

This chapter has outlined the moral and economic conditions that bound refugee farmworkers to *shawīsh* throughout the war in Syria. By securing the recruitment and reproduction of a highly precarious pool of migrant labor, the *shawīsh* system helped ensure that the costs of labor remained low for Lebanese employers in agriculture. At the same time, Abu Sharif provided critical services for Syrians who were coping with the wartime loss of social benefits from the Syrian state and the subsistence they derived from their land in Syria. Thus, despite being an exploiter of labor, he was also tied up in complex paternalistic relations with the camp residents, who depended on his capacity to provide *amāna*—protection, security, and care—in a context of long-term displacement. This role was riven by contradictions: his efforts to maintain a reputation for generosity among farmworkers were in ongoing tension with the economic imperative to calculate workers' debts, maintain liquidity in the camp's bank account, and maximize profit.

These dilemmas are historically specific, but not wholly exceptional. As a distinct network made by and for displaced people, *shawīsh* camps offer a vivid window onto the political economy of rural debt relations and their reverberating contradictions in everyday life. Exemplifying the tenuous process by which temporary migration networks are remade into long-term sites of refuge, Abu Sharif's work was emblematic of the widening networks of private patronage that have taken up the mantle of accommodating refugees in the face of limited state resources and dwindling humanitarian aid. Fundamentally unsettling the presumptive opposition between "forced" refugees and "free" labor migrants, these camps also reveal the impossibility of understanding Syrians' predicaments without centering their labor conditions and the moral obligations that animate them.

Ultimately, for Abu Bassam and his family, the encumbrances of debt in the *shawīsh* camp were a burden they were unwilling to endure any longer, even if this meant being subjected once again to the risks of eviction and underemployment, as well as the material pressures of paying back an interest-bearing loan to an NGO. In contrast, for those who remained in Abu Sharif's camp even after they worked off their debts, dependence on a patron was the price to pay for a sense of minimum security and a familiar face with whom to negotiate. As I heard time and again in one form or another from workers, "Even if the *shawīsh* exploits me, at least I know that, with him, my livelihood is guaranteed."

As camp residents navigated between the tenuous prospects of return to Syria, becoming "free" workers, or staying put throughout the tumultuous summer and fall of 2019, including during those uncertain weeks that Abu Sharif was stuck in prison, what seemed to be at stake for most of them was not primarily an ideal of "freedom" but rather how to build a semblance of home in the face of an increasingly uncertain future. Caught between two nations spiraling into financial ruin, many farmworkers came to see indebtedness as an almost unavoidable fact of life. Whether their plan was to stay in the camp, leave for another, or return before the next season, the question that dominated everyday talk among most families in the camp was not ultimately *if* they expected to be in debt but, rather, to whom and on what terms.

FIGURE 14. Faux fur and a potholed road ahead, my view from Abu Sharif's truck.

Four

REFUSAL AND RETURN

I WAS JOLTED OUT OF A DEEP SLEEP BY THE SOUND OF VIGOROUS honking blasting from Abu Sharif's pickup truck. It was 4:30 a.m.

I sat up on my floor mattress and fumbled for my contact lens case in the semidarkness. Rawia, who was sleeping next to me, rolled over with her eyes still closed. "Lissa bakīr" (it's still early), she grumbled sleepily. "Go back to bed." It was so cold inside the tent that I could see her breath rising in thick plumes. I pulled the heavy wool blanket around my shoulders and curled up for a few more precious minutes of sleep.

Another round of honking. "Yalla ya banāt!" (Come on, girls!) Sharif, the eldest son of Abu Sharif, and Abu Nader, a camp resident, were calling in unison from the central meeting area of the camp as the appointed overseers for that day. Rawia sat up and reached for her cosmetic bag and dress sitting in a crumpled pile between us. To Rawia's left, her younger sister, Bouthaina, was still fast asleep with a blanket tucked tightly over her head to keep the cold air out. Their older brother, his wife, and their four small children were sleeping in the second room of the tent. Their mother, father, and younger brother were asleep in the third room. Their father's snoring was faintly audible, since there was only a thin wall of tarpaulin between us.

"Gūmī!" (Get up), Rawia barked tersely at Bouthaina, who stirred slightly at the sound. It was March, the end of winter, which Syrians refer to as the season of "sitting" (*gaʿidīn*)—a euphemism for unemployment. After spending the past several days "sitting" without work, Bouthaina had gotten used to sleeping in.

Rawia headed to the tent's kitchen chamber to prepare breakfast while I got dressed. I stacked our mattresses to make space for us to sit cross-legged on the floor. A few minutes later, Rawia returned carrying a bowl of fresh sheep's milk yogurt and a boiling pot of black tea on a silver tray. A bag of leftover pita bread was hanging over her right arm. Shoving aside the wool blankets with her foot, she placed the tray on the floor in front of me.

"Gūmī, Bouthaina!!!" Rawia shouted, more forcefully this time, "It's time to eat!"

"Menī jūʿāna!" (I'm not hungry) Bouthaina shouted back equally forcefully, her voice muffled under the covers.

Rawia switched to a gentle tone when addressing me, graciously pouring the tea into a small glass cup for me before pouring one for herself. "Drink, *ḥabibti*," she said sweetly, placing the freshest piece of pita bread on my lap, while reserving a stale, half-eaten piece for herself to scoop up the yogurt. The tea was so sweet that I could barely stomach it first thing in the morning, but I drank it anyway because I knew we had two five-hour work shifts ahead of us.

"Yalla ya banāt!" we heard again in the distance, set against a growing chorus of teacups clanking on their trays, murmurs in the other tents, and the creaking corrugated iron doors of outhouses opening and closing throughout the camp.

Rawia pulled out her compact mirror and effortlessly drew her eyebrows in the *Raggāwiyya* (Raqqa girl) style: two thin, long lines that nearly met at the center, framing a tiny dot permanently tattooed between her eyes. "How do I look?" she asked me, batting her eyelashes, as she placed a baseball cap over her strawberry blonde dyed hair, leaving a few strands loose to frame her face.

That particular morning took place in early 2019, just a few months after I started regularly sleeping over in Rawia's camp. Over subsequent months, the rhythm of the wakeup call became so familiar to me that I can still conjure its sequence in my head with almost eidetic precision. Like that of other women in the camp, Bouthaina and Rawia's work "uniform" consisted of a brightly colored, floral-patterned polyester dress layered on top of tight-fitting leggings. Women in Abu Sharif's camp took great pride in selecting the patterns for their dresses, which were hand-sewn and embroidered with plastic sequins, lace, and pearls by Imm Khaled, the seamstress of the camp. When at home in the camp, women wore their dresses loosely hanging to the ground with plastic sandals and headscarves. When working in the fields, they tied the bottom portion of their dresses around their waists to form a skirt, sturdily fastened with a knot on their bellies. Wearing their dresses this way created a large makeshift pocket in front to hold their mobile phones and snacks. On harvest days, it also formed a perfect cover for surreptitiously stuffing a few fruits or vegetables to take home to their families, even though gleaning was technically not permitted.

Bouthaina finally crept out of her bed to belatedly perform *ṣalāt al-fajr* (dawn prayer). As Bouthaina prostrated on the floor beside us, Rawia stood up to face a plastic mirror suspended on the tarpaulin wall of the tent. She carefully wrapped her black-and-white scarf over her baseball cap, covering her face so that only her eyes were visible.

It was now nearly 5:00 a.m. Abu Nader honked the horn in long, droning bursts, a sign that it was time for roll call. Rawia, Bouthaina, and I took turns guarding the outhouse for each other before quickly walking over to the center of the camp. The sky was dark blue, with the moonlight faintly illuminating the winding paths between the tents. Looking out across the vast plain on which the camp was situated, the first glimpses of sunrise were barely visible on the horizon. Light purple framed the mountains' undulating silhouette, dotted with glittering light from the distant villages nestled in the foothills.

Rawia, Bouthaina, and I were among the last to join a circular formation of about sixty workers standing side by side. The majority were women from teenage to their late forties, alongside a handful of young men and about a dozen children. Those assigned to weeding work on the Salam family's vineyard were carrying worn-out hoes.

Abu Nader was holding a piece of cardboard torn from the bottom of a Cedars-brand cigarette carton. On the backside, there were about twenty-five names scrawled in the *shawīsh*'s handwriting, with different numbers listed after each name.

"Abu Ali, three," Abu Nader called out. A teenage girl, a ten-year-old boy, and their mother stepped forward in unison.

"Abu Khaled, two." A teenage boy and his older sister stepped forward.

"Imm Fadi, two." A young woman and her mother stepped forward.

"Abu Brahim, two." Bouthaina stepped forward. Rawia's gaze remained fixed upon the mirror compact in her hand as she took a half-hearted step. She put the last touches on her winged eyeliner before stuffing the compact into the front pocket of her dress.

When roll call was finished, the workers gathered around Abu Sharif's two pickup trucks, taking turns helping each other climb up onto the cargo beds. They stood shoulder-to-shoulder with their arms hanging over the guardrails, as there was barely enough room to fit everyone onto the back of the trucks. I climbed into the front passenger's seat next to Sharif who was running the heater on full blast—a welcome relief from the cold. Rawia squeezed in next to me and then propped me playfully onto her lap, since there was room for only one person next to the driver. I asked Sharif if I could take a look at the roll call list, which he was now holding in his hand. Trying to decipher Abu Sharif's handwriting in the dim light, it occurred to me that, except for Imm Fadi who was a widow, practically all twenty-five names listed were those of men. Yet curiously, not one of these men was physically present in the lineup of workers that morning, except for Abu Nader, who was working as an overseer.

From her pencil-thin eyebrows to her carefully wrapped scarf, woven within Rawia's elaborate morning routine were subtle claims over her capacity for desire and femininity within an agricultural system that often reduced her body to its labor-power. Quintessentially Jazīran in style, her colorful patterned dresses and bold makeup conveyed a sense of pride in rural eastern Syrian cultural tastes and an insistence that one can be beautiful and expressive even while engaged in hard labor. Yet these acts of subtle rebellion and daily self-care remained inseparable from Rawia's obligations to support her family, the stakes of which only grew further as Lebanon's financial crisis deepened throughout 2019. Considered the most indebted household in Abu Sharif's camp, her parents continued delaying her marriage, despite her desires to find true love after a tumultuous divorce some years earlier, because they critically depended on her wages as a farmworker.

That Rawia's routines were enacted within the intimate confines of her tarpaulin home was significant, for they expressed both the brief moments of private fantasy that this space afforded to her as well as the weight of familial attachments and labor obligations that the camp's debt regime had placed upon her shoulders. Organized according to the names of men who did not go to work with them, the work of female farmworkers like Rawia was vital to Lebanon's low-waged economy of agricultural production. As the previous chapters have shown, *shawīsh* camps not only supply the largest and least remunerated labor force within Lebanon's agricultural system; these camps also became the chief source of affordable housing and services for rural refugees throughout the war in Syria, especially those like Rawia who hail from the Jazīra region.

Focusing on the inner life of Syrian farmworker families, this chapter examines how indebted farmworkers like Rawia negotiated the possibility of returning to Syria or imagining longer-term refuge in Lebanon. Set against the backdrop of Lebanon's autumn 2019 protests and its mounting public debt crisis, the chapter charts the distinct trajectories of two women who refused their debts to Abu Sharif through the limited means available to them: Rawia, a divorcée who ultimately remained bound to Lebanon, and Imm Hassan, a widow who eventually returned to her village in the countryside of Raqqa.

As a system of debt-based labor recruitment structured on a "family wage" model, *shawīsh* camps epitomized a long-standing feminist observation about the politics of domestic life: the household is not simply a refuge but also a site of struggle that regulates and sustains capitalism's most valuable commodity—labor-power—on the backs of feminized work, both paid and unpaid.[1] By "refusal," then, I mean the various acts of contention, both individual and collective, over how labor was valued within and beyond the home, including the power to withhold labor. This included the everyday tactics by which members of Abu Sharif's camp sought to renegotiate, alleviate, or refuse the obligations associated with their debts, whether by shirking work, striking, labor sharing, growing their own food, appeals to Abu Sharif's piety, or prayer. While often taking the form of highly individualized repertoires of contention, the stakes of such struggles were deeply relational, tied as they were to the present and future stability of their displaced multigenerational families. These reproductive binds, as I refer to them, encompassed the daily processes through which the burdens and affordances of debt were redistributed and negotiated among kin, down to the most minute scale of the gendered body.[2]

To demonstrate how these everyday acts of refusal were linked to a broader set of economic conditions, the chapter begins by recounting the early weeks of Lebanon's 2019 "October revolution" from the vantage point of Abu Sharif's camp. While this popular uprising filled many Lebanese with hopeful optimism, I seek to make sense of the more somber and pessimistic mood that permeated Abu Sharif's camp throughout this period. Having lived through the violent aftermaths of their own revolution-turned-war, a mounting currency crisis in Syria exacerbated by international sanctions, and concerned about long-term prospects of survival in Lebanon, my Syrian friends presciently observed the looming signs of economic collapse that plunged Lebanon into a financial ruin and decimated the livelihoods of countless people from 2020 onward.

The chapter then shifts to Rawia, analyzing the circumstances that kept her attached to Abu Sharif's camp throughout this period of economic crisis and political upheaval. Because bridewealth was so central to rural Syrian households, her labor was weighed against two competing values: the longer-term benefit of her agricultural wages and unpaid contributions to the household, and the more immediate influx of cash her family could secure through her bridewealth at marriage. As Rawia's brothers faced waves of criminalization and underemployment, *shawīsh* camps became a safe place for them to wait out slack periods in the urban labor market, avoid the looming threat of detention by Lebanese authorities, and shield themselves from the indignity of what was often understood as "girls' work" in agriculture. Meanwhile, Rawia's labor sustained the family's baseline everyday survival, including absorbing the costs of her male kin's underemployment, through her continuous labor in the fields and in the home. Her response was to reclaim her labor time, including foot dragging at work, hatching intricate plans to obtain a personal phone, leaning on her female kin through informal work rotations, and eventually striking for several months.

The second half of the chapter follows Imm Hassan's successful efforts to work off her debts to Abu Sharif. By squeezing her family's consumption, refashioning her aid networks, and reclaiming her capacity to provision her household through her unremunerated labor, Imm Hassan was able to return to her village in Raqqa, where she remains until today. In the end, this came with a heavy cost, as she returned to Syria with her sons but made the difficult decision to leave her two daughters behind to get married in Lebanon. Her daughters' bridewealth helped cancel out the family's debts and allowed Imm Hassan's son—whose marriage was long deferred throughout the war in Syria—to finally get married.

The question of when and how to return was also a reproductive battleground. Though return remained an ideal aspiration for most families in the camp, it became a fraught terrain of negotiation not only between camp residents and the *shawīsh* regarding the terms and conditions of their credit-debt obligations but also among family members themselves regarding how to carry on with key life transitions while ensuring the stability of their livelihoods. This raised a host of difficult questions regarding, for example, who should get married and when; of what it meant to provide for a family; of how wages were allocated and distributed; of what kinds of work were considered secure, valuable, dignified, or demeaning; and, ultimately, of who should stay in Lebanon or go back to Syria.

Whether they were still in debt or not, returning to Syria as a *united* family was ultimately a dream that very few camp families entertained as a concrete possibility within the near future. The reasons for this varied from family to family depending on their circumstances. For many, the difficulties surrounding return came down to the seemingly banal but deeply significant question of how to secure a living wage. As was the case even before the war began, it was difficult for multigenerational families in rural Syria to sustain themselves in their villages without at least a few family members sending cash remittances from abroad. Many families were also avoiding mandatory military conscription for their male relatives in Syria, while others could not afford to lose the UN aid on which their families vitally depended in Lebanon. Return, in other words, was a painful and often maddeningly uncertain process of negotiation and speculation about how family members would be divided or stay together.

WITNESSING THE *THAWRA* FROM ABU SHARIF'S CAMP

October 23, 2019. It seemed, at first glance, to be a morning like any other in Abu Sharif's camp. I was seated on the floor of the camp store preparing lunch with Rawia's mother, Imm Brahim, as I often did when there was no work in the fields. Rawia and I were helping her remove the cores of zucchini for making *kūsā maḥshī*. They were planning to stuff them with canned mortadella—the halal equivalent of Spam—because freshly ground meat was getting too expensive.

Abu Ali, one of the camp residents, appeared at the door. But before he even had a chance to greet us, Imm Brahim blurted the same refrain that she had repeated all morning: "Don't ask about bread. We don't have it."

Save for the faint sounds of the news buzzing on camp residents' television sets, one might have hardly noticed from the camp's characteristically sleepy rhythms that Lebanon's streets had been filled with protesters for five days straight. Yet as the encounter between Imm Brahim and Abu Ali showed, even basic daily routines and fixtures of daily life like bread were starting to break down amid an unfolding public debt crisis.

Abu Sharif paid Imm Brahim a daily wage at the equivalent to a five-hour agricultural shift for managing daily food deliveries and documenting the camp residents' daily purchases, which she tallied up at the end of each month. Most of the camp residents' purchases, including those at the *dukkāneh*, were not paid in cash but rather were added each month to Abu Sharif's ledger of assets and liabilities. A local wholesaler usually delivered pita bread every morning, but bread deliveries were delayed on that day because protesters were blocking the roads.

In the midst of this upheaval, Imm Brahim had still somehow managed to gather a veritable feast's worth of zucchini and insisted that I join the family for lunch. "Come! You need to eat!" she texted me repeatedly over the previous days.

Three months pregnant, I was still catching my breath from a harrowing morning spent trying to find a ride to the camp from my friend Abdullah's apartment in a nearby village. Normally a short trip in one of the shared minivans that traverse the valley, that day I looked in vain for a driver willing to dodge the impassioned demonstrators, burning tires, and overturned garbage dumpsters blocking the main roads to virtually every village across the Bekaa. I ended up taking a significant part of the journey by foot.

Despite the hopefulness of those early weeks of Lebanon's 2019 "October revolution"—*al-thawra*, as it came to be known—Syrians like Imm Brahim and her neighbors remained skeptical. In part, this was because the camp residents were still reeling from the shock of Abu Sharif's imprisonment; he was released not long before the protests began. His detention weighed heavily on everyone in the camp, a grim reminder that no Syrian, no matter how well connected, would be spared in the growing backlash against them. In this context, many Syrians ultimately felt that Lebanon's popular uprising was not theirs to claim.

Moreover, almost a decade into their own uprising-turned-war, Syrians understood all too well that revolutionary situations have enormous social costs and unintended outcomes. "If things get violent . . . if there are clashes, more people are going to die," Imm Brahim whispered to me later that night as we watched footage of riot police attacking protesters in downtown Beirut. As she saw it, it was no coincidence that the first two casualties of the protests were Syrian workers. They had died of smoke inhalation in a building that protesters had set on fire, unaware that there were people trapped inside. "God chooses the good [*Allāh ykhtār al-khayr*]. May God have mercy on them," she muttered.

Syrian farmworkers' skepticism of the protests also stemmed from the practical question of how they would get to work. Alongside the daily street demonstrations, one of the main tactics of popular contention throughout the *thawra* was blocking roads with burning tires, makeshift caravans, and cars. For noncitizens like Rawia and Imm Brahim who had little direct stake in Lebanese national affairs, their primary experience of the protests was as a disruption of their ability to reach their jobs, and therefore to get paid. This was a particularly critical loss at that time of year, as the agricultural season ended in November. Several families hoped to settle their debts with Abu Sharif and return to Syria or move to a different camp. But the loss of work and rising costs of living throughout these restive weeks was unsettling their carefully laid plans.

Having struggled for years with the wartime devaluation of the Syrian pound just across the border, Imm Brahim and other members of the camp were also highly attuned to the looming signs of economic collapse. They wisely predicted that Lebanon's currency was headed in a similar direction and were increasingly preoccupied with how to pay for basic staples like bread, tea, sugar, and rice in Lebanon's import-dependent economy. As the protests continued for weeks, the deepening contradictions of Lebanon's trade deficit and public debt crisis were becoming increasingly apparent. Across the Bekaa Valley, banks were closed for days on end. When they were open, banks imposed strict withdrawal limits. Employers were struggling to pay their workers on time, as hours-long queues outside of banks were quickly becoming a familiar feature of everyday life.

Although the Lebanese lira remained officially pegged to the US dollar, its value on the black market and in everyday transactions was rapidly diminishing. This was an especially difficult challenge for Syrian farmworkers, whose already pitifully low credit-wages were accounted in lira. Until that point, many had managed to survive by carefully combining their wages with different sources of humanitarian aid. But even these basic pillars of their income were beginning to diminish, as increasing numbers of Syrians were being randomly removed from the UN High Commissioner for Refugees' monthly cash installments and food aid rations due to budget cuts. I remember well when one of the camp residents flashed her phone in my direction while we watched the news to reveal a perfunctory message from the UN. Due to her limited literacy, she could only partly decipher the technical language. "This means that they cut us off, right?" she asked, with tears in her eyes.

Lebanon's deepening financial crisis brought to light a long-standing contradiction within Lebanon's food system: rising land rents coupled with a declining rate of profit, as well as import dependency for most inputs and manufactured goods. Many *shawīsh* camps were becoming overleveraged, a problem that became more pronounced as the agricultural season was coming to a close. According to the seasonal payment schedule, *shawīsh* camps were obliged to renew their annual rental agreements and settle the balance of payments with employers by late November. In Abu Sharif's case, the camp's annual ground rent was supposed to be paid in dollars to the absentee landlord who owned the property. But his workers' wages were paid in lira, which meant the camp was threatened with bankruptcy unless he could convince the landlord to accept payment at the official exchange rate. It was against this backdrop that members of the camp began talking in earnest about leaving Abu Sharif's camp or returning to Syria at the end of the season, depending on their circumstances.

As Lebanon's economic circumstances became grimmer by the day, I asked Rawia and Imm Brahim if they were also planning to leave, knowing that their response would probably be the same as always. They exchanged an amused look, smiles tinged with pain.

"No, *ḥabibti*, you know we're staying. We're not going anywhere," Rawia replied.

"Unless you find a groom for Rawia in America!" Imm Brahim giggled.

THE GENDERED ECONOMY OF DEBT IN *SHAWĪSH* CAMPS

The residents of Abu Sharif's camp knew very well that Rawia's family was one of the most indebted households in the camp. It was easy enough to spot which families were in debt without looking at Abu Sharif's ledger. They were not necessarily those with the most modest tents, frugal habits, or humble clothing. Indebted families were usually those with the fewest women. Specifically, they were the households with few unmarried women, few teenagers, and a high number of adult men, small children, nursing or pregnant women, elderly people, or disabled people.[3] With Rawia's three brothers caught between cycles of unemployment and stints in Beirut and her sister-in-law only intermittently working because she was still nursing an infant, Rawia's family had only two members of the household working regularly in the fields: Rawia and Bouthaina.

Their father, Abu Brahim, was not only known as one of the most indebted members of the camp; he was also considered the most generous. Soft-spoken, quietly charismatic, and beloved by his neighbors for his hospitality, he was often contrasted in everyday talk against a former camp resident jokingly referred to as "Abu Nuṣṣ Farūjeh"—the father of half a chicken. It was a reference to Abu Nuṣṣ Farūjeh's apparent stinginess with food: despite having a large family, he was notorious for buying a whole roasted chicken at the market and cutting it in half for dinner, saving the other half for the next meal instead of letting his family eat as much as they wanted in a sitting.

These kinds of sentiments showed that, within the camp's hierarchical structure of labor, expectations of patriarchal power and paternal provision applied not only to Abu Sharif but also to male elders in multigenerational families who found themselves under constant pressure to perform the masculine ideal of "heads of household"—gracious, unburdened, authoritative—despite their starkly diminishing capacities to do so.[4] Among camp residents, thriftiness was always regarded with suspicion. In contrast, spending generously on one's family and guests was a mark of virtue, even if this meant going deeper into debt.

The camp's "family wage" system reinforced such ideals of masculine provision. The implicit understanding was that male elders like Abu Brahim were the primary decision-makers about household expenditures and credit requests, while their female and younger kin took on the bulk of waged and unwaged work. Mothers, in turn, were usually responsible for the actual process of household accounting. Those with high literacy, like Imm Brahim, carefully documented their families' daily earnings and expenditures in spiral notebooks from the dollar store.[5] Mothers wielded these notebooks, their edges worn from years of daily use, as durable proof to Abu Sharif whenever there was a discrepancy in his balance sheet. Those with limited literacy did this careful accounting work through memorization instead, making constant mental notes about the overall balance between their debts, assets, and flows of credit.

Camp residents, for their part, often justified these conditions through gendered claims about bodily comportment and the proper contours of "men's work." Throughout my fieldwork, it remained an unquestioned principle that married men in the camp should not engage in the drudgery of weeding, planting, spraying herbicide, and harvesting—tasks that were cast as "girls' work." Among men and women alike, this gendered division of labor was often narrated as a matter of basic propriety. As many camp residents put it to me matter-of-factly, "Men don't weed."

These gendered divisions of labor were also encoded in employers' everyday speech. Lebanese contract farmers and landlords who hired farmworkers from *shawīsh* camps usually referred to workers collectively as "girls." For example, a typical way that Lebanese employers requested workers for the next day was to say to Abu Sharif, "Bring us fifty girls tomorrow." While indexing the gendered association between "girls" and hard labor, designations of certain tasks as "girls' work" were not merely attributes of sex or age. After all, the workers recruited to these jobs also included adult women, teenage and young adolescent boys, and some young men. This family credit-wage system thus signified a much more systemic problem facing migrant farmworkers across the world: how wage differentials are normalized along gendered and generational lines.[6]

Within agricultural work, only one job was deemed appropriate for married male heads of household: the *wakīl* (overseer), whose responsibility was to oversee their female kin's tasks, pressure them to work faster, and manage the timing and duration of their breaks when working in the fields. The value of a female worker's wage was only two-thirds of the wage of the male *wakīl*. The designation of certain tasks as "girls' work" and others as "men's work," thus very clearly contributed to wage repression, though camp residents rarely narrated this to me in such terms. Abu Nader, who often worked as a *wakīl*, explained this distinction to me as a matter of dignity (*karāma*). "Abu Sharif doesn't expect us to work all day bent over with a hoe like girls," he once told me.

Within this gendered and generationally mediated regime of waged labor, one of the key lines of disagreement within families revolved around the threshold between childhood and adulthood. Young men who had reached puberty often claimed that they were too old for girls' work. Their tactics of contesting those conditions took many forms, including shirking work and protracted negotiations with their mothers, who, in turn, tried to convince Abu Sharif to pay their sons at the higher paid rate for overseers whenever this work was available. Unmarried young women like Rawia, in turn, found reprieve throughout those grueling working days by setting their sights upon marriage: singing wedding songs, imagining their wedding day, and describing in vivid detail what they imagined their life as a *sitt bayt* (lady of the house) would look like.

"One day, I'll marry a man so rich, he'll give me a card with money on it," Rawia once told me as she packed onions in crates, without looking up, since we were on a piece rate. Her scarf was pulled taut over her mouth, but I could see from her eyes that she was smiling.

"You mean a credit card?" I asked her.

"Yeah. When I get married, I'll just show up to any store and buy whatever I need. Like a rich lady! I'll *never* have to work again!"

Buoyed by dreams that vacillated between pragmatic plans and wishful fabulation, young women like Rawia held tightly to the fantasy of marrying someone whose income was sufficient to support them, thereby alleviating them from the burden of waged work after marriage. The ultimate goal, as Rawia and others saw it, was to marry a well-paid restaurant worker who could afford renting an apartment in the city rather than living in a camp. In *shawīsh* camps, by contrast, most married women were regularly recruited to work as a condition of their family's collective debt obligations.[7]

Young women's expectations of domesticity were built upon ideals of masculine provision that predated the war.[8] But under the compounding pressures of long-term displacement and criminalization, these ideals became ever more difficult to uphold. In the absence of "respectable" work, male elders often stayed "sitting" (*ga'idīn*) in their tents. Most men over the age of fifty-five, like Abu Brahim, opted to retire early rather than endure the indignity of working on another's land for a paltry wage. Younger unmarried men, meanwhile, sought out work in restaurants, taxi driving, or construction in the Bekaa Valley or Beirut, though this was becoming an increasingly risky endeavor as Syrian men were being stopped and detained arbitrarily with increasing frequency.

This predicament was especially acute for Rawia's twenty-three-year-old brother, Maher, who struggled to find work in Beirut as businesses hiring Syrians came under increasing pressure to regularize their paperwork, pay prohibitive fines, or shut down completely. Maher spent almost four months out of work toward the end of my fieldwork. Most of the time, he confined himself to one dark corner of the tent. Day and night, we knew when he was awake from the sound of guns popping on the popular battle royale video game, PUBG. Imm Brahim occasionally lost her temper with Maher, but there was still a tacit understanding between them that he would not be required to go to work in the fields with his sisters, Rawia, Bouthaina, and Brahim's wife, Leila—even though the family's debts were mounting.

BATTLEGROUNDS OF BRIDEWEALTH: RAWIA'S DOUBLE BINDS

I always knew when Rawia's eldest brother, Brahim, was visiting from Beirut, because there would be a new car parked behind the family's tent. The car's mint-green license plate clearly distinguished it from the handful of other cars that passed through the camp from time to time, indicating that it was a temporary rental. Initially, I found it curious that he would incur the high cost of renting a car for the one-hour drive from Beirut to the Bekaa. But the more time I spent in the Bekaa, the more I understood that this was a carefully crafted technique of safely moving from one place to another as the wave of criminalization against Syrians, especially young men, made traveling within the country riskier by the day.

One December evening toward the end of my fieldwork, Brahim appeared at the entrance to the family's tent wearing new clothes, smelling of cologne, with several plastic bags filled with fresh fruit and candy draped over his arms. It had been more than a month since he had visited, as the protests had made road closures a daily reality and his ability to move more precarious. "Assalamu ʿalaykum!" Brahim called out, as he removed his polished leather loafers, placing them among the dozens of plastic sandals, rubber boots, and mud-caked sneakers lined up outside of the tent. He was wearing a crisp white button-down shirt with his hair slicked back in the typical Syrian *shabāb* style, his mustache neatly trimmed and his face clean shaven. His five-year-old son and three-year-old daughter charged toward him, showering him with kisses as they reached into the bags to see what he'd brought for them. His wife, Leila, was crouched on the floor over the propane gas stove in the kitchen, preparing a pot of sweetened tea.

We gathered that night until past midnight in one room of the tent, keeping warm next to the *ṣōbiyya* heater over many cups of tea, as the notoriously harsh Bekaa frost was just beginning to set in. Brahim didn't say much, spending most of the evening doting on his youngest daughter, who had just turned one. He briefly mentioned that he and his two brothers were looking for a different apartment. Like many of Beirut's poorest populations, they were living on the outskirts of a Palestinian refugee camp in the southern suburbs of the city alongside migrant workers from Sri Lanka and Ethiopia.

At one point, Brahim wordlessly handed a few 50,000 lira notes to his father, each worth around $20 at that time, depreciating from $33 just a few months earlier. Abu Brahim took the cash from Brahim's hand without comment, tucking it under his phone to put in a safe hiding place later that evening. Though I never felt it appropriate to ask how much Brahim and his two brothers gave to their family, I sensed that they gave as much of their earnings as they could whenever they came to visit. Alternating between stints as delivery workers in Beirut's restaurants and periods of unemployment, the brothers sometimes barely broke even with the rising cost of living in the city. The family was well aware that Brahim was saving up to marry a second wife, while his two younger brothers were saving up for their first.

As usual, the Lebanese television station, al-Jadid, was blaring in the background. Two months into Lebanon's uprising, the constant footage of violent clashes revealed the darkening mood of the once-hopeful protests. Rawia was particularly distressed that night, though not because of the news. She was upset because her father had sold her phone that day to pay off a debt to the local grocer. For Rawia, this was a devastating loss of her connection to the outside world. "What am I going to do?" she whispered to me that night as we went to sleep.

A few months earlier, Rawia had asked me to buy her a phone, which I did willingly. For all my Syrian friends, a personal phone was an enormously significant lifeline, a means of connectivity to far-flung relatives, and, for women especially, a vital source of personal autonomy.[9] But like most electronics in Lebanon, mobile phones were imported, which made them exceptionally expensive, especially as the lira was losing its value. Despite their costliness, phones were considered a basic need of any household, and I never encountered a Syrian family that did not have at least one phone. In Abu Sharif's camp, usually every married member of the camp household, men and women alike, had their own phone. Less commonly, unmarried young men had their own phones. Though some unmarried women had their own phones that they shared with their sisters, this was the least typical. But Rawia—brazen, headstrong, and deeply determined to find true love after being divorced—saw the phone as the antidote to, as she always put it to me, "the hundred problems in my life."

Underlying the different elements of this scene—the rental car, Brahim's work in Beirut, Rawia's fixation on a phone, the cash—was the centrality of marriage and bridewealth to the political economy of debt in Abu Sharif's camp. Not only in Rawia's family, but among all families in the camp, marriage and flows of bridewealth payments were the most significant expense around which plans for return, requests for credit, and the distribution of labor responsibilities in each household were oriented. Known as *mahr* in Arabic, this practice refers to the forms of payment—cash, gold jewelry, home goods, furniture, dwellings, or land—that the groom's family makes to the bride's family upon marriage.[10] Within Islam, *mahr* is supposed to be paid directly to the bride and is considered her legal property, but the actual practice varies significantly across the region. Contrary to orthodox Islamic ideals, in the eastern Syrian context, all or part of the *mahr* is usually claimed by the bride's father. Many of my middle-class urban friends from Syria regarded this tendency for bridewealth to be appropriated by the father as an un-Islamic trading in women's bodies and indicative of eastern Syrians' attachments to "backward" practices. However, when viewed in the context of eastern Syrians' dependence on agricultural provisioning, bridewealth was also an important claim to the value of working women's labor within multigenerational patrilocal households.[11]

As their debts proliferated, the question of how to finance young men's bridewealth payments, and when to marry their daughters, became a constant preoccupation among camp residents. The burden of bridewealth payments, which ranged from $2,500 to $4,000 or more at that time, was indeed a crushing expense for eastern Syrians who were coping with long-term displacement as refugees. I remember how Imm Hassan's twenty-five-year-old son, Karim, started working night shifts as a DJ at weddings across Lebanon to save up for the bridewealth payment. Much like Rawia's brothers, he gave as much as he could to his family, but saving was his priority. "Everything I do is for the *mahr*," Karim told me one evening before a gig. "I just want to get married. I'm ready. But it feels like I'll never make enough."

Meanwhile, unmarried women in the camp were keenly aware of how the timing of their marriages was based on a difficult trade-off between the short-term infusion of cash their family could obtain from the bridewealth payment and the long-term loss of the value of their wages as agricultural workers. As a divorced woman, Rawia was caught in an especially difficult temporal conundrum. She yearned to get remarried, but with each year that she grew older, her marriage prospects dwindled. At twenty-seven, she had already passed the prime marriageable age for rural women from eastern Syria. Getting married soon would both ensure that Rawia's marriage prospects would not "expire" and provide a solution to her family's short-term liquidity problems by providing cash in the form of a bridewealth payment. At the same time, Rawia's labor was indispensable to maintaining the delicate balance of liabilities and assets that her indebted family was negotiating. The daily wages she conferred through agricultural work supplied much-needed regular income, chipping away at the debts her family had taken on to finance her eldest brother Brahim's bridewealth payment years earlier and the costs associated with raising his four children, all of whom were under the age of six.

Equally importantly, Rawia's position as a full-time working member of her household also secured their right to housing in Abu Sharif's camp. Under patrilocal custom, if Rawia were to get married, she would be obliged to move to her husband's home, which would mean the loss of her wages and unremunerated labor for her family. Without Rawia, Abu Brahim's family would only have Bouthaina as a daily agricultural worker. Their youngest brother was still too little to work throughout the year, Imm Brahim was not in physical shape to engage in heavy agricultural labor, and Brahim's wife, Leila, was nursing an infant and only intermittently able to go to work. By deferring Rawia's remarriage, Abu Brahim and Imm Brahim were prioritizing the value of Rawia's wages as a vital source of long-term solvency, even as her value in the marriage market was depreciating.

Ensuring her family's survival thus placed Rawia in a double bind. First and foremost, she remained bound to the *shawīsh* system in which her family was deeply indebted. Second, and more tacitly, she was obliged to support her precariously underemployed brothers. Within this terrain of familial interdependencies, Rawia's remarriage prospects thus hung in an ambiguous state of constant deferral, caught between the narrowing temporal horizon of finding a partner and the enduring imperative of helping her family work off their debts.

Stubborn and vivacious, Rawia found ways to cope with this indeterminacy through small, everyday acts of defiance and self-assertion, from immersing herself in fantasies of romance to an outright refusal to work on some occasions. Every time I visited the camp, Rawia seemed to be hatching a new plan to find her new "true love." Elopement (*khaṭīfa*) was an alluring fantasy, but neighborly talk in the camp was filled with cautionary tales of women who had married for love against their parents' wishes who were eventually abandoned by their husbands. For Rawia, already divorced, to lose her family's trust was a risk she could not take. Her dilemma showed how, despite her stated desire for autonomy from her parents, her tactics of contention were inextricable from her obligations to them.

It was in this context of battling interdependencies that Rawia's unrequited desires for romantic partnership and independence became channeled into a particular act of refusal: a relentless pursuit of a phone for herself. Like most unmarried women in the camp, Rawia did not have a phone of her own when I first met her, both because it was an expense her family could not afford and because it posed a risk to the proprietary transparency between an unmarried daughter and her family. If Rawia wished to use the Internet or catch up with friends or family over WhatsApp, she was expected to use her mother's phone. My phone was Rawia's safest route to indulge in her fantasies of connectivity, as Imm Brahim's incredible capacity for surveillance within the household did not apply to me as an honored guest.

Eventually, Rawia was able to convince her family to let her have a personal phone. She did so by claiming that she had unexpectedly received one as a "gift" from me. It was true that I had purchased a phone for her when she asked for one, but she told me to pretend that it was an unprompted gift that she was obliged to accept. When I expressed concern about lying to her parents, Rawia laughed. "Take it easy [*ʿādī*]. It's just a white lie."[12]

Rawia's elaborate plot to get a phone was one among many repertoires of refusal, including feigning illness whenever possible. Another was shirking and foot dragging, as she seized every opportunity to scroll through her new phone while working in the fields. Like other workers from Abu Sharif's camp, Rawia was highly attuned to the fact that not all their overseers were the same. She knew very well that her ability to claim a measure of joy and reprieve during a long workday depended on her overseers' position within the labor process, which varied from crop to crop. She knew, for example, that contract farmers (*ḍammān*)—like Ibtissam whom we met in chapter 1—were directly invested in turning a profit, which meant that they closely monitored the workers' productivity and were more likely to impose steep piece rates to maximize workers' output. Every evening, when Abu Sharif made the rounds in the camp to give workers their assignments for the next day, Rawia invariably protested when assigned to work with *ḍammān*. She didn't always get her way, as sometimes the entire camp was assigned to the same job. But on days when there were several different assignments, Rawia often succeeded—through her combination of incredible charisma and pushiness—in persuading Abu Sharif to assign her to whichever was the most "easy-going" (*aryaḥ*) job for the next day.[13]

Beyond these more individualized repertoires of contention, she also found refuge in the support of her female kin, especially the wife of her eldest brother, Leila. Rawia's parents often cited Leila's bridewealth payment as a main source of the family's debts—and thus, deferral of Rawia's marriage. But instead of succumbing to the forces that could have pitted them against each other in this context, they often worked to relieve each other's burdens through the limited means available to them. They did so by flexibly rotating responsibilities throughout the day. Leila's one-year-old was still breastfeeding, which meant Leila was not obliged to go to work in the fields except on peak harvest days. The family's daily work assignment was usually set at two "girls" from their household, with occasional *wakīl* opportunities for Maher. As long as two "girls" showed up each day, Abu Sharif was willing to accommodate rotations. Within this shifting nexus of paid and unpaid labor, Rawia, Leila, and Bouthaina developed a tacit rotation between them. If Leila's children were sick or fussy, it was agreed that Rawia and her little sister should go to work. If, alternatively, Rawia or her sister needed a break from hard labor, Leila was usually willing to go to the fields instead.

In this context of growing male precarity, bridewealth thus played an ambivalent role in Rawia's household. On the one hand, it reinscribed gender hierarchies by stalling Rawia's transition to feminine adulthood, keeping her bound to her family because they needed her wages. On the other, bridewealth appeared to be one of the few material and symbolic resources at women's disposal for making the gendered value of their labor visible to each other and their kin. In Leila and Rawia's case, it furnished the grounds of sisterly solidarity to help alleviate their labor burdens on a day-to-day basis. Rawia sometimes described this as Leila's unpayable debt to her. Leila, an exceptionally stoic woman whose calm reserve was the mirror inverse of Rawia's fiery capriciousness, affirmed this ongoing debt in her actions more than words, particularly in the ways that she carefully attended to Rawia's complaints and consistently took on the bulk of household labor.

When it became clear to Rawia that her family was endlessly deferring her marriage, she started to actively avoid work. Work assignments had slackened throughout the fall of 2019, as the Lebanese uprisings led to unpredictable road closures and deferred payments. Abu Sharif was becoming concerned about losing more workers at the end of the season. His nephews' camps, like many other *shawīsh* camps, were on the verge of closure, as dozens of workers had moved to other camps or back to Syria in the previous season. Within the camp system's balance of assets and liabilities, maintaining a certain scale of production was central if his camp were to remain profitable. Shrewd and deeply perceptive, Rawia understood very well that she had unusual leverage over Abu Sharif at that moment, even though her family was deeply indebted to him. It was against this backdrop that Rawia announced to me in early November 2019 that she was going on strike. She came to this decision after Abu Sharif, in her words, "insulted" her.

"He came to our tent the other night to give us our assignment for the next day," she explained to me one night over many cups of tea. "I told him I didn't feel well and couldn't go to work. He was in a bad mood, very stressed as usual, and he shouted at me. . . . It was *totally* insulting. Tasteless and disrespectful [*bala ṭʿame, bala iḥtirām*]. I can't accept that kind of treatment."

"Why do you think he did that?" I asked her.

"Because he's despicable [*ḥaqīr*]. Anyway, I told him that I'm not going to work anymore. I told him, 'I'm not going back to work until you apologize to me.'"

"Can he kick you out of the camp?"

"Don't worry. He can't do anything. Not a *single* thing."

"Really?"

"He wouldn't dare. And anyway, I'm one of his favorites. He won't stay angry for long."

Though Rawia did not say so, I knew that one of the reasons that Abu Sharif could not evict Rawia or force her to work was that her father, Abu Brahim, was one of the most important figures in the camp. Alongside a handful of others, Abu Brahim was considered one of the original members of the camp and served as one of the main points of contact who recruited neighbors and extended kin from his village. At a time when Abu Sharif was concerned about losing workers, Abu Brahim's family was thus in an unprecedented position to stake their claim to the camp, no matter how indebted they were and whether Rawia went to work or not.

Notably, Rawia's emphasis on "respect" (*iḥtirām*) was related to the idea of dignity that her male neighbors and relatives often invoked. Yet, for Rawia, the stakes of dignity were not simply what *kind* of labor she was engaged in, but how she was treated. Indeed, one of the primary ways that residents of Abu Sharif's camp often expressed their misgivings with their work conditions was by discerning between "good" and "bad" treatment (*muʿāmla*). Still, Rawia was not asserting a claim to dignity qua political equality in the camp, in the agricultural labor system, nor within her family. She was, rather, affirming the power of gendered hierarchies by calling attention to the kinds of ethical obligations that inhered in them.

With her family's unspoken blessings, Rawia's strike continued for several months, until the new agricultural season began in March 2020, after I had left Lebanon. I sensed that her family was able to support her strike because it coincided with the low winter season. They thus had little, materially speaking, to lose from it. Day jobs were much more intermittent during that season, and Bouthaina and Leila agreed to take Rawia's place on the rare day that two "girls" from the house were assigned to a job.

Although I never was able to find out if Rawia received an apology from Abu Sharif, she did conscript me into another web of lies to purchase her a new phone sometime later, which is how we have kept in touch to this day. All the while, she prided herself on being Abu Sharif's "favorite" and the most "pampered" (*mdallala*) member of the camp.

REFUSING CHARITY: IMM HASSAN'S SACRIFICE

Just as Rawia's repertoires of refusal were deeply bound up in her status as an unmarried woman, so too were the experiences of mothers in the camp embedded within the binding pull of their generational and gendered familial obligations. This was particularly so among widows who not only bore the extraordinary responsibility of caring for their children on their own but also were chiefly responsible for managing plans for a possible return to Syria. Abu Sharif went to great lengths to demonstrate his magnanimity to all the mothers of the camp, but especially widows, given their unique status within Islamic almsgiving. Yet, the question of whether and how to receive Abu Sharif's "gifts" was a fraught terrain for camp mothers. Much as Rawia refused to be mistreated or reduced to her status as an unmarried farmworker, Imm Hassan sought to affirm her sense of dignity by steadily refusing to be dependent on Abu Sharif and those in the camp community whom she deemed untrustworthy.

Like Rawia's father, Imm Hassan's late husband, Abu Hassan, was known as one of the original members of Abu Sharif's camp. When he suddenly passed away from a stroke in early 2019, I had only recently started regularly staying overnight in the camp. Though I had met Abu Hassan on a few occasions before his death, I eventually felt that I knew him well from the countless occasions that he visited Imm Hassan in her dreams.[14] From the moment he passed, he came to her practically every night, reassuring her that his soul was finally at rest in his homeland.

Imm Hassan remained indebted to Abu Sharif because of an extraordinary favor he had extended to her earlier that year. In addition to convening a large three-day mourning reception (*ʿazza*) in the camp in Abu Hassan's honor, he made a special effort of working with a Lebanese border guard to safely transport Abu Hassan's body back to Syria for a proper burial in his village. He also arranged for Imm Hassan to be smuggled across the border in both directions so that she could attend her husband's burial and mourn with her relatives.[15] This profound gesture nevertheless left her in debt in many senses—emotionally, morally, and economically—not least because she lost over a month's worth of credit-wages during her period of mourning.

Right before Ramadan began in May, Abu Hassan's dream visitations took on an increasingly ominous tone. He began warning Imm Hassan that Lebanon was becoming dangerous and insisting that she return home to Syria. At first, she was unsure of how to interpret his exhortations. "Does he mean I should go home after this November? How am I supposed to go?" she asked me. The problem was that she and her children were still thousands of dollars in debt to Abu Sharif. She knew that it would take much more than a season to work off this debt, unless she resorted to drastic means, such as marrying off her daughters, squeezing her family's consumption to a minimum, or finding a new benefactor.

Imm Hassan's initial uncertainty about returning gave way to iron clarity after she had a fight with Abu Sharif's eldest son, Sharif. From that point forward, she understood the urgency of Abu Hassan's message and resolved, no matter what, to return to Syria at the end of the season. I remember well how she recounted the fight to a few neighbors who were visiting from another camp.

"The other day, Sharif came over to give us our work assignments. I told him that I couldn't work because my legs are swollen," Imm Hassan explained to us as she rubbed her thighs. "He got so angry and shouted awful things. Dirty words. . . . My daughters were crying and said 'Don't talk like that. Don't curse us.' It was not good [*mū zayn*]."

"What a shame. Immoral people [*sha'b fasgān*]," one of the neighbors scoffed.

"The worst part was that no one from the camp came to help," Imm Hassan continued. "Have you seen the guys from our camp? All of them were hiding in their tents. Everyone buried their heads while Sharif attacked us! Not a single man showed up to defend us [*wala waḥad bibayyan*]. They stayed sitting [*ga'idīn*] and just pretended it wasn't happening!"

"Those guys wouldn't know their own funeral if it hit them" (*zūl ḥata al-'azza mā ya'rafūnu*), one of the women scoffed. "Lifeless, bloodless, like a piece of wood!"

"Look," one of the neighbors interjected, "It's May. There are six months left in the season. You need to leave this place, Imm Hassan."

"Yes, Abu Hassan told me so," she replied. "He came to me right after the fight, in my dream. My God! He never left me since he passed. He told me, 'I saw that you were fighting with Sharif.' I swear to God, he saw what was happening. *Subḥān Allāh*. He said, 'We're going to Syria.' And then he and I packed up our bags."

Imm Hassan then stood up, as though she were on a pulpit. "I'm done here. I've made up my mind!" she shouted. "I'm not staying here!" (*mā 'ād aḍal hīna*).

This conversation vividly underscored the importance of dignity and respectability to all camp members' concepts of sociality, and, in turn, the ways that these social expectations became a gendered battleground, especially as Lebanon's economic crisis deepened. Imm Hassan's claim that the men ought to have "defended" her against Sharif revealed the ways that she, like Rawia and most other members of the camp, did not necessarily seek to overturn the gendered norms that structured the camp's moral life and economy. On the contrary, she had expected the men to uphold the normative ideal of paternal provision and protection that the *shawīsh*'s family wage system implied. These expectations, to be sure, were not expressions of false consciousness but rather demonstrated the ways that gendered and patriarchal norms were inhabited and rearticulated over time, becoming overdetermined precisely at the moments when they were in crisis.[16]

These expectations were also symptomatic of a brewing generational divide between men who had reached adulthood in Syria and those who were raised in Lebanon throughout the war, where many of the traditional rites of passage for Syrian "manhood"—army service and gainful employment—were upended. When Imm Hassan's neighbor referred to the men of the camp as "lifeless," she was alluding to their growing lethargy and depression in the face of underemployment and waves of criminalization. Camp elders often described young men as a "lost generation" of interminable bachelors addicted to escapist fantasies, video games, and late-night hangouts, despite their vigorous efforts to secure gainful employment and save up for marriage.

Imm Hassan's extraordinary determination to leave Abu Sharif's camp nevertheless ran up against the deeply hierarchical concepts of moral neediness that structured the camp. Along with Rawia's family, her household was known to be one of the most indebted, in addition to her status as a widow, which meant that she was in an especially vulnerable position and uniquely deserving of protection and aid from Abu Sharif.[17] But Imm Hassan resolved to refuse this aid precisely by claiming her own capacity for reproductive and distributive labor. Knowing that the "upper" hand of the giver is held in higher moral regard than the "lower" hand of the receiver within Islam, she refashioned herself as a giver rather than a receiver of alms, despite being a widow herself, through her own limited means. She did so by giving away some of the food aid she received from her monthly UN rations—rice, oil, flour, beans, and the like. Though she accepted hot meals that were donated to her by a range of local charities (and anything I or her family members brought to her, after much insistence), she reduced her borrowing from Abu Sharif to the bare minimum.

Over the course of the subsequent months, she reduced her borrowing further, as her family subsisted almost entirely on her family's *mouneh* reserves and vegetables from a small garden that she had cultivated next to her family's tent. More than an ephemeral act of resistance, this was a painstaking process of belt-tightening and slow sacrifice—labor that would have been scarcely visible to me had I not spent countless days working with her in the fields and in her home.[18] Imm Hassan's refusal was not a wholesale rejection of her status as a debtor and widow—this would be materially impossible—but rather an effort to refashion the moral and economic obligations embedded in this status through her own labor.

Her profound capacity to stretch her limited means epitomized Abu Ayman's dual invocation of the "stomach" that came up in the previous chapter. When speaking of the *shawīsh*, Abu Ayman argued that "a person with a full stomach doesn't know anyone," a reference to the antisocial connotations of wealth accumulation. At the same time, he also warned Imm Hassan that "a person with an empty stomach" cannot fight back against injustice. He was cautioning her against the risks of self-exploitation, as she was squeezing her family's consumption to reduce her dependence on

FIGURE 15. Imm Hassan's vegetable garden.

cash loans from Abu Sharif, including cutting meat out of her family's diet. Indeed, while she had cooked elaborate meals for breaking fast with her family throughout Ramadan, I noticed that, apart from meals donated by local charities, most of the meals were vegetarian or made with canned mortadella.

Abu Sharif was aware of Imm Hassan's intentions to leave the camp, but he initially found her plans quite implausible, even laughable, given the extent of her debts to him. I still recall how he approached her as we sat in front of her tent right before ʿEid, the feasting day marking the end of Ramadan. He was making the rounds to other tents in preparation for the holiday. He had clearly been planning to speak to her for a while, but he acted nonchalant, as though it were a spontaneous visit.

"Imm Hassan, what sweets do you want me to bring you for ʿEid?"

"Nothing. I don't want anything," she replied tersely.

Abu Sharif raised his eyebrows incredulously. "What, is someone helping you? Do you have someone sending you money from Beirut?" he asked.

"By the Prophet Muhammad, I don't beg anyone [*mā amad īdī la-waḥad*]," Imm Hassan replied. The phrase literally means "I don't extend my hand to anyone." She was referring to the fact that she had barely borrowed any money from Abu Sharif for the entire month of Ramadan. Abu Sharif knew this, but he assumed that she must have been getting assistance from elsewhere.

"Listen, Imm Hassan, people are talking [*kalām ṭāliʿ u nāzl*]," Abu Sharif replied, pivoting to the underlying issue that was simmering between them. His tone was brusque but caring. In Arabic, the expression he used meant "Words are going up and down." He was implying that he was aware that she was speaking negatively about him to the other camp residents.

She stared back at him, her blue eyes like steel. "I swear to God, I never cursed you."

"Then what have you been saying?"

"Every morning, I wake up and pray," she replied calmly. "When I think of you and this camp, I say, 'For us God sufficeth, and he is the best disposer of affairs [*ḥasbunā Allāh wa niʿma al-wakīl*].'" She was referring to verse 173 of Sūrat Āl ʿImrān (3:173) of the Holy Qur'an, a prayer that is often recited to remain steadfast in the face of transgressions or injustices committed by those in power. She was, in her own way, accusing Abu Sharif of being an unjust leader.

Abu Sharif was clearly offended but maintained his composure. Instead of trying to contest her claim, he reminded her of the hierarchical obligations that kept her bound to the camp. After all, Imm Hassan was still thousands of dollars in debt to him.

"Imm Hassan, don't you need money? Don't you need food? Haven't we been bringing you food for the iftar?"

Imm Hassan ignored his question and instead insisted on her own capacity to claim her labor within the camp's distributive networks. "I have given the *fiṭra* throughout all of Ramadan," she told him matter-of-factly, meaning that she had donated food to the less fortunate. Though she did not say so, I knew she was referring to her modest food donations to the two other widows of the camp and a neighbor from a different camp whose husband was in prison.

Abu Sharif chuckled mockingly. "Huh? *You* distributed the *fiṭra*? I thought everyone was giving food to *you*." His derisiveness was a reference to her lowly status as a widow and a debtor. He was insisting on the ontological nature of her position as a needy person, implying that her efforts to fashion herself as a "giver" were a contradiction in terms.

But Imm Hassan was unwavering. "Like I told you," she replied. "I don't ask for anything from anyone [*mā agūl la-waḥad anṭīnī*]."

Abu Sharif shook his head and walked away, as if to suggest that she was just wasting his time. But it was clear that he was annoyed and quite stunned.

The conversation powerfully expressed the ethical stakes of Imm Hassan's efforts to refuse her debts. From a voluntarist perspective, one could think of this scene as an expression of Imm Hassan's willful capacities for autonomous, self-directed action. Yet, as Saba Mahmood influentially argued, conceptions of power focused on women's individual autonomy delimit how ethical forms of life can be approached.[19] Concepts like "resistance" or "refusal" cannot be treated as self-evident norms outside of the historical conditions within which they assume meaning. Viewed as such, Imm Hassan's appeals to pious norms of moral conduct, respect, and dignity exemplified a "discourse of piety," wherein the force of her claims was not about her intentionality, but rather about how they were linked to historical traditions of Islamic ethical life.[20] When Imm Hassan insisted that she "never cursed" Abu Sharif and recited the supplication "For us God sufficeth, and he is the best disposer of affairs," she was making a claim about the moral obligations of respectful leadership and virtuous conduct through a shared discourse of piety that was legible to Abu Sharif as a Muslim.

She was also inhabiting and affirming a set of gendered power hierarchies, even as she was refusing certain obligations connected to them—as was the case for Rawia. Understanding very well that she was both a widow and a debtor, which consigned her to a specific status of neediness, she sought to refashion this status not by claiming she was something else, but through her redistributive labor. She *gave* through the limited means available to her. Giving alms within Islam is not strictly understood as charity in the Christian sense but rather is a mandatory redistribution of a portion of one's surplus income. Surplus, in this context, is defined as that which exceeds the *niṣāb*, which is the vital minimum income one needs to meet household subsistence.[21] For this reason, the vast majority of faithful Muslims, even the very poor, give alms as a matter of pious obligation. At the same time, those who are too poor to give are never to be pitied. Giving to the poor is considered an act of redistributing God's divine sustenance, that is, passing on a gift that is ultimately not the property of the giver.[22] Given the plasticity of gift giving within these pious economies of circulation, Imm Hassan ensured her survival by taking some gifts and passing on others. In this way, she refused to be treated as a beggar or object of Abu Sharif's pity.

Imm Hassan's efforts to refashion her status as a needy person stemmed from not only her disenchantment with Abu Sharif but also a deepening sense of alienation from the camp as a community. In part, this disillusionment reflected how the crushing impact of Lebanon's financial crisis was eroding the trust that once existed between them. Camp residents often reminisced about the times when mothers could safely store their valuables at home.[23] But a spate of tent robberies throughout the summer and fall 2019 left residents stunned and distrustful. Imm Hassan described this to me as a loss of *al-raḥma*, a Qur'anic concept that means mercy or grace, but more literally "ties of the womb" (*ṣilat al-raḥim*).[24] Over time, this disenchantment hardened her sense of the boundary between "relatives" (*qarāyib*) and "foreigners" (*ajāneb*). From Imm Hassan's perspective, most members of the camp were becoming consigned to the latter. "I swear, see this whole camp?" she told me. "I'm done with them. Ever since they didn't come to help me after the fight with Sharif, I have cut my connections to them [*qaṭ'at ṣilatī*]."

Yet even as Imm Hassan was seeking to cut her relations with untrustworthy people and narrow her circle of kin, the conditions of her indebtedness shaped those relational possibilities in significant ways. While often staked as a matter of dignity, her return to Syria was, in an important sense, not an unmediated assertion of autonomy. It was inspired, first and foremost, by what she understood as a divinely ordained message from her late husband. It was, secondarily, motivated by a sense of alienation from the camp's unwinding moral fabric. Within this battleground of binding interdependencies—to God, to her late husband's spirit, to her children, to the camp, and to herself—there was no rarified sphere of willful political agency that worked separately from these obligations.

Not unlike Rawia's attachments to her family, Imm Hassan's efforts at refusing her debts and returning to Syria ultimately demanded difficult sacrifices that were, to a significant extent, tied up in her kinship obligations. At ages nineteen and twenty-two, her daughters Halima and Omnia were of prime marriage age, while her twenty-five-year-old son, Karim, had been saving up for years for the bridewealth payment. Given the immediacy of Imm Hassan's liquidity problems, she and her children understood that the time had come for her daughters to get married. The value of her daughters' bridewealth payments from their grooms helped dramatically offset her debts, without which she would have been unable to return. But this meant the pain of separating from them: Halima and Omnia were obliged to stay in Lebanon with their husbands under patrilocal custom.

Imm Hassan's "gift" to her daughters was a greater sense of flexibility about their marriage partners. While romantic love remained a fantasy of virtually every young woman in the camp, they were usually expected to marry within their tribal clans, and cross-cousin marriages were quite typical. Though Halima and Omnia stuck to their obligation to marry within their clan, Imm Hassan allowed them to marry men whom they knew. In the end, Halima married the lover whose name—as we might recall from chapter 1—she had once asked me to write on her glove while at work earlier that year.

AN UNCEREMONIAL DEPARTURE

December 15, 2019. Imm Hassan's last evening in the camp was remarkable precisely in its unremarkability. Earlier that afternoon, I had left the camp for a few hours to purchase gifts for her, which had turned out to be quite a lengthy ordeal as I needed to withdraw cash and nearly every ATM was empty due to the economic crisis.

When I returned to the camp with the gifts, it was nearly sunset. Abu Sharif was standing in front of his guesthouse with several men from the camp, grilling kabobs over a barbeque. They invited me to join, but I was eager to see Imm Hassan, so I politely declined and rushed straight to the tent of her neighbor, Imm Muhammad. I knew Imm Hassan would be there, because she had vacated her tent earlier that day to make room for the new tenants, a family originally from Rawia's father's village.

Like most women in the camp, Imm Hassan was extremely effusive about greetings and very unsentimental about farewells. When visiting neighbors, her habit was often to simply stand up and walk out the door with a perfunctory "God be with you" when it was time to go. True to this unsentimentality, there was no moment in the evening when hugs or tearful goodbyes were exchanged. Instead, we bid her farewell by gathering in a manner that resembled any other evening in the camp.

When I arrived at Imm Muhammad's tent, the living room was full of people seated on the floor. Imm Hassan; her two daughters, Halima and Omnia; her ten-year-old son, Hussein; her adult son, Karim; and her nephew from Beirut were gathered around the *ṣōbiyya* heater, along with Imm Muhammad, her daughters, and a handful of other women from the camp. Imm Hassan had a plastic bag wrapped over her head, as she was dyeing her graying hair dark red to celebrate the occasion. Imm Muhammad poured me a cup of tea as I sat down next to Imm Hassan, who was sorting through a pile of papers, carefully laying out the essential paperwork she would need in Syria: Abu Hassan's death certificate, her family's UN registration paperwork, as well as photocopies of her children's identification cards.

"Is that barbeque out there for you, Imm Hassan?" I asked her, wondering if Abu Sharif had organized a special occasion in honor of her departure.

She and Imm Muhammad burst out laughing.

"For me?" Imm Hassan replied between chuckles. "No way."

"The only thing they're celebrating out there is their growing stomachs!" Imm Muhammad added, holding out her hands in the shape of a potbelly. The two women burst into another fit of laughter.

Imm Hassan's daughter Halima scrolled through videos and photographs of her recent wedding celebration on her phone, showing me an image of herself dressed in a bejeweled, bright teal dress. In the typical eastern Syrian style of weddings, her face was caked with a thick layer of white powder, her hair was mounted in a stiff crown-like updo, and her eyes were lined heavily with kohl and eyeshadow. She seemed genuinely happy, but it was obviously a bittersweet occasion, as she and her sister were unsure of when they would see their mother again.

At around 10 p.m., after washing the dye out of her hair and sorting through her paperwork, Imm Hassan was ready. She stood up unceremoniously, followed by her nephew, daughters, and sons, and they all made their way to the door. They hovered for a moment to bid us all farewell collectively. From there, her nephew drove them to another camp to gather with their extended relatives. Some hours later, they met with a smuggler who took Imm Hassan and her two sons across the border, and from there, they took a series of minivans and buses to their village in the countryside of Raqqa to reunite with her two eldest sons who had stayed behind throughout the war, as well as her brothers and their children.

The following day, Abu Sharif's younger brother, who lived in one of the tents next to Abu Sharif, spoke of Imm Hassan with great affection. "She's been with us for so long. I can't believe she went back. The poor woman. She was still in debt [*madyūna*] until right before she left," he added.

"What do you mean?" I asked him.

"Well, you know her daughters got married. And then she sold her tent to the new family for 600,000 lira. But she still owed 1,600,000 lira[25] to Abu Sharif at the end."

"So what did she do?"

"She transferred her remaining debts to Imm Muhammad."

It was then that I understood why Imm Hassan's last evening in the camp was spent in Imm Muhammad's tent. Imm Muhammad was one of the families with the highest number of working women and girls; her family was thus one of the few that was completely debt free and had built up savings. I remembered how Imm Muhammad told me a few days earlier that her family was planning to stay in Lebanon for another season, which had surprised me at the time, as I knew they had originally planned to return. Their change of plans now made sense.

I walked over to Imm Muhammad's house to find out more.

"Imm Hassan was still about 2,200,000 lira in debt right before she left," she explained to me. "Abu Sharif sold her tent to the new family. Imm Hassan had expected she would get back what she paid. But Abu Sharif only got 600,000 for her. He couldn't find anyone willing to pay more. So she was in a bad situation."

"So you decided to take her debt?" I asked her.

"We transferred her debt to our house. We will stay here in Lebanon for another season."

"Will Imm Hassan pay you back?" I asked.

"I don't think she can. You know the economic situation is tired [*taʿbān*] in Syria. Where would she get the money?"

As I later found out, Imm Muhammad neglected to mention that Imm Hassan had, indeed, reciprocated through the limited means available to her. Imm Hassan arranged for her nephew to transfer the value of her UN cash aid card and food aid card to Imm Muhammad's family on a monthly basis until their debt was paid off. Because her daughters were now married, they were eligible to receive aid from their own husbands' families, which alleviated Imm Hassan of the obligation to transfer her aid to them, and she repurposed this aid as an opportunity to pay off her debts instead.

Imm Hassan's creative use of UN aid brought to my mind David Graeber's well-known argument about the "everyday communism" that exists between people, especially friends, which he suggests is different from what economic anthropologists conventionally think of as reciprocal exchange, in that accounts are never taken.[26] Yet, interestingly enough, accounts *were* taken between Imm Hassan and Imm Muhammad. Ultimately, Imm Hassan's insistence on settling accounts was not so much a measure of her trust, or lack of trust in Imm Muhammad, as Graeber might conceive of it. It was, rather, emblematic of the reproductive battlegrounds that she was negotiating.

Knowing the longevity of Imm Hassan's relationship to the camp, I couldn't shake a sense of sorrow at the marked unceremoniousness of her departure, especially when compared to the elaborate mourning reception that Abu Sharif arranged earlier that year in honor of her husband's passing. Imm Hassan's departure, by contrast, was a comparatively austere affair that merited practically no gesture from him at all, other than the banalities of finding new tenants. Despite her growing frustration and disillusionment in the months leading up to her return, I sensed that Imm Hassan nevertheless wished to honor what the camp represented to her in its best moments: a space of stability and mutual support.

Like other women in the camp, it was never lost on Imm Hassan that her labor—in the household, among neighbors, in the fields, in negotiations with Abu Sharif, in the family wage system—formed the linchpin and the bellwether that carried camp life forward. Navigating between the flow of familial life transitions, household debt obligations, and long-term plans, this labor became all the more significant as the financial crisis unfolded in Lebanon throughout the fall of 2019. After months of squeezing her family's consumption and resisting taking loans from Abu Sharif, Imm Hassan's final act of repurposing the UN card was her own way of laying claim to the value of this reproductive labor through her limited means. Placing her remaining debts in the hands of her neighbors and nephew was as much a refusal to be dependent on Abu Sharif as it was an affirmation of her enduring interdependencies with others.[27]

REFUSAL AND RETURN

Imm Hassan's trajectory as a widowed mother would seem, at first, the flip side of Rawia's experience as an unmarried divorcée. Imm Hassan, after all, returned to Syria, while Rawia remained in Lebanon. So too, as debtors, they seemed distinct. One remained indebted to the camp and the other was free to go. Yet the binding obligations they faced were deeply intertwined. As the centrality of bridewealth to both women's familial trajectories made clear, domains of social reproduction—marriage, parenting, caregiving, honoring the dead—were the most intense yet least visible sites through which Syrian farmworkers negotiated the conditions of their indebtedness. For Rawia, what was at stake was an ideal of romantic marriage and feminine domesticity, understood as the antidote to her grueling life as a farmworker, set against her family's ongoing need for her labor. For Imm Hassan, it was the difficult balance between the needs of her adult children and what she understood as God's calling to reunite with her deceased husband's soul in Syria. Despite their seemingly divergent outcomes, both women's struggles epitomized the binding power of reproductive obligations in conditions of displacement, whether that meant holding life transitions in abeyance, separation from family members, or subjection to self-exploitation. Acts of refusal, in other words, did not necessarily absolve these women's conditions of debt nor radically transform their labor conditions, but rather brought their reproductive binds and battlegrounds into relief.

In both women's cases, gendered appeals to dignity (*karāma*) and respect (*iḥtirām*) were central to such struggles. While dignity is often understood in terms of its modern secular-humanist connotations, claims about dignity were not staked as a matter of equal rights in this context.[28] On the contrary, they were linked to habituated, embodied ideas about moral obligation and gendered propriety, and more specifically, pious concepts of good treatment. These notions of dignity were also rooted in normative ideals of paternal provision—in the figure of the household head and the *shawīsh* as a father-like patron—that became increasingly difficult to sustain but nevertheless furnished the grounds of women's grievances and expectations.

Rawia, through her pursuit of a phone, her individual strike, and her penchant for shirking agricultural work, refused to be reduced to a pitiable spinster, yet she also refused to abandon her family to fulfill her desires for marriage. Her actions showed that romantic fantasies and dreams of finding love were essential to her life but ultimately remained subordinate to the more immediate material needs of her indebted family. Rawia's relationship to her sister-in-law, Leila—one formed through the binds of bridewealth, labor sharing, and patrilocal marriage—revealed the tacit kinds of gendered political contention that can emerge in contexts of indebtedness. Lacking a union or state protections, their efforts to improve their circumstances were often directed primarily toward their kin. Within the family wage system, women's well-honed capacities to rotate between tasks became a safety valve that could be stretched in times of need. Instead of strikes or other forms of collective organizing, these were contingent strategies of mutual aid and care work, whose stakes were vital but whose outcomes were not necessarily emancipatory nor wholly transformative.[29]

Imm Hassan, in turn, refused to be reduced to a beggar and refused to remain stuck in Lebanon, but, like Rawia, her refusal was one made in and through her binding attachments to others. For Imm Hassan, a devout Muslim, this was a labor of pious cultivation and painstaking sacrifice, as she sought to emancipate her family from their debts while doing so virtuously. This raised a host of difficult ethical dilemmas: about how to accept or refuse a gift, of what ought to be passed on to the needy, of what should be reserved for her children and herself, and how to determine who really counts as kin. Above all, her refusal was rooted in the conviction that divine beneficence supersedes worldly oppression. But as she heeded her late husband's messages beseeching her to return to Syria, she incurred another set of debts: specifically, the pain of separation from her daughters who stayed in Lebanon.

Return itself was a reproductive bind. As the backlash against Syrians grew throughout 2019, calls for Syrians' mass repatriation abounded, while humanitarian organizations pushed back to insist that Syria was still not safe so long as Bashar al-Asad remained in power. The latter certainly held true for countless Syrian refugees, including those who were actively opposed to the regime and those who were avoiding military conscription. But what the humanitarian logic seemed to miss was that return, like displacement, was a far more complex material predicament that exceeded a calculus of violence, physical safety, or ideological persuasion.

That most members of Abu Sharif's camp did not consider themselves political dissidents no doubt positioned them differently than those threatened with persecution, but this was not, in itself, any guarantee of their mobility. Even for those who deemed it "safe" to return, the war's reverberating effects had left their mark: Syria's infrastructure, food system, and state institutions were decimated, the Syrian pound was rapidly losing its value under the combined impacts of war and international sanctions, and many basic goods and services were scarce, prohibitively expensive, or impossible to find. The Kurdish-led Autonomous Administration of North and East Syria had consolidated in eastern Syria, but there were no assurances that this would translate to long-term stability nor an equitable future for members of non-Kurdish Arab clans like Imm Hassan's family. It was *despite* these uncertainties that Imm Hassan made the weighty decision to return.

Return, like refusal, was not an individual assertion of free "agency" or resistance, but rather a process of struggle steeped in collective obligations. Leaving her daughters in Lebanon with hope that they would be adequately supported by their husbands, Imm Hassan's return offered only a partial sense of closure to the years of displacement that she and her family had endured. This displacement began long before the war, rooted in her family's origins as poor agro-pastoralists and sharecroppers in eastern Syria, followed by their dispersion as the paradoxical beneficiaries and victims of land reform and dam building. While bringing untold relief to Imm Hassan and her family, her return offered no easy remedy to the more intractable problem of familial separation, driven by decades of dependence on waged work as migrant farmworkers and deepened by the pragmatics of survival in the face of wartime uncertainty. Both for those who stayed in Lebanon and for those who went back home, return was ultimately more than a one-time event: neither an end nor a resolution, nor an antidote to displacement, but rather as a web of familial obligations and debts that endured across borders.

FIGURE 16. **Taking a break from potato planting on a cold afternoon in March.**

Conclusion

DEBT AND REFUGE

JULY 5, 2022. THE FAMILIAR SMELL OF SOIL GREETED ME AS WE turned onto the unpaved road leading to Abu Sharif's camp, a path that I'd followed so many times that my body still remembered when to expect the jolt of every pothole. Only this time, I was not in Abu Sharif's truck, but in the back of a minivan; Imm Brahim had asked her nephew, who worked as a driver between Beirut and the Bekaa Valley, to take a detour to pick me up as part of his daily afternoon circuit. The other difference from 2019 was that I had no free hands to write in my notebook. My toddler son was sitting in my lap, his two years of age the most palpable proof of the time that had passed since I left.

A dozen children from the camp were gathered expectantly at the entrance, cheering and waving. Their faces were all familiar, but everyone was a bit taller and leaner: the infants were now toddlers, the toddlers were kids, and the adolescents now looked like young adults. As we entered the camp grounds, I could hear the crackle of wheels hitting gravel set against the children's excited shrieks and screams charging alongside us until we reached a halt next to Rawia's tent.

Rawia, Bouthaina, Leila, Imm Brahim, Abu Brahim, and Leila's children were already waiting outside when we pulled up. Imm Brahim rushed to embrace us with kisses as we descended from the van. Standing behind them were two young women whom I did not know personally but recognized from the wedding photos that Imm Brahim had shared over WhatsApp a year earlier: Maher's first wife and Brahim's second. Rawia was dressed head-to-toe in a shiny royal blue polyester dress adorned with pearls and a matching hijab for the occasion. She was never the type to be sentimental, but I could see that her eyes were glossy with a sheen of tears.

Inside their tent was a characteristically generous but unusually elaborate feast: a large silver tray piled with tender grilled meat over rice, which we scooped by hand with rounds of fresh pita bread. Abu Brahim was the only adult male present: their three eldest sons, Brahim, Maher, and Bilal, were all working intermittently as delivery guys in the city. Despite the obvious traces of the economic crisis unfolding across Lebanon, they had managed to find work that summer; restaurants catering to expats and wealthy diaspora with access to US dollars were still thriving, and the pandemic had driven up demand for delivery services.

Toward the end of our meal, one of Abu Sharif's daughters stopped by to let us know that her father was ready to receive us. She walked us over to the family's tent, which struck me as unusual since he always used to meet me in his guesthouse. His wife greeted us with kisses and promptly laid out a floor mattress for us to sit on the ground outside next to his sons, placing a *rikwa* of coffee and several cups in front of us.

After a few minutes, Abu Sharif emerged from the tent wearing his house clothes, a flowing charcoal *jalabīyya* rather than his usual all-black ensemble. I could see that he had lost weight, as his once youthfully round, ruddy face had given way to a gray pallor. He greeted us warmly and then reclined on his side with his head propped over one arm, as though he were relaxing, but he was obviously exhausted. We exchanged a few pleasantries and updates over coffee before he slipped back into his tent to take a rest. As his wife explained to me, he had recently been diagnosed with cancer, and the prognosis was not looking good.

Witnessing the rapid devolution of Lebanon's economy from afar, I was not entirely sure what to expect when I returned in 2022. From the moment we landed in Beirut, it was clear that many things had changed dramatically. We were staying in a friend's apartment in Gemmayze, where the devastating port explosion in August 2020 still felt like an open wound. The streets were dimmer, the electricity cuts were longer, there were more people begging on the streets, and empty storefronts loomed on every corner. And yet, coffee shops, pubs, and restaurants charging New York City prices were still booming across Beirut, some of them newly opened. The high-level humanitarian workers who frequented these spots—one of the best jobs a Lebanese citizen could hope for amid the crisis, because they were paid in dollars—stood in stark contrast to their languishing beneficiaries. Many Syrian families had been removed from UN food aid and cash aid over the past several years, and those who were still receiving this aid were struggling with the latter's precipitous devaluation.

Abu Sharif's camp was also a scene of contradictions, but one where the forms of labor that sustained them were more palpable, despite their seeming marginality to the city's changing landscape. By that point, at least half of the families who were living in the camp had moved elsewhere in Lebanon or gone back to Syria. Some of the young women had gotten married and had moved to other camps to live with their husbands' families. Many of the young men, like Rawia's three brothers, had migrated to the city to try their hand at delivery work, enticed by the prospect of getting tips in dollars. Meanwhile, a few families, including Imm Bassam, Abu Bassam, and their children, had moved back to their villages in Syria in hopes of staying for the long term. No matter their circumstances, virtually everyone had at least a few relatives who remained in Lebanon to try to find gainful employment and remit whatever they could.

As in Abu Sharif's case, several elders and middle-aged members of the camp and neighboring camps had died or were battling cancer. No one was sure why it was happening, but some surmised that it was connected to the camp's drinking supply, contaminated by years of runoff from chemical inputs and fertilizers across the Bekaa. Bottled water was prohibitively expensive for most farmworkers, so camp families resorted to filling empty bottles with water from a spring about a half kilometer away. As I listened to residents grappling with how the ravages of cancer had become so pervasive as to even afflict their camp's patron, I thought of the many mornings when they were hired to spray herbicide—the only job they insisted I could never do with them precisely for this reason. I was also reminded of the winters we spent huddled around *ṣōbiyya* heaters powered by diesel fuel (*māzūt*), its unmistakable neon yellow-green color and foul smell still seared in my memory as we all ingested its toxic fumes without ventilation to keep tents warm.

But the camp was also colorful and unusually bustling that summer—in some ways even more than when I left in 2019. Many residents had replaced the ragged white UN High Commissioner for Refugees tarpaulin with a patchwork of tarpaulin pieces—some purchased, some scavenged,

FIGURE 17. New tarpaulin walls on Imm Brahim's home.

some donated—bearing various images and advertisements from private companies like Burger King. The hodge-podge of logos and images gave the camp a festive feel, if eerily dissonant, as my son and I walked along its winding paths.

Most families, like Imm Brahim's, had also grown. Brahim's wedding to a second wife offered indeed an important glimpse into the more subtle ways that Syrian farmworker families coped with the financial crisis. Bridewealth, which was once valued at up to $4,000, had dipped to as low as $500 for some brides throughout the pandemic, according to camp members' estimates. "Women's bodies have become the cheapest thing around," Rawia huffed, enumerating the list of young men in the camp and neighboring camps who were no longer bachelors. In practical terms, what this meant was that her prospects of marriage had become even slimmer, while her brothers found themselves in an unusual position to get married earlier than they expected, using the cash savings they'd gathered over the years.

As the crisis wore on, businesses in Lebanon began to dollarize throughout 2023, meaning that prices were set in US dollars rather than Lebanese lira and customers were obliged to pay in dollars accordingly. This was, of course, prohibitive to the many workers who were still being paid in lira. Bridewealth payments also became dollarized, rising eventually to rates closer to $2,000. Taken together, what these dynamics revealed was that, under the crushing macrostructural effects of Lebanon's sovereign debt crisis, the value of women's labor within Syrian farmworker families had become, once again, a tense battleground.

True to her convictions, Rawia did eventually get her way. In early December 2023, my phone buzzed with two dozen images sent over WhatsApp from Rawia. She was dressed in a sparkling white dress, her blonde dyed hair mounted with a crown of pearls and a sequined lace veil trailing down her back. In one of them, she was hugging her groom tightly around his waist. As she later explained to me, he was from her father's tribal clan in Raqqa and had been introduced to her family through his job as a delivery worker with Rawia's brothers. Tall and lean, he was dressed in a tight-fitting white shirt, gray vest, and matching gray slacks, with his hair slicked back with a thick layer of gel. They were standing in their rented apartment, a modest room in

Dahieh on the outskirts of a Palestinian refugee camp—the very region of Beirut that would be pummeled a year later by the Israeli military.

"How do I look?" she asked.

It felt like a sisterly throwback to the countless mornings we had spent getting ready together and putting on makeup before work. But it seemed, at least for now, that her days as a farmworker were finally behind her.

To conclude an ethnography imposes the pretense of taking leave or offering some kind of synthesis or closure. But as my Syrian farmworker friends know too well, closure is difficult to narrate in a place that has witnessed such extraordinary losses and convulsive transformations over the past six years: currency crises on both sides of the Lebanese-Syrian border; the chemical explosion at the port of Beirut; a global pandemic; the genocide in Gaza; Israel's devastating military incursions that have killed thousands and displaced countless others in Lebanon, culminating in the assassination of Hizbullah's iconic Secretary General Hassan Nasrallah; and, finally, the stunning fall of Bashar al-Asad's regime on December 8, 2024.

I left Lebanon in December 2019 with the expectation that I would return the following summer. Nearly five months' pregnant, I had a teaching fellowship lined up in New York, and my husband, then a graduate student like me, had been offered the opportunity to teach a few classes that spring. We could not have known what 2020 had in store just a few months later; I gave birth on April 30 at the height of the pandemic. By then, the Lebanese lira was trading at around 4,000 to the US dollar—a threefold devaluation. By the time I returned to Lebanon in the summer of 2022 with my husband and son, the lira had lost more than 90 percent of its value.

Plotting reproductive life events alongside currency fluctuations might seem strange for readers based in the United States who may not have as much experience thinking about such matters. But for the billions of people in the world whose local currencies and livelihoods are devalued relative to the dollar's long-standing preeminence in the global financial system, this is a daily reality, most acutely felt in the dozens of countries currently facing public debt crises.[1] In Lebanon, charting the downward spiral of the lira became a total fact of life from late 2019 onward. As Lebanese families from across the socioeconomic spectrum grappled with the shocking loss of their life savings practically overnight, Syrians and other noncitizen workers struggled with the devaluation of their already low wages, putting into question whether to stay in Lebanon at all.

Witnessing this crisis unfold while becoming a mother deepened the feminist commitments that first inspired me to write this book: namely, to understand how debt and displacement are deeply intertwined, from the macro scale of national economies and global financial systems, down to the minute scale of how reproductive labor is mobilized and reorganized in times of crisis. Being bound to my own caregiving obligations in the United States while grappling with how to support friends in Lebanon and Syria broke the illusion of mobility that so often underlies ethnography as a method—the assumption that the ethnographer can always move freely between worlds—confronting me with a challenge that is likely familiar to many anthropologists: how to remain in solidarity from a distance.

The immersive period of research that formed the core of this project had arguably reached a certain conclusion by late 2019, but many of the most important relationships that made it possible endured, as did my material accountability to them. By virtue of having access to US dollars, I understood very well my responsibility to offer support to my Lebanese and Syrian friends from abroad. I was, in other words, far from immune to the credit-debt relations that I set out to understand in this book.

A few months before my family and I returned for a visit to Lebanon, Imm Brahim wrote to me in early 2022 asking for a loan to start her own business in the camp. By then, Abu Sharif had drastically scaled back his lending, while the value of workers' wages had diminished precipitously. Like other employers across Lebanon, Abu Sharif was obliged to raise their wages to adjust for the lira's depreciation, but their dollar value remained well below the pre-2020 rate. As Imm Brahim explained to me, the daily wage he paid her for running the camp store was now barely enough to cover the cost of pita bread.

Imm Brahim decided to take matters into her own hands and open her own store, which she planned to run out of her family's tent in the camp. She was already in direct contact with the local wholesalers who delivered bread, fruits and vegetables, spices, canned goods, and household items to the camp on a regular basis, as well as a family of shepherds who lived nearby and supplied fresh milk, cheese, and clarified butter to camp families and local Lebanese villagers. As she explained to me, she had all the necessary connections to open a store but could not afford the initial costs of investing in an inventory. "I need $500 to get the business going, *ya binti*," she told me over WhatsApp, using the affectionate address "my daughter."

My husband and I sent the money to Imm Brahim via OMT, the Lebanese equivalent of Western Union, which by then had become the chief means by which most people in Lebanon could access dollars. Out of respect for her vigorous commitment to the principle of mutual aid among women—that she *would* pay me back when she could—we carried on with the idea that it was a temporary loan for some time until we quietly let it pass, though I was sure from the outset that I could never accept repayment. As the scale and severity of the crisis wore on, these material obligations also grew to cover many other things: Rawia's new phone, her emergency root canal, several tooth extractions, surgery for Halima's postpartum complications, cash to cover Ramadan meals and wedding expenses, and the list goes on. Eventually, my friends did away with the pretense that these were "loans" as my role steadily evolved into one akin to a relative abroad with access to dollars who sends money regularly.

I mention these not to give the reader an account of any particular generosity on my part, for they are completely banal and routine for everyone who is connected to Lebanon and Syria, a mere instance of much larger networks of private money transfers that have emerged to fill the material void that the ongoing economic crisis has left in its wake. They include the many forms of charity that attract donors in far-flung locations, from formalized networks of NGOs to GoFundMe campaigns. But their material baseline is remittances, the invisible but vital flow of cash among kin across borders. While no doubt motivated by feelings of familial obligation, love, and ethical duty, they are symptomatic of the more enduring and pernicious problem of austerity, as highly privatized forms of aid and remittance flows are all that is left to keep war-torn and economically devastated regions afloat in the absence of public resources or more collectivized alternatives.[2]

The nearly two years I spent living and working among Syrian farmworkers—and coming to terms with my obligation to support them

FIGURE 18. My son visiting Imm Brahim's new store.

materially as I wrote this book throughout multiple crises—helped me understand the sheer scale of such predicaments across the world. The dependence of whole countries upon remittances, valued at $685 billion in 2024, not including the billions of undocumented transfers, is a direct outcome of austerity and currency devaluation. So, too, is mass migration; those who risk dying at the border to work in Europe and the United States are often migrating to escape the effects of austerity on their economies, unfavorable terms of trade, and the devaluation of their local currencies relative to the dollar.[3] The iconic yellow-and-black Western Union signs and varieties of local money transfer companies that dot every corner of immigrant communities across the US make that much apparent.

This is doubly true for the ordinary people who struggle daily with the effects of sanctions or siege warfare on their economies: Syria, Iran, Cuba, Gaza, Venezuela, among others. After a lifetime of witnessing my father's somber phone calls with our relatives fretting over the devaluation of the Iranian rial, I was already conditioned to see the economic violence that Lebanese and Syrians were enduring. Indeed, one key aspect of Syrians' predicaments that has often been overlooked are the ways that the devaluation of the Syrian pound has devastated people's livelihoods and undermined their future prospects of return.[4] While the recent agreement to lift sanctions is a welcome change that has brought a sense of relief to many, the accumulated impacts of war and sanctions on the country's infrastructure, health system, agriculture, industry, and finances will likely take years, if not decades, of reconstruction. Facing currency devaluation on both sides of the border, Syrians in Lebanon have found themselves in a difficult bind, caught between two nations decimated by war and economic crisis, neither of which offer the promise of stability that they desire.

Over the years, I have found myself continually returning to the sentiments of a dear Syrian friend, Abu Khalil, whose life story did not make its way into this book but whose words appeared early in my introduction and bear repeating: the spectacle of what he calls "bloody war" (*ḥarb dāmiyya*) is always accompanied by a less spectacular but equally devastating "economic war" (*ḥarb iqtiṣādiyya*).

From austerity measures to the dull force of poverty, the power of economic war is drawn precisely from its unspectacular, long-term, and less visible effects, confined as they are to the privatized sphere of households. These effects are evident in how family relations are squeezed and stretched to accommodate otherwise unlivable material constraints, whether by reducing consumption, taking on debt, accelerating or delaying marriage and other life transitions, or sending a relative on a deathly journey across the

Mediterranean in hopes that they might survive, pay off their smuggler, and eventually make enough money to remit. They are also evident in long-term bodily afflictions and rising morbidity; cancer rates in Beirut have increased by an estimated 30 percent annually since the financial crisis began in late 2019.[5] On both sides of the Lebanese-Syrian border, economic war in all its guises has subjected countless people to illness, displacement, familial separation, and premature death.

Economic warfare is also manifested in how Lebanon's debt crisis has come to be regarded as a uniquely "Lebanese" problem: of mismanagement, of corruption, of lawlessness, and so on.[6] But Lebanon's debt crisis, like all public debt crises, cannot be reduced to national-level policies, nor the exigencies of the present. The roots of this crisis partly date back to the 1990s in the aftermath of Lebanon's fifteen-year civil war, a period that marked a global US-led push toward liberalized trade agreements and neoliberal fiscal policies after the fall of the Soviet Union.[7] Not coincidentally, this is precisely the period in which Lebanon's ailing agricultural sector became increasingly dependent upon cheap labor from Syria through the *shawīsh* camp system. Under pressure from its international creditors, the Lebanese government engaged in a series of austerity measures and anti-labor measures, including imposing a freeze on the minimum wage from 1996 to 2008. It is in this context that Lebanon's economy became increasingly dependent on migrant workers from Syria, Egypt, Sri Lanka, Sudan, Ethiopia, and the Philippines, who make up the vital backbone of Lebanon's low-waged economy. Wealth inequality soared throughout these decades, with Lebanon boasting one of the highest numbers of billionaires per capita in the world alongside an increasingly impoverished population.[8]

In short, Lebanon's current predicaments are a particularly acute expression of *global* inequalities that extend down to the intimate domain of families and households. It is this global perspective that stands to be forgotten if Lebanon's crisis is understood as exceptional or confined to the national scale, where recourse to policies of "good governance" may enable yet another round of neoliberal, market-led austerity. And it is this global perspective that calls attention to how Lebanon remains firmly situated within the renewed Western-led consensus toward externalized border security under US President Trump, as low-income and middle-income postcolonial nations—including those facing acute debt crises—continue to host the vast majority of the world's displaced people, even as their material capacities to guarantee for them a decent livelihood are diminishing.

In Lebanon, Syria, and beyond, how displaced people are narrated on the global stage today ultimately lays bare a deeper set of contradictions shaping the governance of mobility across borders. It also reveals the all-too-common tendency for the figure of the "refugee" and the "migrant worker" to be pitted against each other in the process. Who is left out in a global refugee system that demands proof of political coercion and persecution in order to be deemed worthy of refuge? And how can the free mobility of people—refugees and migrants alike—be imagined without reproducing the logic of "free" labor under capitalist globalization?

While the scale of Syrians' displacement is staggering, their struggles to secure work, repay debts, and sustain family life are hardly unique. The experience of displacement—ranging from the acute experience of being forcibly uprooted to the slow violence of indebtedness and housing insecurity, to the maddening uncertainty about how to move or stay put—is now arguably the condition of our global majority. Many feminists rightly insist that these compounding crises express a central contradiction within capitalism itself at this phase of global history: the endless drive to grow and accumulate undercuts the very conditions that allow life to be sustained and reproduced on our planet.

Thinking about debt, displacement, and refuge together illuminates the politics of solidarity and interdependence that structure our contemporary world.[9] Debt, both at the macro level of national economies and at the intimate level of household budgeting, is a powerful lever that shapes how people act politically and relate socially, whether as a force of constraint, division, or as a basis for collective action. It may enable the pursuit of a home and livelihood in some ways and undermine its long-term stability in others.

In the United States, we can see parallels to the ways families make decisions about how to pay for healthcare, or the way younger generations are continuously deferring or altogether abstaining from childbearing and other life transitions due to their crushing student loans. Debt is present in unequal morbidity and mortality rates and in the structural invisibility of caregiving for the ill, elderly, disabled, and children. It is present in the ways that farmworkers harvest food that they can barely afford to eat.

Refuge, like debt, is not a metaphor but a social relation—someone needs it, someone provides it, and someone's labor sustains it. These relations unfold across multiple scales and implicate all of us in some way, wherever we are located. At the broadest level, they reveal the limits of the global humanitarian regime to accommodate the world's displaced, a responsibility that continues to fall disproportionately on postcolonial nations on the periphery—countries like Lebanon—even as migrations to the United States and European Union command the most attention. They also lay bare the uneven local terrains of refuge that emerge amid austerity and the retrenchment of public welfare, where privatized networks of charities, NGOs, communities, patrons, and employers—places like *shawīsh* camps—take on these obligations. And at the most intimate scale of the household, it is the feminized labor of indebted workers like Rawia that most often bears the material weight of securing refuge for others, day after day.

Syrian farmworkers have taught me many lessons, and one of them is that refuge is a struggle. As in the potato fields where this book began, refuge reveals itself not in grand gestures but in the daily toil of working people. Refuge is labor—sustained through the undervalued and often invisible tasks of food provisioning and care. It is a battleground, fought over in the spaces of family and home. It is the embodied burdens of debt, of moral obligation, of the past itself. Yet it is also persistence: the capacity to continue amid crisis, to make life possible in conditions not of one's choosing.

There is little that is romantic in this endurance, yet there is power in recognizing that these struggles, while fragmented and unequal, do not stand alone. Years removed from the research that formed the heart of this book, what moves me still are not the extraordinary aspects of these farmworkers' predicaments—it is their familiarity. The pressures that bear down on Syrians in Lebanon reverberate far beyond the camps: they are woven into the global circuits of labor, debt, and care that sustain everyday life elsewhere.

The struggle for refuge, then, is not a distant or lofty utopian project. Its stakes are enormous and its possibilities concrete—lodged in the daily rhythms of labor, in the solidarities that emerge under duress, in the fight for mobility, and in the potential for change residing, quite literally, in every worker's hands.

EPILOGUE

ON DECEMBER 8, 2024, I RECEIVED A FLURRY OF WHATSAPP MESSAGES from Rawia. At the time, she was visiting her relatives in the countryside of Raqqa. Two months earlier, Rawia had asked me to send her money to flee the terrifying Israeli military bombardments that surrounded her newlywed husband's modest apartment in South Beirut and her family's tent in the Bekaa Valley. And now, two months later, she was asking for money to cross in the other direction. The ceasefire in Lebanon had been declared, Asad's regime had fallen, and her first impulse was to cling to the life she had precariously built in Lebanon throughout the war in Syria.

In striking contrast, many of my Syrian friends who did not live in the camps, including Abdullah and his family, were completely elated. "We'll see you in Syria, *inshallah*!" Abdullah cried out over WhatsApp, as his usually cool-tempered manner gave way to pure joy, set against the clamor of horns honking and cheering in the background. In all the years that I had known him, it was the first time that he sounded unreservedly optimistic.

Between Abdullah's hopefulness and Rawia's consternations, another round of messages began to trickle in from members of the camp soon thereafter. But, as it turned out, these messages were not about the political situation. They were about Abu Sharif. After his long battle with cancer, he succumbed to his death that night.

That Abu Sharif's passing paralleled the fall of Asad's regime was both tragic and deeply unsettling. "May God forgive him," everyone repeated in their messages, which is the appropriate ritual expression among Muslims upon someone's passing. But it also felt like a strange commentary on the moment and the broader historical tensions latent within it: about the intimate transitions that mark epochal events; about what it meant to memorialize a patron who had exploited their labor but who ensured that they had shelter and their basic needs fulfilled in exile; about indeed their fraught attachments to the promises and losses associated with the Syrian state itself.

In the most painfully concrete sense, his death conveyed how joy and mourning coexisted in this moment for Syrians, and not all in the same way. Syrians in Lebanon, after all, were still reeling from the wreckage of the war with Israel throughout the fall of 2024. The very day that the ceasefire between Israel and Hizbullah went into effect, Hay'at Tahrir al-Sham emerged from their base in Syria's northern province of Idlib and proceeded to push the regime out of Aleppo, followed by Hama and Homs, and, finally, Damascus. After enduring Israel's airstrikes and sonic booms for months, many of my Syrian farmworker friends were initially stunned by the dizzying swiftness of this victory mere days after the ceasefire, especially those who had fled back to Syria, as Rawia had done, in search of refuge.

The monumental fall of the Asad family's fifty-four-year regime on December 8, 2024, was undoubtedly a watershed. Its profound significance—to all those who lived in fear and languished in the regime's prisons, to the families of the dead and the disappeared, to those who were besieged and subjected to relentless aerial bombardments, and to those who were forcibly displaced not only throughout the war but across generations—cannot be underestimated.

But moments of transition are also moments of inheritance, no matter how seemingly profound the break with the past. For working-class and rural Syrians like Rawia, inheritance is invariably a material question of how change proceeds, for whom, by whom, and under what circumstances. In short, it is a question of how life may be, as they often put it, "guaranteed" (*maḍmūn*). These are not abstract questions: they determine their conditions of their survival, safety, and prospects of long-term return. As a combination of euphoria, relief, uncertainty, and fear has set in over the months that have followed Asad's fall, it is indeed the seemingly mundane material factors of everyday life—labor conditions, the devaluation of the Syrian pound, and how to rebuild and secure a livelihood in Syria—that linger on the minds of many of my Syrian farmworker friends.

Using the savings she built up from running her own store for the past several years, Imm Brahim decided in February 2025 to move back to Syria, at least temporarily, to begin rebuilding the family's home, along with her two eldest sons, Brahim and Maher, their wives and children, and her youngest son, Mahmood. Meanwhile, Abu Brahim, their son Bilal and his wife, and Bouthaina have remained in the camp. Despite deepening anti-Syrian sentiment taking hold across Lebanon, Imm Brahim emphasized to me that they are not ready to relinquish their claims to refuge there, given the many uncertainties that lie ahead in Syria. Rawia and her husband, for their part, are still living in their modest apartment in South Beirut, bracing for the possibility of more bombardments from Israel.

What does the current transition mean for Syrian farmworkers like Rawia and her family? While it is impossible to speak in all-encompassing terms, a few factors stand out at this momentous juncture. One is that although return has become a compelling prospect for many Syrians living in exile, the need for remittances and ongoing instability in Syria will likely mean that many families must maintain some form of translocal householding across borders in the months and years to come. Beyond the real possibility of further unrest and violence, there are also many underlying economic factors. Particularly for those lacking any cash savings, return offers few material guarantees to those struggling with the costs of rebuilding their livelihoods and homes in Syria's war economy. Exacerbated greatly by the devaluation of the Syrian pound, many farmworker families are reluctant to make plans for long-term return to an economy where building materials and many basic goods remain costly or difficult to find and, equally importantly, where the possibility of a stable income remains far from guaranteed.

Here, the complex inheritances of Baʿthism matter in both a material sense and as a contested reference point about what should change, what public entitlements should be revived or maintained, and what model of economic development will take hold in Syria moving forward. It is telling that virtually every farmworker I met throughout my fieldwork held tightly to the concept of a strong welfare state, affordable healthcare, free schooling, and equitable land distribution—part of an older Baʿth Party ideal of

"Arab socialism" that even those who were very critical of the regime seemed to embrace. In practice, as this book has shown, the Syrian state had been steadily retreating from this role for decades before the 2011 popular uprising began, especially throughout its liberalized transition to a "social market economy" under Bashar al-Asad. It was precisely in this period of liberalization that Rawia's family, and many others, became dependent on labor migration to meet their basic needs. Farmworkers nevertheless continuously invoked this ideal of state-backed "guarantees" when explaining to me the sense of uncertainty they felt about returning.

Such attachments to a strong welfare state are as much a commentary on Syria's prewar past as they are a testament to Syria's fraught history of class division and transformation, which is itself inseparable from the political economy of Baʿthist rule since the party took power in 1963, followed by Hafiz al-Asad's coup against left-wing factions in 1970.[1] The 74 percent of Syrians who identify as Sunni Muslims, for example, encompass enormous class diversity: middle-class business owners and traders in Aleppo, small farmers in the Damascus hinterlands, wealthy landlords and their descendants whose vast properties were confiscated and redistributed throughout the land reforms from 1966 to 1970, and the diverse beneficiaries of these reforms, including displaced farmworkers from Syria's Euphrates region with whom I worked closely, among many others. Pushing past the media punditry that often reduces Syria's complexities to neat sectarian mappings or, conversely, the ways that the Hay'at Tahrir al-Sham's calls to Syrian "unity" might operate as a cover for neoliberal market-led austerity, a critical political economy perspective of the various class forces at work in the post-Asad transition will prove invaluable to understanding the challenges that are to come, particularly as the early revolutionary ideals of the 2011 uprising are today being resurrected with a provisional sense of hope and determination.[2]

Another important factor concerns the politics of refuge and asylum. From Lebanon to Germany to Türkiye, millions of displaced Syrians are facing unprecedented pressure to repatriate from their host governments, as evidenced by the German government's swift decision to suspend all pending asylum cases from Syria almost immediately after Asad's fall. Here, the pernicious distinction between "refugees" and "migrants" may prove detrimental to Syrians who struggle to garner persuasive "proof" of political persecution now that Asad is not in power. As is the case in Lebanon, underlying this backlash against Syrians is also the fluctuating demand for their labor.

Finally, there is the ongoing question of revolutionary change, a struggle that may have its most proximate antecedents in the 2011 uprising, but arguably began much earlier in the heyday of global anticolonial struggle in the 1960s and 1970s. By carefully considering Syria's internal contradictions and external pressures throughout its incorporation into the global economy, this book has sought to take seriously what revolutionary change might mean from the perspective of Syria's most precarious workers, whose struggles for a more equitable food system, collective guarantees, and stable conditions of social reproduction are far from over, but which they share in common with low-income workers across the world.

Looking more closely at the women featured in this book—Rawia, Imm Hassan, Imm Brahim, and Imm Bassam—what they all seemed to share is a refusal to be pitied, demeaned, or devalued. This is an important form of revolutionary subjectivity that should not be ignored nor minimized. From Rawia's labor rotation with Leila to Imm Hassan's *mouneh* garden, to Imm Brahim's successful efforts to establish her own store, each worked within enormous constraints to achieve some measure of freedom and control over their labor time, even as those efforts remained subordinate to their binding obligations to family members. There is a long and radical feminist history of such efforts across the world, from enslaved Caribbean women's attempts to remake themselves into sellers of their own products through their provisioning grounds to Vietnamese women's *co so* care networks throughout the Vietnam War to Bolivian women's efforts to refuse bank debt and reestablish mutual aid through Mujeres Creando.[3]

To speak of inheritances in this time of transition, thus, does not mean denying the real sense of hope for a different future that many Syrians feel at this moment. Rather, it means paying careful attention to how rural and working-class Syrians like these women bear the weight of historical transformations and contradictions as they unfold. And it is to take seriously that, beneath the spectacle of elites jostling for power in Lebanon, Syria, and elsewhere, it is ordinary people's daily struggles that continue to endure and demand our solidarity.

Acknowledgments

This work is greatly indebted to many people, places, and institutions across several continents. None of this research would have been possible without my interlocutors and beloved friends in the Bekaa Valley, who generously brought me into their lives throughout my fieldwork and beyond. While they must remain anonymous, they include those pseudonymously known as Rawia and her family, Imm Hassan and her family, Imm Bassam and her family, Abu Sharif and all the members of his camp, Ibtissam and everyone working on the Salam estate, Abdullah and his family, Abu Charbel and his work team, as well as many others who were named and not named in this book. My gratitude for what they shared with me far exceeds what can be expressed here. There are many ways that this book surely falls short, but I hope it stands as a small testament to their truly life-changing impact on me.

Numerous fellowships gave me the vital gift of time to write and revise, including the American Council of Learned Societies Fellowship, the Mellon/American Council of Learned Societies Dissertation Completion Fellowship, the Mellon Committee on Globalization and Social Change Dissertation Fellowship, and the Center for Place, Culture, and Politics Dissertation Fellowship. My field research was supported by the National Science Foundation (Doctoral Dissertation Improvement Grant 1823380), the Wenner-Gren Foundation (Dissertation Fieldwork Grant 9773), and the Max Weber Foundation (Orient-Institut Beirut Doctoral Fellowship). Preliminary research was supported by funding from the CUNY Graduate Center, including the Interdisciplinary Research Fellowship in the Service of Public Knowledge and summer grants from the Department of Anthropology and the Office of the Provost. At Vassar College, generous start-up funds and multiple research awards from the Environmental Research Institute supported my participation in conferences and invited talks to present this research, followed by a Faculty Research Committee award from the Lucy Maynard Salmon Research Fund to support publication costs. I thank all of these institutions for their support and recognition.

At Stanford University Press, I am deeply grateful to Kate Wahl for her deft editorial wisdom, mentorship, and unflagging support for this project at every stage. I offer many thanks to the two anonymous reviewers and to the Middle Eastern and Islamic Societies and Cultures Series editors, Sherene Seikaly and Lara Deeb, for their thoughtful engagement and incisive feedback, which helped me navigate the final stage of revisions and bring this book to full fruition. I owe special gratitude to Laleh Khalili for seeing potential in this book early on and encouraging me to develop a proposal. And a big thank you to the entire team at SUP and Newgen, especially Thane Hale, Kristine Hunt, Tiffany Mok, Bailey Odom, Larkin Paddack, Adam Schnitzer, and David Zielonka, for their skillful support throughout the production process; to Michele Wetherbee and Martyn Schmoll for designing the book's beautiful cover.

At Vassar, I have had the immense privilege of working with faculty, staff, and students who inspire me every day. I wholeheartedly thank my current and former colleagues in the Department of Anthropology for their support and intellectual engagement: April Beisaw, Mark Chatarpal, Zach Cofran, Colleen Cohen, Aviva Cormier, Becky Dinkel, Deanna Johnson, Martha Kaplan, Candice Lowe Swift, Dana Patota, Tom Porcello, Louis Römer, Ryan Rybka, and David Tavárez. Beyond my department, I am grateful to the following colleagues and friends for making Vassar such a dynamic and inviting place to live and work: Carlos Alamo, Tagreed Al-Haddad, Stephane Andrade, Omar Badessi, Veronica Brownstone, Leroy Cooper, Andy Davison, Azra Dawood, Maria Hantzopoulos, Diane Harriford, Katie Hite, Bill Hoynes, John Hulsey, Jonathon Kahn, Arpitha Kodiveri, Timothy Koechlin, Ryan LaBrozzi, Montse Madariaga-Caro, Candy Martínez,

Taneisha Means, Mootacem Mhiri, Amanda Munroe, Himadeep Muppidi, Hiram Perez, Shivani Radhakrishnan, Mariam Rashid, Michael Reyes Salas, Johanna Römer, Claire Sagan, Josh Schreier, Logan Stapleton and Ana Diaz, Jasmine Syedullah, Catherine Tan, Josh Tan, Kirsten Wesselhoeft, Kimberly Williams Brown, Eva Woods Peiró, Klaus Yoder, and many others. I am particularly grateful to Claire, Kirsten, Klaus, Catherine, Josh, Louis, Johanna, and Zach for supporting my family in countless ways and for making Poughkeepsie truly feel like home. In addition, I offer many thanks to Sa'ed Atshan for providing helpful counsel during his fellowship at Vassar, and to the Office of the Dean of Faculty (Brian Daly, Demetrius Eudell) and President Betsy Bradley for generously granting me a much-needed research leave as I completed this book. Last but not least, I thank my wonderful students, especially those who joined my Revolutionary Subjects seminar, for inspiring me to write and teach with clarity and conviction.

At Smith College, I gratefully acknowledge the support and professional development that the Eveillard Postdoctoral Fellowship provided to me. Thank you to Lisa Armstrong, Fernando Armstrong-Fumero, Elif Babül and Robert Samet, Omar Dahi, Yoav Elinevsky, Susanna Ferguson, Matthew Ghazarian, Suzanne Gottschang, Steven Heydemann, Colin Hoag, Pinky Hota, Elizabeth Klarich, Caroline Melly, Anna Mwaba, Javier Puente, Jorge Vásquez, Gregory White, and Mariyana Zapryanova for welcoming me into the Five College community—it was a thrilling experience to return after so many great memories from my years there as a Smith undergraduate. And thank you to Tara Goldberg and Christopher Hellwig for being such wonderful friends and neighbors!

To my comrades and mentors at the CUNY Graduate Center, I offer endless appreciation. I feel extremely fortunate to have pursued my doctoral training under the guidance of scholars who embody intellectual dynamism, integrity, and commitment in every sense: Mandana Limbert, Marc Edelman, Karen Strassler, Gary Wilder, Ilana Feldman, and Katherine Verdery. Through their thoughtful feedback, reading suggestions, and constant support, each of them has made their mark on this book in immeasurable ways.

In addition to these valued mentors, I thank the following faculty members and colleagues who made the GC such an enriching place to study and develop my scholarship: Anny Bakalian, Beth Baron, Caity Bolton, Avi

Bornstein, Michael Blim, Jillian Cavanaugh, Hazal Corak, Gerald Creed, Ellen De Riso, Mark Drury, Scott Erich, Jessie Fredlund, Ola Galal, Nick Glastonbury, Ruth Wilson Gilmore, Samira Haj, Thayer Hastings, Nour Hodeib, Shima Houshyar, Zehra Husain, Omnia Khalil, Marnia Lazreg, Louise Lennihan, Romm Lewkowicz, Elliot Liu, Stephanie Love, Zeynep Oguz, Yasemin Ozer, Jeff Maskovsky, Sam Novacich, Jeremy Randall, Amir Reicher, Angela Reyes, Paloma Rodrigo, Douaa Sheet, Julie Skurski, Cihan Tekay, Miriam Ticktin, and Liang Wu, among many others.

In Lebanon, there are numerous people who made this work possible. The Lebanon Dissertation Summer Institute, led by Nadya Sbaiti and Ziad Abu-Rish, made my first two weeks of fieldwork welcoming and exciting. The last four months of my fieldwork were greatly enriched by my fellowship at the Orient-Institut in Beirut, and I thank Birgit Schäbler, the OIB staff, and the fellows for many memorable discussions. I offer many thanks to the staff at Bissan Bookstore, Dār al-Fārābī publishing house, Halabi Bookstore, Maktabet al-Sa'eh, the American University of Beirut library, the Zahle municipal library and newspaper archive, the Lebanese University Faculty of Arts and Humanities in Beirut, and the Lebanese University Faculty of Letters and Human Sciences in Zahle for patiently attending to my inquiries about texts on agrarian and labor history, many of which were obscure, out of print, or difficult to find. In addition, I gratefully acknowledge the following scholars and experts for generously taking the time to share with me their insights on agrarian history, migration, and labor in the Levant during my time in Lebanon and beyond: Malik Abisaab, Lynn Abdouni, Seda Altuğ, Estella Carpi, Jake Cassani, Karim Eid-Sabbagh, Cynthia Gharios, Muhammad Hachicho, Kanj Hammade, Guita Hourani, Joseph Hourani, Nidal Khaled, Rima Majed, Giuliano Martiniello, Katharina Lange, Abdullah Said, Elizabeth Saleh, Mayssoun Sukarieh, Diana Sarkis Fernández, Father Ibrahim Sarrouj, Jamal Wakim, and Rami Zurayk.

I offer most sincere thanks to my dear friend and Arabic tutor, Ali Baba, whose vast knowledge of the eastern Syrian dialect, culture, and history improved my research in every way. We spent countless hours going over interviews, and Ali's brilliant capacity to richly contextualize colloquial words and expressions brought this project to another level.

Many other friends have made Lebanon a second home for me over the years. I thank Nadine Abdallah, Raji Abedsalam, Jackson Allers, Isaac Blacksin, Marta Bogdańska, Greg Burris, Esther Chang, Zack Cuyler, Hannah Scott Deuchar, Sam Dinger (and the *shabāb*!), Aaron Eldridge, Brent Eng, Hisham Esper, Kareem Estefan, Clothilde Facon, Rabih Fakhri, Foroogh Farhang, Robert Haddad, Salah Hamzeh, Pardie Karamanoukian, Hussein Kazoun, Nikolas Kosmatopoulos, Owain Lawson, Bruno Marot, Rida Mawla, Molly Oringer, Natasha Pesaran, Nova Robinson, Anna Reumert, Naima Shalhoub, Sally Shamas, Samee Sulaiman, Stefan Tarnowski, Vasiliki Touhouliotis, Rebecca Whiting, the Younes family, Gabriel Young, and many others for the great times together.

I have had the honor and privilege of presenting chapter drafts in a range of workshops, invited talks, and colloquia over the past five years. For the sake of brevity, I must list these events, their organizers, and key discussants in a manner that does not adequately capture just how much I benefited from them, but I wish to thank everyone who participated and shared their feedback. They include: the Committee on Globalization and Social Change year-long seminars on "Debt" and "Borders" (Gary Wilder); the Center for Place, Culture, and Politics year-long seminar on "The Agrarian Question" (Ruth Wilson Gilmore, Peter Hitchcock, David Harvey, Mary Taylor); Brown University's Center for Middle East Studies (Paul Kohlbry); the Moise A. Khayrallah Center's "New Perspectives on Middle East Migrations" workshop (Akram Khater, Stacy Fahrenthold, Andrew Arsan, Fadi Bardawil); the American University of Beirut "Labor in the Middle East and North Africa" workshop (Rima Majed, Elizabeth Saleh, Anne Alexander, Joel Beinin, John Chalcraft, Seda Altuğ, Joseph Daher); McMaster University's Anthropology colloquium (Basit Iqbal, Yana Stainova); the Franz Boas Seminar at Columbia University's Department of Anthropology (Naor Ben-Yehoyada, Nadia Abu El-Haj, Beth Povinelli); University of Barcelona's Anthropology colloquium (Susana Narotzky); the Yale MacMillan Center Program in Agrarian Studies colloquium (Shivi Sivaramakrishnan, Elizabeth Wood, Eda Pepi); Syracuse University's Anthropology colloquium (Amanda Hilton, Lauren Woodard, Julia Jong Haines); the CUNY Graduate Center's Anthropology colloquium (Jeff Maskovsky), and the Leibniz-Zentrum Moderner Orient colloquium

(Katharina Lange, Samuli Schielke). I have also had the privilege of joining many conference panels and roundtables over the years, far too numerous to name here; I am grateful to all who convened them and offered their insights.

Several colleagues deserve special mention for the depth of their feedback and engagement. Caity Bolton, Stephanie Love, and Yasemin Ozer pored over every piece of my writing when it was still in its earliest stages through our weekly Zoom calls. Caity, Stephanie, and I have continued to share our work regularly as we have navigated each stage of the book revision process—their brilliant ideas, encouragement, and friendship have buoyed me through the highs and lows of writing. I thank Stephanie and her graduate students at the University of Pittsburgh for reading the whole manuscript just before submission. I would also like to thank Amiel Bize, Sam Dinger, Paul Kohlbry, Amir Reicher, Anna Reumert, Aarti Sethi, Kate Wahl, and especially Gary Wilder for offering helpful comments on drafts of chapters at various stages of revision.

In addition to those already mentioned, I thank the following colleagues, mentors, and friends for inspiring conversations that have enriched my sensibilities as a writer and scholar: Lila Abu-Lughod, Hadia Akhtar Khan, A. Haroon Akram-Lodhi, Hilal Alkan, Salam Alshareef, Kellan Anfinson, Rasha Arabi, Nader Atassi, Andreas Bandak, Sarah Besky, Natalia Buier, Dean Chahim, Matan Cohen, Max Cohen, Adrian Comly, Maria da Silva, George DeMartino, Samuel Dolbee, Deniz Duruiz, Jaume Franquesa, Samer Ghaddar, Ariana Gunderson, W. Nathan Green, Seth Holmes, Hazem Jamjoum, Morgan Jenatton, Don Kalb, Matan Kaminer, Sinem Kavak, Rashid Khalidi, Gabi Kirk, Winnie Lem, Martin Lemberg-Pedersen, Anna Levy, Candace Lukasik, Elisa Marvena, Nikhita Mendis, Alessandra Mezzadri, Timothy Mitchell, Ahmad Moradi, Mnqobi Ngubane, Graham Pitts, Sonia Prelat, Shozab Raza, Arpan Roy, Kali Rubaii, Sayres Rudy, Sahar Sadjadi, Quincy Saul, Sophie Schrago, Aditi Sen, Diana Shikaki and Ibrahim Shikaki, Alice Speri, Luisa Steur, Sara Stevano, Alesandra Tatić, Michael Taussig, Stefan Voicu, Daniel Zhubin Younessi, Ruslan Yusupov, the Levant POLLEN node members, and my comrades on the board of the Friends of the Freedom Theater in Jenin, among others.

Within and beyond academia, I offer heartfelt thanks to my cherished circle of close friends and kin—many of them named here—for bringing joy to my life. My chosen sisters, Dorit Price-Levine and Noelle Ghoussaini, have been there through the best times and the hardest of times, offering wisdom and companionship when I have needed it most. My beloved Uncle Bob and Aunt Phyllis have been my vital anchor both in New York City and in the Hudson Valley—I am deeply grateful for their generosity and constant encouragement.

This research flourished through the loving support of my husband, Oriol Vallès Codina, my parents, and Oriol's family. It is only after becoming a mother that I started to truly grasp the many sacrifices of my parents, Holly and Cyrus. My father's vivid stories of his childhood in Iran, my mother's artistic ways of seeing, and their devotion to progressive causes are among the many ways that they cultivated my passion for anthropology. No words can adequately convey the depth of my love, respect, and appreciation for all they have given me.

Mateu was born just as I started writing the manuscript that eventually became this book, while Oriol was finishing his PhD. My parents took care of him for many hours every day so that we could write. Oriol's parents, aunts, brother, and grandmother did the same during winters and summers in Barcelona. And when I began the difficult journey of revising the manuscript while juggling the demands of a tenure-track job, a team of loving caregivers was there to support me at every stage, including our family members and a circle of dedicated teachers at Mateu's schools. This book would not exist without them. Estimats Esther, Josep Maria, Màrius, Nati, Isabel, Àvia, Lídia i tota la família de Berga: moltíssimes gràcies per tot. Us estimo!

Oriol has been my steadfast partner, comrade, and confidante throughout. We have discussed practically every idea found within these pages over the course of countless evening walks and morning coffees. He has patiently listened to me repeat myself over and over for the better part of a decade and somehow has managed to remain enthusiastic, while always making me think—and laugh! For his love and devotion in a world that so often feels unbearably bleak, I am forever thankful.

Conceived alongside the birth of my first child and concluded with the birth of my second, this book owes much of its feminist perspective to the practical wisdom gained through the challenges and joys of writing and mothering at once. Nurturing Mateu as he grows into a spirited, loving, and fiercely intelligent five-year-old has taught me more than any other experience of my life. And just as I put the finishing touches on this book, luminous baby Sol came into the world, lighting each day like an eternal sunrise. Their brimming curiosity and vitality know no bounds, and their tender hearts are my refuge.

I most lovingly dedicate this book to Mateu, Sol, Oriol, and my parents.

Notes

Prologue

1. The 2006 Lebanon War—known in Arabic as *Ḥarb Tammūz* ("July War")—lasted for thirty-four days, from July 12 to August 14, and claimed the lives of more than one thousand people, the vast majority of them Lebanese civilians. See Khayyat 2022 for a stunning ethnographic account of this period and its aftermaths, narrated from the perspective of villagers in Southern Lebanon.

2. By "social reproduction," I mean it in the broadly feminist materialist sense: the wide range of activities, institutions, and relationships through which people struggle to sustain life—from housekeeping to childrearing to subsistence work—and, in turn, how capitalist relations are renewed and reconfigured through these processes (Katz 2001). Variously supported by families, communities, state and public institutions, nongovernmental and charitable organizations, and private market relations, social reproduction encompasses childbearing, childcare, child socialization, education, care for the elderly and disabled, the provision of food, shelter, clothing, healthcare, and welfare, subsistence work and household labor, and sexual and conjugal relations.

Introduction

1. Located at the northern edge of the Syrian steppe, at the foot of the Anatolian Plateau between the Tigris and Euphrates rivers, the fertile Jazīra region encompasses what is today northeastern Syria, western Iraq, and southeastern Türkiye. On the history of the Jazīra, see Altuğ 2011, 2024; Dolbee 2023.

2. United Nations High Commissioner for Refugees Refugee Data Finder, https://www.unhcr.org/refugee-statistics/

3. Veltmeyer and Wise 2016, 1.

4. On the migrant-refugee divide, see De Genova 2013; Holmes and Castañeda 2016.

5. Janmyr 2016, 61.

6. Throughout Lebanon and Syria, the term *'arab* is polysemous. While it literally means "Arab," in colloquial usage it often refers specifically to Bedouin populations, who may also be called *Bedu*. In this context, the term marks not only an ethnic distinction (for example, between Kurds and Arabs) but also connotes tribal and genealogical lineage.

7. For overviews of critical agrarian studies, see Akram-Lodhi et al. 2021; Akram-Lodhi and Kay 2010a, 2010b; Bernstein et al. 2018; Borras 2023; Edelman and Wolford 2017; Levien et al. 2018; Sajadian 2020a.

8. What is today commonly referred to as "social reproduction theory" comes out of a broadly Marxist tradition rooted in decades of feminist writing that sought to draw attention to the labors of childrearing, housekeeping, and subsistence work that vitally sustain the labor force under capitalism, which are often rendered invisible by virtue of being unpaid or underpaid and relegated to the domestic sphere. While associated strongly with the Italian Operaismo autonomist movement in the 1970s (Federici 2020), feminist theorizing and activism surrounding the politics of social reproduction was and continues to be internationalist, carried forward not only by feminists based in Europe and North America but arm-in-arm with pioneering anticolonial activists and Black feminists like Andaiye and Selma James, among many others (Andaiye 2020; Dalla Costa and James 1975). For overviews of social reproduction theory, see Bhattacharya 2017; Federici 2020; Fraser 2016; Mezzadri 2020; Katz 2001; Morgan and Weinbaum 2024; Weiss 2021, 2022. For more on this topic from a specifically agrarian perspective, see Mezzadri et al. 2024; O'Laughlin 2022; Ossome and Naidu 2021.

9. On agrarian debt, see Agarwal 2021; Arango Vásquez 2020; Gerber 2013, 2014, 2021; Green 2022, 2025; Natarajan and Brickell 2022; Prosnitz 2023; Sajadian 2024; Sethi 2018. On feminist approaches to debt, see Cavallero and Gago 2021; Federici 2014; Han 2012; Guérin et al. 2023; Petchesky and Alexander 2014; Schuster 2014, 2015; Stack 1983; Zaloom and James 2023.

10. Under the banner of "Unity, Freedom, Socialism" and "One Arab Nation with an Immortal Mission," the Ba'th (Resurrection) Party was founded in 1947 by two urban middle-class intellectuals, Michel 'Aflaq and Salah al-Din al-Bitar, as part of a broader wave of Arab nationalism spreading across the Levant throughout the

interwar period. In the 1950s, the Baʿth Party amalgamated with the Arab Socialist Party of Akram Hourani, which substantially expanded the Baʿth movement's peasant base. For more, see Batatu 1999; Devlin 1991.

11. The term *ʿashīra* (pl: *ʿashāʾir*) refers to a segmentary lineage within a tribal confederation. As will be discussed further in the next two chapters, the residents of Rawia's camp hailed from a wide variety of tribal clans in the Jazīra plateau of eastern Syria. *Shāwi* (pl. *shawāya*) refers to pastoralists who herd sheep as their main source of livelihood, usually of a lower status than camel herders, residing in northeastern Syria and western Iraq (Dukhan 2022a, 2022b; Lange 2005, 2015). Though it has pejorative connotations among Syrian urbanites, the word *shāwi* was a common self-designation among farmworkers from this region of Syria, who referred to their dialect of Arabic as *shāwi*. On the *shāwi* dialect of Arabic, see Jastrow 2012. For more on tribal politics and history in Syria, see Alhamd 2022; Dukhan 2018; Lange 2014.

12. On dispossession by displacement, see Araghi 2008, 2009.

13. The size of these camps varies widely, some consisting of a single patrilocal family unit and others hosting hundreds of people from diverse backgrounds. Though some *shawīsh* are Lebanese, most of them are enterprising Syrian labor migrants with prewar migratory ties to Lebanon. Not all camps are run by *shawīsh*, and the role and function of the *shawīsh* depends on the scale, geography, and history of each camp (Cassani 2021, 2023; Dziadosz 2020; Nassar 2025; Sajadian 2020b; Sender 2024; Stel 2020; Zuntz et al. 2022; Zuntz 2023). This system of labor recruitment is present in various forms throughout Syria, Jordan, and Türkiye as well (Abdelali-Martini and Pryck 2015; Chatty 2017; Duruiz 2019; Kavak 2016; Pelek 2019, 2022).

14. For more on this seasonal economy of cross-border labor and remittances, see Lange 2007; Rabo 2017; Sajadian 2024; Zuntz 2021.

15. In fact, the UN High Commissioner for Refugees reports that currently less than 1 percent of the world's refugees are successfully resettled in third countries each year. Even for those who do receive resettlement or asylum, it is often a path mired in economic precarity and instability. See Allan 2020; Besteman 2016; Fassin 2005; Gowayed 2022; Nguyen 2019; Ticktin 2011.

16. Owen 2020.

17. Malkki 1995b, 503.

18. For more on this history, see Long 2013; Robson 2023.

19. It should be noted that the 1951 Convention is only one instrument among a broad array of international and transnational frameworks addressing the conditions of displaced people, migrant workers, and rural populations. These include, among others, the UN General Assembly's 1990 International Convention on the Protection of the Rights of All Migrant Workers and Members of Their Families; the

International Labor Organization's 1949 and 1975 Conventions concerning migrant workers; the Convention on the Elimination of All Forms of Discrimination Against Women (including Article 14 on rural women); the 1984 Convention Against Torture and Other Cruel, Inhuman or Degrading Treatment or Punishment; the 1966 International Covenant on Civil and Political Rights; the 1966 International Covenant on Economic, Social and Cultural Rights; and the 2018 United Nations Declaration on the Rights of Peasants and Other People Working in Rural Areas. For a detailed account of Lebanon's status with respect to many of these frameworks, see Janmyr 2016. For discussions of transnational agrarian frameworks, see Edelman and Borras 2016; Edelman 2024. For more on the ILO conventions on migrant workers, see Böhning 1991.

20. United Nations, *Convention Relating to the Status of Refugees*, Geneva, July 28, 1951. Quoted from Owen 2020.

21. Benard 1986.

22. See, by way of example, Besteman 2016; Cabot 2019; Cabot and Ramsay 2021; De Genova 2013, 2016; Fassin 2005; Feldman 2018b; Haralambous 2020; Holmes and Castañeda 2016; Lubkemann 2008; Nguyen 2019; Ticktin 2011; Malkki 1995a, 1995b, 1996; Monroe 2023; Ramsay 2017, 2020; Rosenthal 2023.

23. Anthropologists have addressed the dilemma of ahistoricism and refugee exceptionalism in several ways. A significant body of scholarship has approached refugees in terms of broader genealogies and regimes of humanitarianism. This literature emphasizes how the space of the refugee camp—as a quintessentially modern technology of governance and containment—critically shapes the ethical and political subjectivities of refugees (Agier 2010; Feldman 2018b; Malkki 1995a and 1995b; Peteet 2005). Contesting depoliticized or reductive depictions of refugees, there is also a rich range of ethnographic research that approaches protracted displacement as an everyday social condition, charting the complex forms of improvisation and survival, material practices, networks of mutual support, and ethics of care that shape refugees' daily lives (Abdi 2005; Alimia 2022; Allan 2013; Belloni 2016; Dinger 2022b; Oka 2014; Perdigon 2015, 2018), including the role of refugee brokers within these communities (Ozer 2024; Zuntz 2023). Another way of thinking beyond the refugee paradigm is by delving deeper into regionally embedded vocabularies and practices associated with displacement, as shown in Farhang's (2025) fascinating genealogical and ethnographic analysis of the *gharīb*.

24. As many scholars have noted, refugees do not occupy a unique temporality but rather reside within the "shared rhythms" of labor, precarity, and uncertainty with which all displaced people contend in various ways—not least the challenges of building a navigable future (Cabot and Ramsay 2021; Ramsay 2020). Writing of

refugees resettled in the United States, Gowayed (2022) and Nguyen (2019) both demonstrate vividly how refugees are often relegated to networks of low-waged employment as well as insufficient welfare provision and systems of social support.

25. On the agrarian politics of migration and displacement, see Araghi 2008, 2009; Veltmeyer and Wise 2016.

26. McMichael 2021.

27. For more on food regimes, see Friedman and McMichael 1989; McMichael 2009, 2021. For a critical feminist perspective of the food regime framework, see Mincyte 2023.

28. See Davis 2006. Readers in the United States might be most familiar with the predicaments of Mexican villagers who have, since the signing of the North American Free Trade Agreement in 1994, migrated to pursue the lowest paid yet essential work at enormous cost to themselves and their families, as they weigh the risks of detention or death crossing the border and deportation while working in the United States, and endure the harsh daily conditions of precarity (De León 2015; Holmes 2013; López 2011; Striffler 2007).

29. See Hanieh 2013; Zurayk 2011. It was beyond the scope of this study to analyze the historical and political economic dynamics of the 2011 Syrian popular uprising, particularly given the fact that most of my interlocutors did not participate nor did they consider themselves political dissidents. As I have written elsewhere in an unpublished essay on the dynamics of self-organization and local political mobilization, the vigor and swiftness with which popular uprisings spread across Syria throughout 2011 and 2012 were deeply linked to Syria's protracted liberalization process, growing rural-urban inequalities, and a long history of political suppression of Islamist and leftist opposition movements. For diverse accounts of the political, social, and historical conditions that gave rise to the Syrian uprising, its trajectories, and its aftermaths, see Abboud 2018; Abouzeid 2019; Al-Khalili 2023; Al-Haj Saleh 2017; Borri 2016; Daher 2019a; Dahi and Munif 2012; Hinnebusch and Zintl 2014; Hokayem 2013; Ismail 2018; Pearlman 2018; Proudfoot 2022; Salamandra and Steinberg 2015; Tarnowski 2022; Vignal 2012; Wedeen 2019; Yassin-Kassab and Al-Shami 2016.

30. Gilmore 2007, 11.

31. On borders, see Balibar 2002; De Genova 2016; De Genova and Peutz 2010; De León 2015, 2024; Galemba 2017; S. Ghosh 2022, 2023, 2025; Heyman 2001, 2022, 2024; Fassin 2011; Mezzadra and Neilson 2013; Reeves 2014; Reumert et al. 2025; Sur 2021; Walia 2021. In my conceptualization of the border as a mechanism of social control that regulates labor (both waged and unwaged), I am drawing inspiration not only from critical border studies but also the literature on abolition and racial capitalism (Davis and Dent 2001; Gilmore 2007, 2022).

32. Walia 2021.

33. Walia 2021, 84.

34. On Syrian refugees as workers, see Cassani 2021, 2023; Dinger 2021; Kavak 2016; Pelek 2019, 2022; Turner 2015. On the border politics of inclusion and exclusion, see Mezzadra and Neilson 2013. On "inclusion" from a feminist social reproduction perspective, see Mezzadri 2020.

35. The anthropological literature on farmworkers is vast. By way of example, see Benson 2011; Besky 2013; Bourgois 1988; Chatterjee 2001; Duruiz 2019; García-Colón 2020; Griffith 1995; Holmes 2013; Horton 2016; Jayawardena 2015; Jegathesan 2019; Kaminer 2024; López 2007; Narotzky and Smith 2006; Saxton 2021; Salinas 2018; Striffler 2002.

36. For more, see Federici 2014, 2020.

37. On the politics of social reproduction and gendered migration among translocal rural households across the Global South, see Gidwani and Ramamurthy 2018; Green and Estes 2019, 2022; Rao 2021; Shah and Lerche 2020. This point also bears relevance to research on "mixed status" families (Castañeda 2019).

38. For more on this issue, see Sajadian 2024 and chapter 4 of this book.

39. Bourgois 1988.

40. Seth Holmes's (2013) pathbreaking research on indigenous Oaxacan Triqui migrant farmworkers in the United States reveals how the normalization of farm labor hierarchies in terms of gender, class, age, lack of citizenship, regional origins, and racialized characteristics serve to justify lower wages and loosen labor protections. The overrepresentation of minoritized ethnic groups and Indigenous populations in migratory labor is, indeed, an important feature of our globalized food system that merits further historical comparison and analysis—from Dalits and Adivasis in India (Jain and Jayaram 2023; Lerche and Shah 2018) to Hill Country Tamil farmworkers in Sri Lanka (Jegathesan 2019), to Q'eqchi' Maya lowlanders in Guatemala (Grandia 2012), to Thai Isaan farmworkers in Israel/Palestine (Kaminer 2024), to Basotho people in South Africa (Ngubane 2024), and beyond.

41. In their incisive review of scholarship on the Middle East in anthropology, Deeb and Winegar (2012) note the striking neglect of rural areas. More than two decades earlier, Lila Abu-Lughod (1989) lamented a similar problem in her famous review article. Lauding the wealth of studies of peasants in other regional contexts, particularly the field of subaltern studies in South Asia that was emerging at the time, Abu-Lughod asked provocatively, "Are there household economies only in Africa? Is there peasant resistance only in Asia? Is there capitalist transformation of rural areas only in Latin America?" (299). Though Arabic-language research on agrarian history and politics in Syria and Lebanon is robust (Baʿlabakkī 1994; Ḍāhir 1983;

Ḥannā 1975, 1990; Ḥizb al-Shuyūʿī al-Lubnānī 1973; Saʿīd 1995; Ṣalībā 1999, 2004; Smilianskaia 1972), the Middle East perhaps remains the least represented region within the comparative tradition of agrarian studies and peasant studies. Fortunately, a new generation of MENA-focused scholarship spanning agrarian studies and rural political ecology is beginning to emerge (Ajl 2021; Basha 2023; Carneal 2024; Djerbi 2024; Duruiz 2019; Kavak and Eren Benlisoy 2025; Kirk 2024; Kohlbry 2026; Lawson 2024; Martiniello and Kassem 2023; Panosetti et al. 2025; Perosino 2024; Riachi and Martiniello 2023; Rignall 2021; Thomson et al. 2022; Williams 2023).

42. The early decades of the left-leaning Middle East Research and Information Project (MERIP) offer pioneering examples of this work. In her retrospective article on the study of women over the course of the journal's fifty-year history, Judith Tucker (2021) notes a focus on the political economy of rural women's work, such as Friedl 1981; Pfeifer 1987; Taylor 1984, among others. It also is worth emphasizing that some of the classic articles on Middle East women's studies, such as Kandiyoti's (1988) "Bargaining with Patriarchy," were written specifically in the tradition of agrarian studies. The ethnographic literature on gender, sexuality, marriage, and women's worlds in the Middle East is vast and wide ranging. Some examples include Abu-Lughod 1986, 1990, 2008; Adely 2024; Chatty and Rabo 1997; Deeb 2006, 2024; Friedl 1989; Joseph 1983, 1993, 1994, 2018; Limbert 2010; Mahmood 2005; Meneley 1996; Mikdashi 2022; Singerman 1995. Some examples of the excellent historical work on gender and labor include Abisaab 2010; Ferguson 2024; Khater 2001; Seikaly 2015; Thompson 2000. On women and gender in rural Syria, see Abdelali-Martini and Pryck 2015; Abdelali-Martini et al. 2003; Lange 2007, 2014; Rabo 2008; Sarkis Fernández 2015, 2020; and on urban Syria, see Gallagher 2012; Salamandra 2004. On women and gender in rural Lebanon, see Abisaab 2010; Khater 2001; Khayyat 2022.

43. See Sayigh 1979, 1981. On gender and labor in Palestinian camps, see also Abdallah 2009; Allan 2013; Barbosa 2022; Peteet 1997, 2005, 2013.

44. As Fawwaz Traboulsi notes, during the French Mandate period, Lebanese nationalists called for the annexation of the Bekaa Valley to the state of "Greater Lebanon" to ensure sufficient arable land and food supplies for the new nation (2007, 83)—a pressing concern after the massive famine that had devastated the region during World War I (Al-Qattan 2014; Brand 2023; Pitts 2016). Such aspirations were not uncontested, however, given the Bekaa's extraordinary religious diversity. Many, if not most, of the valley's Sunni and Shiʿa Muslim inhabitants, along with a number of non-Maronite Christians, including Orthodox and Greek Catholics, expressed a preference for inclusion in "Greater Syria" (Abisaab 2009; Traboulsi 2007, 81). For more on the cultural, historical, and political history of the Bekaa Valley, see Chatty 1974; Joseph 2013; Naff 1972; Obeid 2019; Saʿīd 1995; Ṣalībā 1999, 2004.

45. Chalcraft 2009, 71.

46. Syria's military and security services maintained a heavy-handed presence in Lebanon from 1976 until the assassination of Prime Minister Rafiq al-Hariri in 2005. This prolonged intervention was a source of deep division within Lebanese society, the consequences of which continue to shape the present. While many Lebanese viewed Syria's presence as a foreign occupation and a violation of national sovereignty, others tacitly or explicitly supported its role in Lebanon's security and political affairs. To understand the complexities of these divisions, see El-Husseini 2012; Salloukh 2005; Salloukh et al. 2015.

47. *Iqṭāʿ* refers to large, landed estates that consolidated in the Ottoman era, though it is often imprecisely translated to "feudalism." Given the presence of servile labor and the historical tendency for some of these properties to be undercapitalized, the *iqṭāʿ* system bears relevance to debates on the latifundio in Latin America (Edelman 1992). Sarkis-Fernandez (2020) aptly characterizes *iqṭāʿ* as "a kind of capitalist serfdom," while, in the Iraqi context, Samira Haj (1997) describes it as a "modern system of sharecropping" that intensified during the British Mandate. As discussed further in chapter 2, the question of *iqṭāʿ* was central to postindependence debates over land reform in Syria. It is important to note, however, that unlike Syria, Lebanon never underwent large-scale agrarian reform, and the country's large *iqṭāʿī* estates were never broken up.

48. Within Islamic jurisprudence, *ḍammān* refers to a contractual guarantee and implies the assumption of risk or responsibility, drawing from the phrase "profit follows responsibility" attributed to the Prophet Muhammad. While the agricultural practice of *ḍammān* extends back to the late Ottoman era, it has evolved today into a form of contract farming, which will be discussed in greater depth in the next chapter. On the role of *ḍammān* in the formation of Levantine joint-stock companies and the expansion of agrarian capitalism in the nineteenth century, see Alff 2018. See also Batatu 1999; Tamari 1983 for discussions of the different forms of *ḍammān* found across the Levant.

49. As the coming pages will show, the rise of contract farming went hand-in-hand with the declining viability of small-scale farming in Lebanon. Since the 1970s, smallholder families have increasingly relied on a combination of off-farm employment (military, healthcare, education, services), flows of cash and remittances from work in cities or abroad, and petty merchant trading (local stores selling mostly imported goods). Symptomatic of the "reproduction squeeze" that has pushed many smallholders into waged work and off their land across the world (Bernstein 2003), today it is rare to find Lebanese smallholder families who can survive from agriculture alone. Among elderly smallholders, a combination of subsistence agriculture

and renting out land to contract farmers remains a source of vital retirement income and old-age social security in a country that offers limited pensions (Zurayk 2011, 28–29). For more on Lebanon's market-led approach to agriculture, see Allam 2011; Martiniello and Kassem 2023; Sukarieh and Arafeh 2023; Turkmani and Hamade 2020; Yaghi 2025.

50. *Warsha* (pl. *warash, warshāt*) commonly refers to a small workshop (such as for furniture making or automobile repair) or a construction site. Within agriculture, it connotes a team or camp of workers.

51. Pitt-Rivers 2017.

52. Here, I mean "learning" in the sense that Talal Asad (2020) describes ethnography. Observation, Asad notes, is the essence of all learning, and ethnography entails the observational work of "learning to do what others do by attending to what is said and not said because it is taken for granted" (404).

53. On externalization, see Lemberg-Pedersen 2019; Moreno-Lax and Lemberg-Pedersen 2019. In the US context, a comparable mechanism was the first Trump administration's "Asylum Cooperative Agreements" (sometimes framed as "safe third country" arrangements) with El Salvador, Guatemala, and Honduras. These agreements were designed to allow the United States to deport asylum seekers to those countries on the premise that they should seek protection there, thereby stemming the flow of refugees and preventing them from reaching the United States. They were suspended or formally terminated during the Biden administration in 2021. Under the current Trump administration, renewed efforts are underway to reconstitute these arrangements—especially with El Salvador—as part of a broader push to externalize asylum processing.

54. For more on the history of Syrian labor migration to Lebanon, see Chalcraft 2005, 2009.

55. Chalcraft 2009; Dinger 2022a; Salloukh 2005.

56. Dinger 2022a.

57. On the politics of hospitality in Lebanon and Türkiye, see Alkan 2021; Babül 2024; Berg and Fiddian-Qasmieh 2018; Carpi 2023; Carpi and Şenoğuz 2018; Thorleifsson 2016.

58. Ashkar 2015.

59. Carpi and Şenoğuz 2018.

60. It is also not a state party to the UN General Assembly's 1990 International Convention on the Protection of the Rights of All Migrant Workers and Members of their Families, nor the International Labor Organization Conventions 97 and 143 concerning migrant workers.

61. Janmyr 2021.

62. Janmyr 2017.

63. Lebanon is state party to the Committee on the Elimination of Discrimination Against Women; the 1984 Convention Against Torture and Other Cruel, Inhuman or Degrading Treatment or Punishment; the 1966 International Covenant on Civil and Political Rights; and the 1966 International Covenant on Economic, Social and Cultural Rights. See Janmyr 2016 for a more extended discussion of these issues.

64. Janmyr 2016, 62.

65. For more on the Lebanon Crisis Response Plan, see Dinger 2022a.

66. Dinger 2022a, 218.

67. Michael Burawoy (1976) classically described this as a "dual dependence," where migrant workers depend upon waged employment in the receiving country while the sending country covers the workers' costs of social reproduction.

68. This was, in a significant sense, exacerbated by the wartime devaluation of the Syrian pound, which made the prospects of rebuilding their homes and livelihoods prohibitive even for those who felt they were in a position to return to Syria. Before 2011, the Syrian pound was valued at close to 50 to the US dollar. By 2019, it had devalued tenfold to around 515 to the dollar under the combined impact of war, reverberating economic crisis, and multiple rounds of Western-led sanctions. For more on the historical roots of the devaluation of the Syrian pound, see Daher 2019b.

69. "Caretaker government" refers to a temporary ad hoc coalition of policymakers who perform governing duties until an election.

70. The incendiary rhetoric of Gibran Bassil, Lebanon's foreign minister at the time of my research, epitomized such ideas. See Wintour 2019.

71. As of January 2015, Syrian refugees are no longer permitted to cross the Lebanese border for humanitarian reasons. Syrians entering Lebanon are now required to invoke one of the seven categories for entry: study, tourism, work, trade, healthcare, embassy consultation, or leasing or owning property. They are also required to have a bank account with a certain amount of cash and a hotel reservation with specific dates, including a date of return to Syria.

72. For an excellent discussion of how Lebanon's post-2015 regulations affected Syrians' residency status and entry requirements, see Janmyr 2016. On the broader history and material effects of the *kafāla* system on labor migrants in Lebanon, see Kassamali 2017, 2022, 2025.

73. The history of the Palestinian resistance in Lebanon and its centrality to the Lebanese Civil War (1975–1990) reinforced these dynamics, as Syrians were sometimes juxtaposed within official and popular discourse as "nonpolitical" migrants, compared to the "politicized" Palestinian refugees. While Palestinian refugees in Lebanon have been subject to a range of discriminatory measures regulating their

participation in the labor market for decades, Syrian labor migrants were valued as an exploitable and flexible labor reserve. This obviously changed in important ways throughout the war, and at various junctures in the decades preceding it.

74. Chalcraft 2009, 15.

75. From Syrians to Palestinians to other noncitizen workers and displaced people, the specter of "foreigners" and "others" has long served as a mobilization strategy among hardline Lebanese nationalists, as Al-Saadi (2014) notes. We can see resonances to this rhetoric in the Maronite League's lamentations over the expanding shantytown of Karantina in eastern Beirut in 1965 (Traboulsi 2007, 147). Citing the masses of proletarianized Lebanese peasants, Palestinian refugees, Syrian migrant workers, and displaced Kurds who had built their homes in this growing urban periphery, the League accused the Lebanese state of "selling out Lebanon" to "foreigners." As Traboulsi points out, "This linked two seemingly disparate groups: those who bought landed property were the rich Arabs of the Gulf and Saudi Arabia, while the Karantina dwellers were poor Lebanese with a minority of Syrians and non-naturalised Kurds" (2007, 147).

76. Critical research on labor migration, for example, has shown how state designations of "illegality" shape the dynamics of inequality not only between citizens and migrants, but also among migrants themselves (De Genova 2002; Gomberg-Muñoz 2010; Heyman 2001; Horton 2016; Horton and Heyman 2020).

77. For more on the historical and structural roots of Lebanon's sovereign debt crisis, see Al-Amine 2020; Daher 2022a; Dibeh 2021; Hakim and Andary 1997; Salti 2019; Safieddine 2019; Srouji 2005.

78. Gilmore 2007, 54. See also Federici 2020. For a Lebanese feminist critique of austerity, see also Akiki 2019. On the effects of Lebanon's financial crisis on migrant workers, see Reumert 2020, 2023.

79. For more on the 2019 Lebanese uprising, see Karam and Majed 2022.

80. As will be discussed later in this book, Lebanon's current public debt crisis was a culmination of three decades of neoliberal monetary and fiscal policies throughout its reconstruction process following its fifteen-year civil war. Its postwar economy was a product of ongoing struggles between an ascendant class of emigree elites enriched by fortunes abroad, an old guard of amnestied sectarian militia leaders, a variety of politicians with tacit or explicit backing by the Syrian state, and the leaders of the Shiʿa Islamist social movement Hizbullah. Meanwhile, a growing class of financial elites from within the liberalizing Syrian political class loomed large throughout Lebanon's reconstruction process, exerting a profound influence over the struggles between these different segments of Lebanon's postwar state formation (El-Husseini 2012).

81. Russia's invasion of Ukraine in February 2022 compounded an already deepening crisis in global fuel and food supplies. Like many countries in the region, both Lebanon and Syria are dependent on Russia and Ukraine for wheat and fodder. As the war in Syria decimated its domestic agricultural production, Russia became the leading supplier of wheat to Syria, particularly following Russia's military intervention in Syria in 2015 (Daher 2022b). Coupled with the international rise in fuel prices, the costs of imported food items and all goods related to wheat and fodder skyrocketed in the region.

Chapter 1

1. As Janet Roitman (2013) asks, "When crisis is posited as the very condition of contemporary situations, is it not the case that certain questions become possible while others are foreclosed?" (10).

2. On the concept of *banāt*, see Sa'ar 2004.

3. For more on Lebanon's approach to refugee governance, see Carpi 2023; Carpi and Şenoğuz 2018; Dinger 2022a; Fakhoury 2021; Janmyr 2016, 2017; Janmyr and Mourad 2018; Nassar and Stel 2019; Sanyal 2017, 2018.

4. On the limits and possibilities of "crisis" as a framework of political action and temporal understanding, see Barrios 2017; İpek 2025; Iqbal 2022b; Koselleck 1988; Roitman 2013. Social historians have also long been attentive to the limits of crisis claims, which often obscure the less visible structural crises and continuities in workers' everyday lives (Hall 1978; Thompson 1978). The stakes of such critiques carry particular significance within the humanitarian governance of refugees. For more on how the humanitarian understanding of crisis delimits the terms of political urgency, worthiness, and visibility among displaced populations, see Asad 2015a; Cabot 2019; Carpi 2023; Fassin 2005; Feldman 2018b; Holmes and Castañeda 2016; Redfield 2013; Ticktin 2011.

5. This encompasses what Diana Allan (2020) evocatively describes as "the long turning," a term she borrows from her Palestinian refugee interlocutors, meaning the ways that crisis and insecurity accumulate and are inhabited over the duration of a life course, across generations, and often across borders. Lauren Berlant (2011) likewise describes such conditions as a generalized condition of "slow death" in our contemporary era: what she refers to as the "crisis ordinary." From "quasi-events" (Povinelli 2011) to "slow violence" (Nixon 2011), to everyday crisis (İpek 2025; Obeid and al-Masri 2021; Shevchenko 2008), these perspectives all seek to capture the durational, mundane, and uneventful politics of crisis in late capitalist conditions. While taking inspiration from these ethnographic approaches, I insist on the feminist formulation of "crises of reproduction" in this context because it holds together the microlevel

phenomenological experience of crises, on the one hand, and the broader macrolevel forces that produce them, on the other. Here, I am drawing from Marxist feminist scholarship that analyzes crises of reproduction as a global, uneven, and ongoing process, expressed in the privatization of caregiving and other forms of reproductive work, a globalized gendered division of labor, feminized mass migrations of rural people to urban areas and across borders, and rising rates of consumer debt (Bhattacharya 2017; Cavallero and Gago 2021; Federici 2020, 2014). On Marxist theories of crisis, see Brennan 2024; Gilmore 2007; Kuruma 2025; O'Connor 1981; Shaikh 2016.

6. For an excellent account of the evictions in Riyaq, see Dinger 2018.

7. On the closure of Syrian-run businesses and waves of criminalization during this period, see Dinger 2021.

8. For critical perspectives on the Lebanese state, see Abu Rish 2026; Hermez 2017; Kosmatopoulos 2011, 2024; Mikdashi 2022; Nucho 2016; Obeid 2019, 2023. On the humanitarian discourse of corruption, see Feldman 2018a.

9. For more on the etymology and genealogy of crisis as a concept, see Barrios 2017; Roitman 2013; Starn 1971; Koselleck 1988.

10. On the humanitarian concept of crisis, see Asad 2015a; Redfield 2013.

11. Feldman 2018b, 3.

12. On the politics of home, inhabitation, and domestic life among refugees, see Abourahme 2020; Dinger 2022b; Feldman 2006; Saad 2019; Scott-Smith 2024.

13. See Rabo 1986, 8–9, for a detailed description of the traditional layout of eastern Syrian households.

14. The colloquial term *mouneh* comes from the Arabic root *mana*, which means "storing." Encompassing methods of pickling, curing, sweetening, jarring, and packing with oil, this laborious process of preparing and conserving seasonal food products is a central pillar of rural life across the Levant. *Mouneh* includes nonperishable pantry staples, such as dried herbs like wild thyme, sage, rosemary, and sumac; cured olives; canned fruit jams; pastes made of red peppers or tomatoes; jarred savory preserves like *makdūs* (eggplants stuffed with peppers and walnuts); and dairy products stored in water or oil, such as *kishk* (balls of cracked wheat and yogurt), *jibneh* (cheese) with black sesame seeds, and *labneh* (strained yogurt). As refrigeration has become a fixture of even the poorest Syrian households over the past two decades, the seasonal preparation of *mouneh* also includes the blanching and freezing of seasonal vegetables like okra, beans, and peas. For more on *mouneh*, see Massaad 2017; Sajadian 2025b.

15. Chalcraft 2009, 89.

16. See Ababsa 2019; Daher 2019a; Hinnebusch 1995; Sajadian 2023; Sarkis Fernández 2020; Wedeen 2019.

17. Federici 2020, 70, 104.

18. As Narotzky (2016) states, "Contract farmers are nominally independent producers, but they often lack control over the production process and become mere hands in a system that, moreover, burdens them with the high risk of volatile product markets" (7). For more on contract farming, see Mazwi et al. 2022; Pérez Niño and Oya 2021; White and Wijaya 2022.

19. It should be noted that the scale of *ḍammān*'s work and the nature of his or her relationship to the landlord depends on a range of factors, including the size of the property they are overseeing. In the case of smaller parcels, I often observed that the landlord was not especially wealthy; these smallholders simply lacked sufficient capital to take on the risk of harvesting. In such cases, the relationship between the landlord and the *ḍammān* was often more horizontal and friendly, as in the case of Abu Charbel, who appears at a few points in this book. In these situations, the labor usually consisted of a smaller team of "free workers" overseen and recruited by the *ḍammān* without a middleman, which they supplemented with *shawīsh* workers for larger jobs.

20. For more on clans in Lebanon, see Chatty 1974, 2014; Chatty et al. 2013.

21. A *dūnam* (*dönüm* in Turkish) was the standard measure of land area in the Levant during the Ottoman Empire, originally defined as the amount of land that could be ploughed in a single day. Its size initially varied by region and was roughly equivalent to about 1,000 square yards. In the late nineteenth century, the *dūnam* was standardized to 1,000 square meters—one-tenth of a hectare—a measure that continues to be used today.

22. In 2019, Ibtissam and her siblings rented 250 *dūnam* (25 hectares), for which they paid $450 per *dūnam* to the Salam family at the beginning of the winter season. Ibtissam and her siblings estimated that their seasonal production costs were about $1,000 per *dūnam,* which included the costs of labor from Abu Sharif's camp, machinery, inputs, and irrigation systems.

23. For more on this history, see Khayyat 2022.

24. For more on the Chihab period, see Johnson 1986; Lawson 2021; Nasr 1978; Safieddine 2019.

25. Picard 2002, 92; Ṣalībā 1999, 337.

26. Nasr 1978, 8.

27. In his magisterial account of the history of syndicalist movements in the Bekaa Valley based on firsthand experience as a labor organizer, 'Azīz Ṣalībā (1999) charts the emergence of an agrarian social movement from the 1950s to the 1970s, directly preceding the Lebanese Civil War. In 1954, the Lebanese Communist Party convened a series of conferences in Lebanon's three main agrarian regions—Bekaa,

Akkar, and the South—representing farmers from over one hundred villages (Ṣalībā 1999, 332). Their demands on the Lebanese state included supplying drinking water and irrigation works to all villages, and establishing an eight-hour workday and minimum living wage for farmers, among others. Though many of their demands were not met, farmers succeeded in establishing a series of cooperatives (*taʿāwuniyyāt*) throughout the 1950s and 1960s (Ṣalībā 1999, 336).

28. As Chalcraft (2009) states, "Lebanese employees had to be registered in the newly created national Social Security system, protecting workers against sickness, job loss, retirement, accidents, and so on. Employers had to defray one-third of the costs of this scheme and complained bitterly. Those employing Syrians took on no such costs, nor even the bureaucracy of work contracts. Workers were hired and fired on the spot. Legal issues were minimal and accident insurance was optional" (83–84).

29. Ḥizb al-Shuyūʿī al-Lubnānī [Lebanese Communist Party] 1973, 36.

30. There are some interesting parallels between Lebanon and California's "post-golden-age" crises of the late 1970s, marked by rural out-migration, increasing rates of farmer indebtedness and bankruptcies, and wage stagnation. Meanwhile, undocumented immigrants—much like Syrians in Lebanon—swelled California's farmworker labor force, especially from Mexico and Central America (Gilmore 2007, 42).

31. Nasr 1978, 9–11.

32. Pearlman 2013, 117.

33. Whereas the public sector provided 20 percent of Lebanon's agricultural credits in 1943–1953, by the mid-1960s, this dwindled to 5 percent. In the mid-1970s, fertilizer imports were concentrated in two Lebanese firms, Unifert and Le Comptoir Agricole (Nasr 1978, 8).

34. Picard 2005.

35. Fargues 2009, 552–3.

36. The signing of the Ta'if Accords in 1989 marked the official end of Lebanon's civil war. Though the accord required the disarming of Lebanon's various militias (with the notable exception of Hizbullah), most Lebanese militia leaders were given amnesty and seamlessly entered the newly constructed Lebanese parliament. The Ta'if Accords also permitted Syria to maintain its military troops in Lebanon for an unspecified period—seen by some segments of the war-weary Lebanese population as a guarantor of security and others as a foreign occupier—which effectively meant that Syria dominated Lebanon's domestic security affairs until it abruptly withdrew its troops in 2005 after the assassination of Lebanese Prime Minister Rafiq al-Hariri.

37. El-Husseini 2012.

38. Allam 2011.

39. Located in the Western Bekaa Valley, the Qab Elias market is one of the largest wholesale agricultural marketing hubs and distribution points for fresh produce in the region. It is one of three major markets in the Bekaa Valley, along with Ferzol and Baalbek. Distributors, truck drivers, wholesalers, farmers, and exporters gather in these markets to negotiate prices, where they ship fresh produce to other major markets in Beirut, Sidon, Tripoli, Akkar, Tyre, and Nabatiya, to the Persian Gulf by air, sea, or ground routes through Syria and Jordan—though ground transportation became increasingly difficult and costly throughout the war. For a commodity-chain analysis of how these markets fit within Lebanon's food system, see Center for the Promotion of Imports from Developing Countries 2018; Environmental and Sustainable Development Unit at the American University of Beirut 2020; Mercy Corps 2014; Ruijs 2017.

40. Berlant 2011, 10.

41. Allan 2020.

42. As Abdelali-Martini and Pryck (2015) note, "Historically and still today, rural [Syrian] women have little control of agricultural land and other assets, despite their rights to inherit or purchase land under civil and Islamic law. They often cede their inheritance rights to their brothers to put moral pressure on them for support should their husbands divorce them" (900). For more on the gendered impacts of land reform in a comparative context, see Deere and León 2001a, 2001b.

43. Writing of the Euphrates Dam project in the mid-1980s, Rabo (1986) states, "The planners of the Euphrates Scheme, like the male villagers, never discuss the importance of women in agriculture. Planners and those in power never view the village economy on a household level, nor in relation to larger economic processes. The Scheme is planned by men for a family economy of which they have only a very vague idea" (57).

44. These gendered divisions of labor were also linked to the increasingly dualistic structure of Syria's agricultural markets following Hafiz al-Asad's coup in 1970. On the one hand, the state maintained a monopoly in wheat, barley, dry fodder, cotton, sugar beets, and tobacco. Cultivators of these crops sold their harvest to the state at fixed prices, and the state took responsibility for selling them locally. On the other hand, most fruits, vegetables, and livestock were dominated by private commerce, despite government attempts to regulate their prices and cap profit margins (Hinnebusch 1989, 147–56). Indeed, one of the unintended outcomes of the Euphrates Scheme was the expansion of sheep rearing in the private market, which became a secondary source of income for most Jazīran villagers and a substantial commercial enterprise for wealthy pastoralists (Rabo 1986, 74–75).

45. The chief ecological problem that eastern Syria has faced for decades is extreme water resource degradation. While it is beyond the scope of this book to explore these factors in depth, see Sajadian 2022 and Selby 2019 for more on links between the liberalization of Syria's economy, drought, and migration.

46. Abdelali-Martini and Pryck 2015, 901.

47. Federici 2020.

48. The concept of *al-qūt* ("daily provision") appears in several hadith, including "Whoever wakes secure in his home, healthy in body, and with his day's provision, it is as if the world has been gathered for him." Imam al-Shāfiʿī (767–820 CE) is reported to have said: "I was born in Gaza, raised in the Hijaz, and my provision is only for the night [*qūtī layla*], yet I have never been in need."

49. As Katharina Lange (2007) notes in her research on Euphrates villagers in the 1990s and early 2000s, "Although the nature of migrant labor is well known in the village, working for others is not *visible* there, since it takes place in an environment far from home—unlike the wage labor practiced by village girls" (76–77).

50. Brought to Syria by the Levantine diaspora in South America around the turn of the twentieth century, yerba maté is a staple of many rural Syrian households in the countryside of Damascus and the coast.

51. Batatu 1999, 10.

52. For more on the devaluation of the Syrian pound, see Daher 2019b.

53. Gilmore 2007, 54.

Chapter 2

Sections of this chapter build on a previously published article, "The Drowned and the Displaced: Afterlives of Agrarian Developmentalism across the Lebanese-Syrian Border," *Mashriq & Mahjar: Journal of Middle East and North African Migration Studies* 10 (1): 9–43.

1. Drawn from the Kurdish word *cemedanî, jimdāna* is the eastern Syrian Arabic dialect term for a black-and-white or red-and-white checkered scarf, most well-known by the Palestinian colloquial term *keffiyeh*.

2. On Arab socialism, see Amin 1994; Guirguis 2020; Kadri 2016; Matar 2013; Takriti and Safieddine 2022.

3. For more on the polyvalent concept of *nuzūḥ*, see McManus 2022.

4. On the liberalization of Syria's economy, see Abboud 2018; Daher 2019a; Haddad 2012; Perthes 2006.

5. Drawn from the critical political economy tradition of migration studies, the concept of the "migration-development nexus" shows how migration is not only about the pursuit of the "good life" or an exit from poverty but also deeply bound up

in processes of capital accumulation and agrarian change. See Veltmeyer and Wise 2016; Wise 2010, 2022.

6. There is a vast range of literature on the controversies, inherited legacies, and struggles shaping dam-building projects across the world, including mass displacement. See, by way of example, Baviskar 2005; Bromber et al. 2014; Darwich and Menoret 2025; Fahim 1981; Hoag 2022; Isaacman and Isaacman 2013; Khneisser 2024; Lonergan et al. 2023; Mitchell 2002; Nixon 2011; Roy 1999; Scott 1998; Tsikata 2006; Weist 1995.

7. The interdisciplinary field of memory studies shows that popular narratives about the past are not simply a transparent window onto "what really happened" but rather a dynamic social relation between past and present that is continuously mediated and transformed by the shifting material circumstances in which memories take form. Moving beyond the binary between "official" and "subaltern" narratives, this research draws attention to the performative nature of memory, including its silences and embodied forms. This approach helps make sense of how Syrian farmworkers' narratives moved back and forth between the official state metanarratives and other registers of telling. See Connerton 2011; Caswell 2014; Gordillo 2014; Han 2020; Haugbolle 2010; Hirschkind 2020; Limbert 2010; Passerini 1987; Seremetakis 2019; Steedly 2019; Stoler and Strassler 2000; Strassler 2009. For an exemplary examination of the contested politics of memory in eastern Syria, see Lange 2019.

8. On the temporalities and aftermaths of revolution, war, mass displacement, and other political struggles, see Al-Khalili et al. 2023; Bardawil 2020; Best 2012; Bissell 2005; Das 2007; Elling and Haugbolle 2024; Ferguson 1999; Harootunian 2019; Koga 2016; Lear 2009; Love 2021, 2023; Pursley 2019; Sajadian 2023; Saleh 2020; Salem 2020; Scott 2014; Sharpe 2016; Thomas 2019; Wedeen 2019; Wilder 2015; Wilson 2023; Winchell 2022.

9. Shah and Lerche 2020.

10. The Raqqa Campaign was a series of battles and offensives launched by opposition groups between 2012 and 2013—most prominently by the militant faction Jabhat al-Nusra—to capture the city of Raqqa and its surrounding countryside from Syrian government forces. It culminated in the Battle of Raqqa in March 2013, when rebel forces fully captured the city of Raqqa from the Syrian army after a three-day battle. In the following months, Jabhat al-Nusra and allied factions were gradually displaced by the Islamic State of Iraq and al-Sham (ISIS), which consolidated control over Raqqa. On June 29, 2014, Abu Bakr al-Baghdadi officially announced the formation of a caliphate called the Islamic State that extended from Aleppo in Syria to Diyala in Iraq. For more, see Rosenblatt and Kilcullen 2019.

11. Throughout the Syrian war, the Kurdish-led People's Protection Units (Yekîneyên Parastina Gel) served as the main ground force combating ISIS while consolidating an autonomous administration in northeastern Syria. In 2015, they became the core of the Syrian Democratic Forces, a multiethnic and multireligious coalition operating under the umbrella of the Autonomous Administration of North and East Syria.

12. On debt as inheritance, see Derrida 1993.

13. Scott 2004, 2.

14. On *shawāya*, see al-Haj Saleh 2012; Dukhan 2022a, 2022b; Jastrow 2012; Lange 2005, 2015; Khalaf 1981; Rabo 1986; Sato 1997.

15. Lange 2005, 104.

16. Lange 2005, 106.

17. For more on this topic, see Anderson 2023.

18. Wedeen 2019.

19. For more, see al-Haj Saleh 2012; Lange 2015, 227–28.

20. For more on the importance of "stability" (*istiqrār*) within Syrian agricultural livelihoods, see Sarkis Fernández 2015.

21. Scott 1977.

22. Wedeen 2019, 25.

23. Berlant 2011, 14.

24. On postsocialist aftermaths, see Shevchenko 2008; Ushakin 2009; Verdery 2013; Yurchak 2005.

25. For more on the role of cotton *shaykhs* in mediating the expansion of capitalist agriculture in the Euphrates region, see Ḥannā 1975; Khalaf 1981; Rabo 1986.

26. Hinnebusch 1989, 87.

27. Lange 2019, 324.

28. Lange 2015.

29. The Walda clan numbers about 150,000 and historically settled in the western areas of Raqqa province along the banks of the Euphrates (Tabler 2018). In contrast to many other Arab tribal populations, the Walda do not claim an eponymous ancestor, and thus the origins of their name are a source of debate. For more on the Walda clan (also transliterated as Welde), see Alhamd 2022; Lange 2006.

30. Lange 2005, 105–6.

31. Rabo 1986, 28.

32. Literally meaning "laying a hand," *waḍʿ* al-yad is the customary process of claiming as private property a piece of land without legal documents extending back to the Ottoman era, generally referring to arable land newly cultivated

by clearing, plowing, and planting that can be claimed as private property so long as it is continuously cultivated. It is one of five different modalities through which private property emerged in the region (Saʿīd 1995, 157). *Waḍʿ* al-yad was an essentially precapitalist institution that emerged to feed Ottoman soldiers, maintain cultivation, and prevent peasant flight. Ottoman land reforms in the mid-nineteenth century formalized *waḍʿ* al-yad, which mandated that whoever undertook planting would be registered with the state and exercise private ownership claims over the land that they tilled continuously. For more, see Saʿīd 1995.

33. Khalaf 1981, 226.

34. Kochuyt 2009.

35. Sato 1997.

36. Lange 2019.

37. Lange 2019, 329.

38. For more on the *maḍāfa*, see Ababsa 2001; Gilsenan 1977.

39. On the "fiction of anteriority," see Derrida 1989; Richter 2011.

40. In making sense of the relationship between Marxism and postcolonialism, the view from South Asia is especially instructive. The question that guided what came to be known as the "India Mode of Production Debate" concerned the extent to which British colonial rule had kept India in a semifeudal state or, conversely, if it had facilitated the emergence of modern agrarian capitalism. By the 1980s, this focus on political economy was increasingly sidelined by a growing interest in postcolonialism and cultural studies. For more on this history, see Chakrabarti and Cullenberg 2003, Ludden 2002; Mohanty 2016; Sanyal 2007.

41. Gidwani 2008.

42. Chakrabarty 1989.

43. Bardawil 2020.

44. Meliczek 1986.

45. Hinnebusch 1989, 91.

46. Hinnebusch 1989, 94.

47. Hinnebusch et al. 2011.

48. For more on this topic, see Sato 1997.

49. Koselleck 2005.

50. Ahmad 1980.

51. Amin 1994.

52. Said 2018.

53. Ismail 2018.

54. Ismail 2018. See also Salamandra 2013.

55. The "Arab belt" refers to a series of state-led policies throughout the 1970s to radically transform the demographic balance of Kurdish-majority regions of Syria's

northeast border with Türkiye. From the time of Syria's independence onward, the pan-Arab orientation of Baʿth leadership became increasingly hostile to Kurdish nationalist aspirations and political organizing. When the Baʿth Party came to power in 1963, the Baʿth chief of police in Hasakah province, Mohamed Talab Hilal, published a report on the Jazīra that proposed a shocking twelve-point plan to disperse Kurds and deprive them of the fruits of citizenship. The "Arab belt" plan included a strategy of *iskān* (settlement) involving the implantation of "pure and nationalist Arabs" in Kurdish-majority regions and a "socialization" policy to promote collective farms populated by these new Arab settlers (McDowall 1993, 215–16). For more on this topic, see Dolbee 2018; Altuğ 2011, 90–94.

56. Ababsa 2004.

57. Tabler 2018.

58. Foy 2013.

59. Rabo 1986, 34–35.

60. Coronil 1997.

61. Rabo 1986, 141.

62. Rabo 1986, 83.

63. Rabo 1986, 86.

64. Rabo 1986, 35.

65. Khalaf 1981, 178.

66. Hinnebusch 1995.

67. According to Lange (2007), young men's migration decisions were strongly linked to the amount of land their family owned. Families with little or no land were more likely to have young male members of the household migrating abroad. On the relationship between bridewealth and labor migration in eastern Syria, also see Khalaf 1981, 248, 294; Rabo 1986, 57, 101–2, 141.

68. Ababsa 2004.

69. As Rabo (1986) states, "It is perhaps ironic that today, with the coming of the Euphrates Scheme and its emphasis on irrigated agriculture, sheep-rearing is—perhaps more than ever—very profitable when conducted on a large scale" (75).

70. Chalcraft 2009, 157.

71. Sarkis Fernández 2020.

72. Ababsa 2004.

73. As Katherine Verdery (2003) observed in property restitution in Romania, unmaking state-led redistributive property regimes generated struggles over different forms of value.

74. The Syrian state commission adopted a strict set of measures that, in practice, appeared quite arbitrary. As Ababsa (2004) states, "Any agricultural engineer present at his working station at the time of the publication of the decision, who

could have left it for various reasons, but who again occupied it at the date of April 3, 2003, had the right to obtain land plots. On the other hand, any temporary worker having had a contract for the agricultural seasons of 1999–2000 and 2000–2001 had the right to obtain lands, but not those employed in the previous seasons. Any farm labourer having worked at least 180 days during 2000 could claim lands, but not those having worked the previous years" (11–12).

75. See Foy 2013, 158; Ababsa 2009.

76. Ababsa 2019.

77. In an age where the specter of "climate refugees" tops headlines, there has been a temptation to make overblown claims linking anthropogenic climate change, mass migrations, and the origins of the Syrian war. Instead, viewed through afterlives of the Euphrates Dam, we see the untenability of isolating a single factor in the emergence of the Syrian uprising, its tragic devolution into war, and the complex ways that Syrian refugees grapple with their displacement until today. Ultimately, these migrations were intimately tied to the role of Syrian state-led agrarian policies and subsequent liberalization reforms in depleting Syria's groundwater reserves and exacerbating rural inequalities. For more, see Ababsa 2013; Barnes 2009; de Châtel 2014; Sajadian 2022; Selby 2019; Selby et al. 2017; Sowers et al. 2013; Zurayk 2013.

78. For more, see Chatty 1974; Joseph 2013.

79. At the time, the combined effects of wartime recession and US sanctions had led to a tenfold devaluation of the Syrian pound, from 52 to the US dollar before the war began in 2011 to over 500 to the dollar in mid-2019.

80. Hinnebusch 1989, 45.

81. For more on ghosts and the mediation of memory, see Kwon 2008; Mueggler 2001; Ng 2020; Zani 2019.

82. Ojeilī 1979, dedication page.

83. Ojeilī 1979, 29.

84. Ṣāliḥ 1999, 9–12.

85. ʿIṣmat 1979, 44.

86. Yassīn 1985, 34.

87. Muhammad Kamil Al-Khatib, quoted in Ṣāliḥ 1999, 11.

88. Derrida 1993.

89. Shanin 2009.

90. See Akram-Lodhi et al. 2007; Patnaik et al. 2011.

Chapter 3

A brief section of this chapter draws on material previously published in "Reproductive Binds: The Gendered Economy of Debt in a Syrian Refugee Farmworker Camp," *Journal of Agrarian Change* 24 (3): 1–23.

1. See Gerber 2013, 2014, 2021; Guérin et al. 2023; Kapadia 2000; Natarajan and Brickell 2022; Sajadian 2024.

2. Federici 2014, 233. For more on the effects of labor brokerage, subcontracting, and other forms of debt-based labor recruitment on migrant farmworkers' organizing power, see Griffith 2009.

3. Federici 2014, 233–4.

4. In framing their claims as such, I am drawing from Ferguson's (2015) emphasis on distributive labor within his influential article on "declarations of dependence." See also Martin 2021; Winchell 2017, 2022.

5. Freedom Fund 2016.

6. As Graeber (2011) notes, it is almost impossible to find a sympathetic representation of moneylender figures across the historical record, underscoring anthropologists' long-standing observation that wealth in money is often perceived as suspect and dishonorable compared to wealth in landed property. See also Hann and Hart 2011; Maurer 2018.

7. Sahlins 1963; Schneider and Schneider 2005.

8. See, for example, Sargent (2019)'s discussion of *thekedars* in India. On labor brokers in migrant farmworker communities, see Alpes 2017; Griffith 2009; Horton 2015, 2016.

9. López 2007.

10. Seth Holmes (2013) makes a similar point about the migrant labor system in the United States in his ethnography of Triqui indigenous farmworkers in the Pacific Northwest. He found that employers and locals from the communities that host these farmworkers often explicitly or tacitly justified their exploitative working conditions according to the racialized logic that they are culturally inferior and that their bodies were "made" for such work. As in the case of Syrians in Lebanon, such notions of bodily comportment often serve to naturalize these labor conditions as unchangeable, long-standing, and culturally ingrained.

11. James 2014.

12. Wedeen 2019, 128.

13. Ferguson 2015.

14. Mahmood also rationalized this as a matter of moral duty. As he put it, "In the end, it came down to his conscience as a Muslim. [The landlord] felt obliged [*mafrūḍ ʿalayh*] because the people are in need [*al-shaʿb miskin*]. We had nowhere else to go. He offered a low rent because he knows the people (in my camp) have nothing."

15. The concept of *maṣlaḥa* has a long lineage in Islamic jurisprudence, though its definition shifted with the rise of the modern nation-state and state-managed property regimes, narrowing over time to connote "public welfare" or "public

interest." See Moumtaz 2021, 196–99, for an excellent discussion of the dense genealogy of this term.

16. For more on *maṣlaḥa* in the Syrian agrarian context, see Sarkis Fernández 2015, 182–84.

17. Gerber 2014.

18. On the risks of sliding down, see Gardini 2020.

19. Marx, quoted in Harvey 2017, 35.

20. Harvey 2017, 35.

21. See Federici 2020; Fraser 2016; Weiss 2021.

22. On the Janus-faced state, see O'Connor 2001; Wacquant 2010.

23. This is a predicament they share with migrant workers elsewhere. Writing of Mexican farmworkers in the United States, Benson (2008) states, "Because labor camps house people who belong to a marginalized social class, government neglect and violation of labor codes are the norm. Workers often lack knowledge of their rights and fear deportation and unemployment" (592).

24. Abu Muhammad was referring to the verse "Worship none save Allah, and be good to parents and to kindred and to orphans and the needy, and speak kindly to mankind; and establish worship and pay the poor-due" (Qur'an 2: 83).

25. "Eating" is a common metaphor for exploitation and self-abasement among rural Syrians, as seen in phrases like "The big eats the small" (*al-kibīr ya'kul al-ṣaghīr*) or "We ate shit" (*akalna khara*) (Rabo 1986, 58). On the metaphor of "eating" people, see also Gilsenan 1996, 132–38.

26. Gerber 2013, 840.

27. See Hartman 1997; Nietzsche 1887.

28. Marx, quoted in Lazzarato 2012, 56.

29. See Asad 2009, 2020.

30. On patronage, see Asad 2018, 29–31.

31. On authority, see Asad 2018; Schmeding 2023. On tribulation, see Iqbal 2022a, 2022b, 2025.

32. Iqbal 2022.

33. Iqbal 2022, 50–55. See also Asad 2015b.

34. Kochuyt 2009.

35. Mittermaier 2014, 527.

36. Kochuyt 2009, 107.

37. For more, see Roitman 2005; Peebles 2010; Schuster 2015; Zaloom and James 2023.

38. For more, see Edelman 1992, 2018; Katz 1974.

39. For more on this topic, see Elyachar 2005; Taussig 1980.

40. Nash 1993, 9.

41. Guyer 2012; Winchell 2016.

42. Winchell 2017.

43. For more on Marx's "double freedom," see Banaji 2003 and chapter 5 of Hartman 1997.

Chapter 4

A brief section of this chapter draws on material previously published in "Reproductive Binds: The Gendered Economy of Debt in a Syrian Refugee Farmworker Camp," *Journal of Agrarian Change* 24 (3): 1–23.

1. For more, see Federici 2020; Weeks 2011. In dialogue with Silvia Federici and other pioneering Marxist feminists, I take inspiration from Lucí Cavallero and Verónica Gago's feminist approach to debt, summarized as follows: "A feminist reading of debt highlights social reproduction as a terrain of struggle, a struggle over valorization and extraction and over how reproduction is organized and to what effect" (2021, xiii).

2. Sajadian 2024.

3. Rawia's family's dilemma gets to the heart of one of the most important and enduring questions within the field of agrarian studies: why some agriculturalists are poorer and more indebted than others. Among agrarian scholars, this question extends back to foundational debates between Karl Kautsky, Vladimir Lenin, and Alexander Chayanov at the turn of the twentieth century (Akram-Lodhi and Kay 2010a; Chayanov 1986; Kautsky 1988; Lenin 1974). In his classic typology of peasant households, Soviet agronomist Chayanov put forth the concept of the labor–consumer balance, meaning the balance between the fulfillment of subsistence needs and the drudgery of labor. This balance hinged on the changing ratio of able-bodied working adults to dependents over the course of generational cycles of family reproduction. Distinct from Lenin and Kautsky's understanding of rural class differentiation in terms of labor exploitation, Chayanov posited that rural inequalities were a demographic phenomenon stemming from family size and household age, wherein households with fewer dependents and more adult children accumulated more wealth. Feminist scholars have drawn upon and reworked the more transhistorical aspects of this Chayanovian framework by drawing attention to gendered inequalities within households and the shifting constellations of waged and unwaged labor that allow agricultural families to survive (Deere 1995; Mezzadri et al. 2024; Ossome and Naidu 2021; Razavi 2009; Sajadian 2024, 2025a).

4. In accounting for these gendered familial dynamics, my emphasis on political economy aligns with a long-standing critique among scholars of gender in the

Middle East who caution against simplistic tropes of "men in crisis," that is, interpreting gendered subjectivities in ahistorical and apolitical "culturalist" or "behaviorist" terms, which bracket the economic and political context in which these gendered relationships take form and transform (Abu-Lughod 1989; Amar 2011; Kandiyoti 1988). This underscores the particular importance of analyzing Syrian gender relations from a historically nuanced agrarian perspective focused on labor conditions.

5. As feminist scholars of household debt note, the task of managing debt payments is often feminized and embedded within other forms of labor, both paid and unpaid. See Cavallero and Gago 2021; Federici 2014; Zaloom and James 2023.

6. For a good summary of how gender and gendered divisions of labor are performed, enforced, and recreated at work, see Weeks 2011, 9–13.

7. It is worth noting that before the war in Syria, it was relatively less typical for eastern Syrian women to work in seasonal agriculture after marriage. As Lange (2007) observed in her research in the early 2000s, "When a girl gets married, she usually stops working 'for others' in agriculture, since it is considered incompatible with the dignity of her married status, and impractical because of her responsibilities as a housewife and mother" (73).

8. As I discussed in chapter 1, Syrians' ability to be paid wages below the living standards of Lebanese was predicated upon their seasonal mobility, as their household incomes were supplemented by subsistence agriculture and the provision of low-cost public services in Syria. Their loss of seasonal mobility throughout the war, thus, put deeper into crisis a delicate set of gendered divisions of waged and unwaged labor that had long structured Syrian rural households yet were shrouded in invisibility. Seasons spent abroad alleviated men from the daily financial and moral pressures of hospitality, and they often endured these poor labor conditions with assurance that their neighbors and female kin did not *see* them. What changed throughout the war was that men and women in Abu Sharif's camp were living in close proximity year-round for the first time. For more on this history, see Lange 2007. For more on the construction of masculinity and the pressures to be a household "provider" in agrarian contexts, see Ragetlie and Luginaah 2023; Rai 2020.

9. In her illuminating dissertation on domestic migrant workers in Beirut, Sumayya Kassamali (2017) insightfully describes the significance of phones for her interlocutors. In fact, she found that many were deeply indebted to local phone stores, an indication of the unique importance of personal phones for migrants' connectivity to relatives in their home countries (102–4). See also Göransson et al. 2020.

10. Rabo 1986, 52–57.

11. As one of the key mechanisms through which rural households meet their labor needs, distribute property, and secure reproductive obligations, marriage transfers are central to the economy of agrarian debt but are rarely analyzed as such. Across the agrarian world, "marriage debt" has become a mounting burden on rural families, especially young men (Estes 2023; Inhorn and Smith-Hefner 2020; James 2014; Reumert 2020; Sykes and Jourdan 2020). The exact value varies across space and time; it is ultimately determined by a process of negotiation between two families regarding culturally mediated standards of familial reputation. Among eastern and northeastern Syrians from tribal backgrounds, there is a preference for village and clan endogamy, especially cross-cousin marriage. Set against the groom's means, the bride's desirability and value are shaped by her family background, age, skills, and appearance.

12. This was indeed a generative "web of lies," as Saleh (2017) puts it so well in her own research on women's labor in Lebanon.

13. While in certain senses, her refusal to work for *ḍammān* was reminiscent of James Scott's influential notion of "everyday forms of resistance" (1985) and "weapons of the weak" (1992), the centrality of gender to these processes was quite distinct. In this way, Rawia's contentious acts spoke to feminist engagements with Scott's work, especially Kandiyoti's (1988) famous concept of the patriarchal bargain, which analyzes how gender inequalities are made and remade through historically specific processes of interfamilial negotiation and struggle, as well as Abu-Lughod's (1990) influential critique of "the romance of resistance."

14. Discussing dreams was a significant component of everyday life in my fieldwork. Much as Diana Allan (2013) describes in her ethnography of Palestinian refugees, I found that "dream talk" in the camp was intimately bound up with the temporality of displacement: a way of working through uncertain futures and unresolved obligations. Many people from Abu Sharif's camp assumed that my doctoral education included dream interpretation (*tafsīr al-manām*), and despite my insistence that I had no skills in this area, they often generously recounted their dreams to me in hopes that I could decipher their symbolic meaning. Such expectations that I would be an expert on dreams might seem quaint, but it was a quite reasonable expectation when viewed in the longue durée of Islamic philosophy. Though the rich tradition of dream interpretation is often downplayed within modern reformist interpretations of Islam, the medieval philosopher Ibn Khaldun listed dream interpretation as one of the "sciences of the religious law" (Mittermaier 2010, 58).

15. For more on funerary rites in eastern Syria, see Lange 2012.

16. For more on this topic, see Joseph 1993, 1994; Kandiyoti 1988.

17. As I explained in the previous chapter, widows, orphans, disabled people, debtors, and the very poor are considered special categories of needy people deserving of alms within Islam. For more, see Kochuyt 2009.

18. For more on rural women's strategies of belt tightening and the ways that their paid and unpaid activities are mobilized to compensate for low wages and enhance the overall level of household production, see Deere 1995.

19. As Mahmood (2005) states, "the meaning and sense of agency cannot be fixed in advance, but must emerge through an analysis of particular concepts that enable specific modes of being, responsibility, and effectivity" (14–15). Such a premise is, as I understand it, not incommensurate with the emphasis on *material* and *embodied* conditions found within agrarian feminist studies, feminist social reproduction theory, and Marxist feminism. Indeed, it is telling that the idea of feminist "agency" against which Mahmood levels her critique are its liberal and poststructuralist variants, not feminist political economy.

20. Mahmood 2005, 17.

21. Kochuyt 2009, 102.

22. Mittermaier 2019.

23. One of the ways that women in the camp saved up for expenses like new clothing or furniture was by setting aside a small amount of cash in piggy banks from the dollar store called *maṭmūra*. Everyone had at least one *maṭmūra* in their tents, and the previous sense of trust in the camp meant that no one had found it necessary to hide them. But a wave of robberies of the *maṭmūra* from people's tents left everyone increasingly distrustful. These elements of community breakdown, anxiety, and mistrust—combined with Abu Hassan's increasingly ominous dream visitations—only deepened Imm Hassan's determination to leave the camp.

24. Perdigon 2011.

25. According to the official exchange rate, 1,600,000 lira was the equivalent of $1,067 in 2019, back when it was pegged at $1 to 1,500 lira.

26. Graeber 2011, 99–101.

27. On kinship, interdependency, and dependency, see Butler 2022; Ferguson 2015; Martin et al. 2021; Martin and Yanagisako 2020; Winchell 2022.

28. For more on dignity, see Asad 2018.

29. This is why, as Cindy Katz (2001) reminds us, social reproduction is a vexed terrain for the politics of radical change. As she states, "social reproduction is vexed because, again almost by definition, it is focused on reproducing the very social relations and material forms that are so problematic. Social reproduction is precisely not 'revolutionary,' and yet so much rests on its accomplishment, including—perhaps paradoxically—oppositional politics" (717–18).

Conclusion

1. Global public debt reached a record high over the last several years, not only in Lebanon, but across the world. Lebanon is one among a fast-growing number of countries that are in default, including Sri Lanka, Zambia, and Suriname, among others. This is not simply an effect of domestic mismanagement, but rather a direct consequence of high interest rates that bear important parallels to the Volcker shock of 1982 that precipitated the Latin American, Caribbean, and African debt crises of the 1980s. Debt Justice UK's Debt Data Portal estimates that, as of March 2025, fifty-four countries are currently facing public debt crises. For a complete map, see https://data.debtjustice.org.uk/. For a rigorously comparative historical account of the root causes of the current global era of acute sovereign debt crises—one that challenges the mainstream narratives found within World Bank, IMF, and UNCTAD reports—see Chelwa and Nhondo Ersko 2023; J. Ghosh 2023. See also Debt Collective and Taylor 2020.

2. As Raúl Delgado Wise asserts (2010), "In a macroeconomic context, remittances serve neoliberal governments that, not bothering to come up with actual development alternatives, use them as a source of foreign exchange income that sustains the country's fragile macroeconomic stability. In some cases, remittances have even been used as a guarantee when incurring foreign debt. In the absence of any kind of project, migrants are now portrayed as the 'heroes of development', an utterly cynical move that renders them responsible for the promotion of said development while the state, opting for the conservative stance of minimal participation, is no longer held accountable" (176–77).

3. This is a dilemma that extends far beyond the Middle East, evident in places facing acute waves of out-migration like Haiti and Venezuela. As Jake Johnson states regarding US-Haiti relations, "The great irony is that our policies seem on the one hand to be very motivated by trying to prevent migration, and yet it is our policies that are also overwhelmingly responsible for creating migration. The two periods of greatest international investment in Haiti, the 1980s and directly following the 2010 earthquake, were also the two periods of highest migration out of Haiti." See Turner and Van Horn 2024.

4. There are many examples of Syrian grassroots activists who supported the 2011 uprising and fiercely opposed the regime but who have long critiqued the duplicitous logic of sanctions, touted by Western leaders as a "soft" means of regime change while, in practice, devastating people's livelihoods (Daher 2019b). On the human costs of sanctions, see Bajoghli et al. 2024 and Mulder 2022.

5. Cheeseman 2024. On this topic more generally, see Agard Jones 2013.

6. In insisting on not exceptionalizing Lebanon, I am drawing inspiration from Michel-Rolph Trouillot's (2020) similar insistence on not exceptionalizing Haiti by highlighting its deep and long-standing embeddedness in our global economy.

7. This went hand-in-hand with Prime Minister Rafiq al-Hariri's postwar reconstruction program, which consisted of a three-pronged strategy of currency stabilization, regressive tax reform, and massive state spending mainly on real estate and construction (Dibeh 2021). While intending to curb wartime inflation and promote economic recovery, these policies came at the expense of productive investment in manufacturing and agriculture. Riad Salameh, a former Merrill Lynch banker, was appointed as head of Lebanon's central bank in this period and was the chief proponent of pegging the Lebanese lira to the dollar. Since then, the central bank's primary objective has been to maintain the peg at any cost. To cover a growing trade deficit and pay off Lebanon's rising foreign debt, while keeping the lira stable, the central bank issued treasury bills and Eurobonds at exceptionally high interest rates, which were enthusiastically purchased by Lebanon's commercial banks and attracted billions of dollars from abroad. Much of this hard currency came from capital deposits by the wealthy Lebanese diaspora, Syrian nationals, and residents of the oil-rich Arabian Peninsula (Al-Amine 2020). While these strategies served as a temporary fix for Lebanon's postwar macroeconomic instability, they progressively deepened Lebanon's debt servicing burden. For more, see Daher 2022a; Hakim and Andary 1997; Safieddine 2019; Salti 2019; Srouji 2005.

8. Daher 2022a.

9. This conclusion owes much to Gary Wilder for countless conversations about internationalism and the politics of solidarity. For more, see Wilder 2022.

Epilogue

1. The historical roots of these class divisions are meticulously documented by Marxist historians, from the prolific works of Abdullah Ḥannā (mostly published in Arabic) to Hanna Batatu's magisterial work.

2. On Hay'at Tahrir al-Sham's neoliberal economic policies, see Daher 2024. On left-wing and worker organizing in post-Asad Syria, see MENA Solidarity Network 2025.

3. See Federici 2004, 112–13; 2014; Galindo 2012; Kwon 2008, 83.

Bibliography

Ababsa, Myriam. 2001. "La madâfa à Raqqa: mutation d'un lieu de sociabilité tribale en attribut de notabilité citadine." *Géographie et cultures* 37: 17–36.

Ababsa, Myriam. 2004. "Privatisation in Syria: State Farms and the Case of the Euphrates Project." Paper presented at the Fifth Mediterranean Social and Political Research Meeting, Florence-Montecatini Terme, Italy, March 24–28.

Ababsa, Myriam. 2009. "La recomposition des allégeances tribales dans le Moyen-Euphrate syrien (1958–2007)." *Études rurales* 184 (2): 65–78.

Ababsa, Myriam. 2013. "Crise agraire, crise foncière et sécheresse en Syrie (2000–2011)." *Maghreb-Machrek* 215 (1): 101–22.

Ababsa, Myriam. 2019. "Syria's Food Security: From Self-Sufficiency to Hunger as a Weapon." In *Syria: From National Independence to Proxy War,* edited by Linda Matar and Ali Kadri. Springer International.

Abboud, Samer N. 2018. *Syria: Hot Spots in Global Politics*. Polity.

Abdallah, Stéphanie Latte. 2009. "Fragile Intimacies: Marriage and Love in the Palestinian Camps of Jordan (1948–2001)." *Journal of Palestine Studies* 38 (4): 47–62.

Abdelali-Martini, Malika, Patricia Goldey, Gwyn Jones, and Elizabeth Bailey. 2003. "Towards a Feminization of Agricultural Labour in Northwest Syria." *The Journal of Peasant Studies* 30 (2): 71–94.

Abdelali-Martini, Malika, and Jennie Dey de Pryck. 2015. "Does the Feminisation of Agricultural Labour Empower Women? Insights from Female Labour Contractors and Workers in Northwest Syria." *Journal of International Development* 27 (7): 898–916.

Abdi, Awa M. 2005. "In Limbo: Dependency, Insecurity, and Identity Amongst Somali Refugees in Dadaab Camps." *Refuge: Canada's Journal on Refugees* 22 (2): 6–14.

Abisaab, Malek. 2009. "Shiite Peasants and a New Nation in Colonial Lebanon: The Intifada of Bint Jubayl, 1936." *Comparative Studies of South Asia, Africa and the Middle East* 29 (3): 483–501.

Abisaab, Malek. 2010. *Militant Women of a Fragile Nation.* Syracuse University Press.

Abourahme, Nasser. 2020. "The Camp." *Comparative Studies of South Asia, Africa and the Middle East* 40 (1): 35–42.

Abouzeid, Rania. 2019. *No Turning Back: Life, Loss, and Hope in Wartime Syria.* W. W. Norton.

Abu-Lughod, Lila. 1986. *Veiled Sentiments: Honor and Poetry in a Bedouin Society.* University of California Press.

Abu-Lughod, Lila. 1989. "Zones of Theory in the Anthropology of the Arab World." *Annual Review of Anthropology* 18: 267–306.

Abu-Lughod, Lila. 1990. "The Romance of Resistance: Tracing Transformations of Power Through Bedouin Women." *American Ethnologist* 17 (1): 41–55.

Abu-Lughod, Lila. 2008. *Writing Women's Worlds: Bedouin Stories.* University of California Press.

Abu-Rish, Ziad. 2026. *The State of Lebanon: Popular Politics and Institution Building in the Wake of Independence.* Stanford University Press.

Adely, Fida J. 2024. *Working Women in Jordan: Education, Migration, and Aspiration.* University of Chicago Press.

Agard-Jones, Vanessa. 2013. "Bodies in the System." *Small Axe: A Caribbean Journal of Criticism* 17 (3 (42): 182–92.

Agarwal, Samantha. 2021. "Indebted by Dispossession: The Long-Term Impacts of a Special Economic Zone on Caste Inequality in Rural Telangana." *Journal of Agrarian Change* 21 (3): 459–84.

Agier, Michel. 2010. "Humanity as an Identity and Its Political Effects (A Note on Camps and Humanitarian Government)." *Humanity: An International Journal of Human Rights, Humanitarianism, and Development* 1 (1): 29–45.

Ahmad, Eqbal. 1980. "Post-Colonial Systems of Power." *Arab Studies Quarterly* 2 (4): 350–63.

Ajl, Max. 2021. "Does the Arab Region Have an Agrarian Question?" *The Journal of Peasant Studies* 48 (5): 955–83.

Akiki, Viviane. 2019. "The Blindness of Political Economy: How Austerity Affects Women." *Kohl: A Journal for Body and Gender Research* 5 (2): 84–88.

Akram-Lodhi, A. Haroon, Saturnino M. Borras Jr, and Cristobal Kay, eds. 2007. *Land, Poverty and Livelihoods in an Era of Globalization: Perspectives from Developing and Transition Countries*. Routledge.

Akram-Lodhi, A. Haroon, Kristina Dietz, Bettina Engels, and Ben M. McKay, eds. 2021. *Handbook of Critical Agrarian Studies*. Edward Elgar.

Akram-Lodhi, A. Haroon, and Cristóbal Kay. 2010a. "Surveying the Agrarian Question (Part 1): Unearthing Foundations, Exploring Diversity." *The Journal of Peasant Studies* 37 (1): 177–202.

Akram-Lodhi, A. Haroon, and Cristóbal Kay. 2010b. "Surveying the Agrarian Question (Part 2): Current Debates and Beyond." *The Journal of Peasant Studies* 37 (2): 255–84.

Al-Amine, Bilal. 2020. "U.S. Sanctions Are Strangling a Lebanon in Crisis." *In These Times*, August 13. https://inthesetimes.com/article/lebanon-beirut-crisis-explosion-sanctions-foreign-debt-imf-trump-maximum-pressure.

Alff, Kristen. 2018. "Levantine Joint-Stock Companies, Trans-Mediterranean Partnerships, and Nineteenth-Century Capitalist Development." *Comparative Studies in Society and History* 60 (1): 150–77.

Al-Haj Saleh, Yassin. 2012. "Ṣūrat al-Shawāya wa-ḥāl minṭaqat al-Jazīra al-Sūriyya" [The image of the Shawāya and the situation of the Syrian Jazīra region]. *al-Ḥiwār*, May 30. http://www.ahewar.org/debat/show.art.asp?aid=309839.

Al-Haj Saleh, Yassin. 2017. *The Impossible Revolution: Making Sense of the Syrian Tragedy*. C. Hurst.

Alhamd, Amar. 2022. "A Study of Raqqa Tribes in Syria Social, Political and Economic Profiles." MA thesis, Hasan Kalyoncu Üniversitesi.

Alimia, Sanaa. 2022. *Refugee Cities: How Afghans Changed Urban Pakistan*. University of Pennsylvania Press.

Alkan, Hilal. 2021. "The Gift of Hospitality and the (Un)Welcoming of Syrian Migrants in Turkey." *American Ethnologist* 48 (2): 180–91.

Al-Khalili, Charlotte. 2023. *Waiting For the Revolution to End: Syrian Displacement, Time and Subjectivity*. UCL Press.

Al-Khalili, Charlotte, Narges Ansari, Myriam Lamrani, and Kaya Uzel, eds. 2023. *Revolution Beyond the Event: The Afterlives of Radical Politics*. UCL Press.

Allam, Nathalie. 2011. "Farming Is Like Gambling: An Examination of the Decline of Produce Farming in Lebanon's Central Bekaa Valley." MA thesis, George Washington University.

Allan, Diana. 2013. *Refugees of the Revolution: Experiences of Palestinian Exile*. Stanford University Press.

Allan, Diana. 2020. "The Long Turning: A Palestinian Refugee in Belgium." *Cultural Anthropology* 35 (2): 225–30.

Alpes, Maybritt Jill. 2017. "Papers That Work: Migration Brokers, State/Market Boundaries, and the Place of Law." *PoLAR: Political and Legal Anthropology Review* 40 (2): 262–77.

Al-Qattan, Najwa. 2014. "When Mothers Ate Their Children: Wartime Memory and the Language of Food in Syria and Lebanon." *International Journal of Middle East Studies* 46 (4): 719–36.

Al-Saadi, Yazan. 2014. "The Diversion Strategy: Lebanese Racism, Classism, and the Refugees." *Al Akhbar English*, June 10. http://english.al-akhbar.com/node/20121.

Altuğ, Seda. 2011. "Sectarianism in the Syrian Jazira: Community, Land and Violence in the Memories of World War I and the French Mandate (1915–1939)." PhD diss., Utrecht University.

Altuğ, Seda. 2024. "Refugees, Labour and Sectarianism in Syria Under the French Mandate (1921–1950)." *Revue des mondes musulmans et de la Méditerranée* 156 (2): 1–19.

Amar, Paul. 2011. "Middle East Masculinity Studies: Discourses of 'Men in Crisis,' Industries of Gender in Revolution." *Journal of Middle East Women's Studies* 7 (3): 36–70.

Amin, Samir. 1994. *Re-Reading the Postwar Period*. Monthly Review.

Andaiye. 2020. *The Point Is to Change the World: Selected Writings of Andaiye*. Edited by Alissa Trotz. Pluto.

Anderson, Paul. 2023. *Exchange Ideologies: Commerce, Language, and Patriarchy in Preconflict Aleppo*. Cornell University Press.

Araghi, Farshad. 2008. "The Invisible Hand and the Visible Foot: Peasants, Dispossession and Globalisation." In *Peasants and Globalisation: Political Economy, Rural Transformation and the Agrarian Question,* edited by A. Haroon Akram-Lodhi and Cristóbal Kay. Routledge.

Araghi, Farshad. 2009. "Accumulation by Displacement: Global Enclosures, Food Crisis, and the Ecological Contradictions of Capitalism." *Review* (Fernand Braudel Center) 32 (1): 113–46.

Arango Vásquez, Lorenza. 2020. "If You Don't Owe, You Don't Own: Debt, Discipline and Growth in Rural Colombia." *Journal of Rural Studies* 78: 271–81.

Asad, Talal. 2009. "The Idea of an Anthropology of Islam." *Qui Parle* 17 (2): 1–30.

Asad, Talal. 2015a. "Reflections on Violence, Law, and Humanitarianism." *Critical Inquiry* 41 (2): 390–427.

Asad, Talal. 2015b. "Thinking About Tradition, Religion, and Politics in Egypt Today." *Critical Inquiry* 42 (1): 166–214.

Asad, Talal. 2018. *Secular Translations: Nation-State, Modern Self, and Calculative Reason*. Columbia University Press.

Asad, Talal. 2020. "Thinking about Religion through Wittgenstein." *Critical Times* 3 (3): 403–42.

Ashkar, Hisham. 2015. "Benefiting from a Crisis: Lebanese Upscale Real-Estate Industry and the War in Syria." *Confluences Méditerranée* 92 (1): 89–100.

Babül, Elif M. 2024. "Compulsory Guesthood, Social Cohesion, and the Politics of Hospitality in Turkey." *Journal of the Royal Anthropological Institute* 30 (2): 379–98.

Bajoghli, Narges, Vali Nasr, Djavad Salehi-Isfahani, and Ali Vaez. 2024. *How Sanctions Work: Iran and the Impact of Economic Warfare*. Stanford University Press.

Baʿlabakkī, Aḥmad. 1994. *Muḥāwalāt fī dirāsāt al-tanmiya al-rīfiyya wa-al-mujtamaʿ al-maḥallī fī Lubnān*. Dār al-Fārābī.

Balibar, Étienne. 2002. "What Is a Border?" In *Politics and the Other Scene*. Verso.

Banaji, Jairus. 2003. "The Fictions of Free Labour: Contract, Coercion, and So-Called Unfree Labour." *Historical Materialism* 11: 69–95.

Barbosa, Gustavo. 2022. *The Best of Hard Times: Palestinian Refugee Masculinities in Lebanon*. Syracuse University Press.

Bardawil, Fadi A. 2020. *Revolution and Disenchantment: Arab Marxism and the Binds of Emancipation*. Duke University Press.

Barnes, Jessica. 2009. "Managing the Waters of Baʿth Country: The Politics of Water Scarcity in Syria." *Geopolitics* 14 (3): 510–30.

Barrios, Roberto E. 2017. "What Does Catastrophe Reveal for Whom? The Anthropology of Crises and Disasters at the Onset of the Anthropocene." *Annual Review of Anthropology* 46 (1): 151–66.

Basha, Zaid Ali. 2023. "The Agrarian Question in Yemen: The National Imperative of Reclaiming and Revalorizing Indigenous Agroecological Food Production." *The Journal of Peasant Studies* 50 (3): 879–930.

Batatu, Hanna. 1999. *Syria's Peasantry, the Descendants of its Lesser Rural Notables, and their Politics*. Princeton University Press.

Baviskar, Amita. 2005. *In the Belly of the River: Tribal Conflicts over Development in the Narmada Valley*. Oxford University Press.

Belloni, Milena. 2016. "Learning How to Squat: Cooperation and Conflict between Refugees and Natives in Rome." *Journal of Refugee Studies* 29 (4): 506–27.

Benard, Cheryl. 1986. "Politics and the Refugee Experience." *Political Science Quarterly* 101 (4): 617–36.

Benson, Peter. 2008. "El Campo: Faciality and Structural Violence in Farm Labor Camps." *Cultural Anthropology* 23 (4): 589–629.

Benson, Peter. 2011. *Tobacco Capitalism: Growers, Migrant Workers, and the Changing Face of a Global Industry*. Princeton University Press.

Berg, Mette Louise, and Elena Fiddian-Qasmiyeh. 2018. "Introduction to the Issue: Encountering Hospitality and Hostility." *Migration and Society* 1 (1): 1–6.

Berlant, Lauren. 2011. *Cruel Optimism*. Duke University Press.

Bernstein, Henry. 2003. "Farewells to the Peasantry." *Transformation: Critical Perspectives on Southern Africa* 52 (1): 1–19.

Bernstein, Henry, Harriet Friedmann, Jan Douwe van der Ploeg, Teodor Shanin, and Ben White. 2018. "Forum: Fifty Years of Debate on Peasantries, 1966–2016." *The Journal of Peasant Studies* 45 (4): 689–714.

Besky, Sarah. 2013. *The Darjeeling Distinction: Labor and Justice on Fair-Trade Tea Plantations in India*. University of California Press.

Best, Stephen. 2012. "On Failing to Make the Past Present." *Modern Language Quarterly* 73 (3): 453–74.

Besteman, Catherine. 2016. *Making Refuge: Somali Bantu Refugees and Lewiston, Maine*. Duke University Press.

Bhattacharya, Tithi, ed. 2017. *Social Reproduction Theory: Remapping Class, Recentering Oppression*. Pluto.

Bissell, William Cunningham. 2005. "Engaging Colonial Nostalgia." *Cultural Anthropology* 20 (2): 215–48.

Böhning, Roger. 1991. "The ILO and the New UN Convention on Migrant Workers: The Past and Future." *The International Migration Review* 25 (4): 698–709.

Borras, Saturnino M. 2023. "Politically Engaged, Pluralist and Internationalist: Critical Agrarian Studies Today." *The Journal of Peasant Studies* 50 (3): 1–41.

Borri, Francesca. 2016. *Syrian Dust: Reporting from the Heart of the War*. Translated by Anne Milano Appel. Seven Stories.

Bourgois, Philippe. 1988. "Conjugated Oppression: Class and Ethnicity Among Guaymi and Kuna Banana Workers." *American Ethnologist* 15 (2): 328–48.

Brand, Tylor. 2023. *Famine Worlds: Life at the Edge of Suffering in Lebanon's Great War*. Stanford University Press.

Brennan, Eugene. 2024. "Crisis as Method: Politics, Temporality, and Agency." *South Atlantic Quarterly* 123 (2): 231–54.

Bromber, Katrin, Jeanne Féaux de la Croix, and Katharina Lange. 2014. "The Temporal Politics of Big Dams in Africa, the Middle East, and Asia: By Way of an Introduction." *Water History* 6 (4): 289–96.

Burawoy, Michael. 1976. "The Functions and Reproduction of Migrant Labor: Comparative Material from Southern Africa and the United States." *American Journal of Sociology* 81 (5): 1050–87.

Butler, Judith. 2022. "Kinship Beyond the Bloodline." In *Queer Kinship: Race, Sex, Belonging, Form*, edited by Tyler Bradway and Elizabeth Freeman. Duke University Press.

Cabot, Heath. 2019. "The Business of Anthropology and the European Refugee Regime." *American Ethnologist* 46 (3): 261–75.

Cabot, Heath, and Georgina Ramsay. 2021. "Deexceptionalizing Displacement: An Introduction." *Humanity: An International Journal of Human Rights, Humanitarianism, and Development* 12 (3): 286–99.

Carneal, Luke. 2024. "A Picture of Farming in Gaza Today: In Remembrance of Youssef Saqr Abu Rabie." *Jadaliyya*. https://www.jadaliyya.com/Details/46334.

Carpi, Estella. 2023. *The Politics of Crisis-Making: Forced Displacement and Cultures of Assistance in Lebanon*. Indiana University Press.

Carpi, Estella, and H. Pınar Şenoğuz. 2018. "Refugee Hospitality in Lebanon and Turkey. On Making 'The Other.'" *International Migration* 57 (2): 126–42.

Cassani, Jacob. 2021. "Bread and Salt: Labour, Reputation, and Trust between Syrian Refugees and Lebanese Hashish Farmers in the Northern Biqa'a." Social Science Research Network.

Cassani, Jacob. 2023. "Before Their Sweat Dries: Labour and Family in the Syrian Refugee Camps of the Biqa'a Valley, Lebanon." PhD diss., University College London.

Castañeda, Heide. 2019. *Borders of Belonging: Struggle and Solidarity in Mixed-Status Immigrant Families*. Stanford University Press.

Caswell, Michelle. 2014. *Archiving the Unspeakable: Silence, Memory, and the Photographic Record in Cambodia*. University of Wisconsin Press.

Cavallero, Lucí, and Verónica Gago. 2021. *A Feminist Reading of Debt*. Pluto.

Center for the Promotion of Imports from Developing Countries (CBI), and CBI Ministry of Foreign Affairs. 2018. *Value Chain Analysis Lebanon Fresh Fruit and Vegetables*. https://www.cbi.eu/sites/default/files/market-information/2018_vca_lebanon_ffv.pdf.

Chakrabarti, Anjan, and Stephen Cullenberg. 2003. *Transition and Development in India*. Routledge.

Chakrabarty, Dipesh. 1989. *Rethinking Working-Class History*. Princeton University Press.

Chalcraft, John. 2005. "Of Specters and Disciplined Commodities: Syrian Migrant Workers in Lebanon." *Middle East Report* 236: 28–33.

Chalcraft, John. 2009. *The Invisible Cage: Syrian Migrant Workers in Lebanon*. Stanford University Press.

Chatterjee, Piya. 2001. *A Time for Tea: Women, Labor, and Post/Colonial Politics on an Indian Plantation*. Duke University Press.

Chatty, Dawn. 1974. "From Camel to Truck a Study of the Pastoral Economy of the Al-Fadl and the Al-Hassanna in the Beqaa Valley of Lebanon." PhD diss., University of Michigan.

Chatty, Dawn. 2014. "The Persistence of Bedouin Identity and Increasing Political Self-Representation in Lebanon and Syria." *Nomadic Peoples* 18 (2): 16–33.

Chatty, Dawn. 2017. "The Syrian Humanitarian Disaster: Understanding Perceptions and Aspirations in Jordan, Lebanon and Turkey." *Global Policy* 8 (S1): 25–32.

Chatty, Dawn, Nisrine Mansour, and Nasser Yassin. 2013. "Statelessness and Tribal Identity on Lebanon's Eastern Borders." *Mediterranean Politics* 18 (3): 411–26.

Chatty, Dawn, and Annika Rabo. 1997. *Organizing Women: Formal and Informal Women's Groups in the Middle East*. Routledge.

Chayanov, A.V. 1986. *The Theory of Peasant Economy*. University of Wisconsin Press.

Cheeseman, Abbie. 2024. "'Where Can You Hide from Pollution?': Cancer Rises 30% in Beirut as Diesel Generators Poison City." *The Guardian*, April 22. https://www.theguardian.com/global-development/2024/apr/22/where-can-you-hide-from-pollution-cancer-rises-30-in-beirut-as-diesel-generators-poison-city.

Chelwa, Grieve, and Mikaela Nhondo Ersko. 2023. "Life or Debt: The Stranglehold of Neocolonialism and Africa's Search for Alternatives." Tricontinental: Institute for Social Research, Dossier 63. https://thetricontinental.org/dossier-63-african-debt-crisis/.

Connerton, Paul. 2011. *The Spirit of Mourning: History, Memory and the Body*. Cambridge University Press.

Coronil, Fernando. 1997. *The Magical State: Nature, Money, and Modernity in Venezuela*. University of Chicago Press.

Daher, Joseph. 2019a. *Syria After the Uprisings: The Political Economy of State Resilience*. Haymarket Books.

Daher, Joseph. 2019b. *The Deep Roots of the Depreciation of the Syrian Pound*. Technical Report. European University Institute.

Daher, Joseph. 2022a. *Lebanon: How the Post War's Political Economy Led to the Current Economic and Social Crisis*. Robert Schuman Center.

Daher, Joseph. 2022b. "The Hellish Cycle Continues for Syria: The Economic Impacts of Russia's Invasion of Ukraine." EUI Middle East Directions Programme Blog. https://blogs.eui.eu/medirections/the-hellish-cycle-continues-for-syria-the-economic-impacts-of-russias-invasion-of-ukraine/.

Daher, Joseph. 2024. "HTS' Neoliberalism Won't Improve Syria's Economy." *The New Arab*, December 18. https://www.newarab.com/opinion/hts-neoliberalism-wont-improve-syrias-economy.

Dahi, Omar S., and Yasser Munif. 2012. "Revolts in Syria: Tracking the Convergence Between Authoritarianism and Neoliberalism." *Journal of Asian and African Studies* 47 (4): 323–32.

Ḍāhir, Masʿūd. 1983. *al-Judhūr al-tārīkhiyya li-al-mas'ala al-zirāʿiyya al-lubnānīyya 1900–1950*. Manshūrāt al-Jāmiʿa al-Lubnānīyya / Qism al-Dirāsāt al-Tārīkhiyya.

Dalla Costa, Mariarosa, and Selma James. 1975. *The Power of Women and the Subversion of the Community*. Falling Wall.

Darwich, May, and Pascal Menoret. 2025. "Asphalt, Water, and Power: The Politics of Infrastructure in the Middle East and North Africa." *Middle East Law and Governance* 17 (2): 199–271.

Das, Veena. 2007. *Life and Words: Violence and the Descent into the Ordinary*. University of California Press.

Davis, Angela, and Gina Dent. 2001. "Prison as a Border: A Conversation on Gender, Globalization, and Punishment." *Signs: Journal of Women in Culture and Society* 26 (4): 1235–41.

Davis, Mike. 2006. *Planet of Slums*. Verso.

Debt Collective, and Astra Taylor. 2020. *Can't Pay, Won't Pay: The Case for Economic Disobedience and Debt Abolition*. Haymarket Books.

De Châtel, Francesca. 2014. "The Role of Drought and Climate Change in the Syrian Uprising: Untangling the Triggers of the Revolution." *Middle Eastern Studies* 50 (4): 521–35.

Deeb, Lara. 2006. *An Enchanted Modern: Gender and Public Piety in Shi'i Lebanon*. Princeton University Press.

Deeb, Lara. 2024. *Love Across Difference: Mixed Marriage in Lebanon*. Stanford University Press.

Deeb, Lara, and Jessica Winegar. 2012. "Anthropologies of Arab-Majority Societies." *Annual Review of Anthropology* 41 (1): 537–58.

Deere, Carmen Diana. 1995. "What Difference Does Gender Make? Rethinking Peasant Studies." *Feminist Economics* 1 (1): 53–72.

Deere, Carmen Diana, and Magdalena León. 2001a. *Empowering Women: Land And Property Rights in Latin America*. University of Pittsburgh Press.

Deere, Carmen Diana, and Magdalena León. 2001b. "Who Owns the Land? Gender and Land-Titling Programmes in Latin America." *Journal of Agrarian Change* 1 (3): 440–67.

De Genova, Nicholas. 2002. "Migrant 'Illegality' and Deportability in Everyday Life." *Annual Review of Anthropology* 31: 419–47.

De Genova, Nicholas. 2013. "'We Are of the Connections': Migration, Methodological Nationalism, and 'Militant Research.'" *Postcolonial Studies: Culture, Politics, Economy* 16 (3): 250–58.

De Genova, Nicholas. 2016. "The 'Crisis' of the European Border Regime: Towards a Marxist Theory of Borders." *International Socialism* 150: 31–54.

De Genova, Nicholas, and Nathalie Peutz, eds. 2010. *The Deportation Regime: Sovereignty, Space, and the Freedom of Movement.* Duke University Press.

De León, Jason. 2015. *The Land of Open Graves: Living and Dying on the Migrant Trail.* University of California Press.

De León, Jason. 2024. *Soldiers and Kings: Survival and Hope in the World of Human Smuggling.* Penguin Books.

Derrida, Jacques. 1989. *Memoires for Paul de Man.* Columbia University Press.

Derrida, Jacques. 1993. *Specters of Marx: The State of the Debt, The Work of Mourning & the New International.* Routledge.

Devlin, John F. 1991. "The Baath Party: Rise and Metamorphosis." *The American Historical Review* 96 (5): 1396–407.

Dibeh, Ghassan. 2021. "The Financial Recovery Plan: Its Impact on Lebanon's Economic Model, Negotiations with the IMF, and Recession." Friedrich-Ebert-Stiftung, Lebanon Office.

Dinger, Samuel. 2018. "Beyond Emergency: The Riyaq Evictions and the Limits of Humanitarian Knowledge." In *al-Lājiʾūn ṣanʿū al-madīna,* edited by Mona Fawaz. Issam Fares Institute for Public Policy and International Affairs.

Dinger, Samuel. 2021. "Dispossessing the Displaced in Lebanon." *Contexts* 20 (1): 15–20.

Dinger, Samuel. 2022a. "Coordinating Care and Coercion: Styles of Sovereignty and the Politics of Humanitarian Aid in Lebanon." *Humanity: An International Journal of Human Rights, Humanitarianism, and Development* 13 (2): 218–39.

Dinger, Samuel. 2022b. "The Sakan Shababiyy, or the World Improvised: Displacement and Masculine Domestic Space in Lebanon." *Ethnography* 27 (1): 272–93.

Djerbi, Dhouha. 2024. "The Social Reproductive Roots of Agrarian Contention: Gendered Labor amid Peasant Struggles in Tunisia." *Antipode* 58 (1): 1–25.

Dolbee, Samuel. 2018. "After ISIS: Development and Demography in the Jazira," Brandeis University Crown Center for Middle East Studies 121.

Dolbee, Samuel. 2023. *Locusts of Power: Borders, Empire, and Environment in the Modern Middle East.* Cambridge University Press.

Dukhan, Haian. 2018. *State and Tribes in Syria: Informal Alliances and Conflict Patterns.* Routledge.

Dukhan, Haian. 2022a. "From Shame to Pride: The Politics of Shawi Identity in Contemporary Syria." *Middle East Journal of Culture and Communication* 15 (4): 377–84.

Dukhan, Haian. 2022b. "The End of the Dialectical Symbiosis of National and Tribal Identities in Syria." *Nations and Nationalism* 28 (1): 141–53.

Duruiz, Deniz. 2019. "Dispossession, Racialization, and Rural Kurdish Labor Migration in Turkey." PhD diss., Columbia University.

Dziadosz, Alexander. 2020. "[Letter from the Bekaa Valley] State of Exception." *Harper's Magazine*, November. https://harpers.org/archive/2020/11/state-of-exception-lebanon-refugee-crisis/.

Edelman, Marc. 1992. *The Logic of the Latifundio: The Large Estates of Northwestern Costa Rica Since the Late Nineteenth Century*. Stanford University Press.

Edelman, Marc. 2018. "'Haciendas and Plantations': History and Limitations of a 60-Year-Old Taxonomy." *Critique of Anthropology* 38 (4): 387–406.

Edelman, Marc. 2024. *Peasant Politics of the Twenty-First Century: Transnational Social Movements and Agrarian Change*. Cornell University Press.

Edelman, Marc, and Saturnino M. Borras. 2016. *Political Dynamics of Transnational Agrarian Movements*. Fernwood.

Edelman, Marc, and Wendy Wolford. 2017. "Introduction: Critical Agrarian Studies in Theory and Practice." *Antipode* 49 (4): 959–76.

El-Husseini, Rola. 2012. *Pax Syriana: Elite Politics in Postwar Lebanon*. Syracuse University Press.

Elling, Rasmus C., and Sune Haugbolle. 2024. *The Fate of Third Worldism in the Middle East: Iran, Palestine and Beyond*. Oneworld Academic.

Elyachar, Julia. 2005. *Markets of Dispossession: NGOs, Economic Development, and the State in Cairo*. Duke University Press.

Environmental and Sustainable Development Unit at the American University of Beirut. 2020. "Overview on Local Agriculture and Food Heritage: Case of West Bekaa and Shouf in Lebanon." Sustainable Networks for Agrofood Innovation Leading in the Mediterranean, American University of Beirut.

Estes, Jennifer. 2023. "A High Price to Pay: Weddings and Waithood in Cambodia." *The Asia Pacific Journal of Anthropology* 24 (1): 1–17.

Fahim, Hussein M. 1981. *Dams, People and Development: The Aswan High Dam Case*. Pergamon.

Fakhoury, Tamirace. 2021. "Refugee Return and Fragmented Governance in the Host State: Displaced Syrians in the Face of Lebanon's Divided Politics." *Third World Quarterly* 42 (1): 162–80.

Fargues, Philippe. 2009. "Work, Refuge, Transit: An Emerging Pattern of Irregular Immigration South and East of the Mediterranean." *International Migration Review* 43 (3): 544–77.

Farhang, Foroogh. 2025. "Death of the Gharīb: A Window towards a Regional Understanding of Displacement in the Middle East." *Comparative Studies in Society and History* 67 (4): 1–24.

Fassin, Didier. 2005. "Compassion and Repression: The Moral Economy of Immigration Policies in France." *Cultural Anthropology* 20 (3): 362–87.

Fassin, Didier. 2011. "Policing Borders, Producing Boundaries. The Governmentality of Immigration in Dark Times." *Annual Review of Anthropology* 40 (1): 213–26.

Federici, Silvia. 2004. *Caliban and the Witch: Women, the Body and Primitive Accumulation*. Autonomedia.

Federici, Silvia. 2014. "From Commoning to Debt: Financialization, Microcredit, and the Changing Architecture of Capital Accumulation." *South Atlantic Quarterly* 113 (2): 231–44.

Federici, Silvia. 2020. *Revolution at Point Zero: Housework, Reproduction, and Feminist Struggle*. PM Press.

Feldman, Ilana. 2006. "Home as a Refrain: Remembering and Living Displacement in Gaza." *History & Memory* 18 (2): 10–47.

Feldman, Ilana. 2018a. "Care and Suspicion: Corruption as Definition in Humanitarian Relations." *Current Anthropology* 59 (S18): 160–70.

Feldman, Ilana. 2018b. *Life Lived in Relief: Humanitarian Predicaments and Palestinian Refugee Politics*. University of California Press.

Ferguson, James. 1999. *Expectations of Modernity: Myths and Meanings of Urban Life on the Zambian Copperbelt*. University of California Press.

Ferguson, James. 2015. *Give a Man a Fish: Reflections on the New Politics of Distribution*. Duke University Press.

Ferguson, Susanna. 2024. *Labors of Love: Gender, Capitalism, and Democracy in Modern Arab Thought*. Stanford University Press.

Foy, Roman-Oliver. 2013. "Enjeux sociospatiaux de la grande hydraulique. Cas de l'Établissement Al-Assad dans le projet de l'Euphrate (Maskané – Syrie)." *Journal des anthropologues. Association française des anthropologues* 132–33: 145–67.

Fraser, Nancy. 2016. "Contradictions of Capital and Care." *New Left Review* 100: 99–117.

Freedom Fund. 2016. *Struggling to Survive: Slavery and Exploitation of Syrian Refugees in Lebanon*. https://cdn.freedomfund.org/app/uploads/2024/03/Lebanon-Report-FINAL-8April16.pdf.

Friedl, Erika. 1981. "Women and the Division of Labor in an Iranian Village." *Middle East Report* 95: 12–31.

Friedl, Erika. 1989. *The Women of Deh Koh: Lives in an Iranian Village*. Smithsonian Institution.

Friedman, Harriet, and Philip McMichael. 1989. "Agriculture and the State System: The Rise and Decline of National Agricultures, 1870 to the Present." *Sociologia Ruralis* 29 (2): 93–117.

Galemba, Rebecca Berke. 2017. *Contraband Corridor: Making a Living at the Mexico-Guatemala Border.* Stanford University Press.

Galindo, Maria. 2012. "La Pobreza, Un Gran Negocio." *Mujer Pública: Revista de Discusión Feminista* 7: 110–31.

Gallagher, Sally K. 2012. *Making Do in Damascus: Navigating a Generation of Change in Family and Work.* Syracuse University Press.

García-Colón, Ismael. 2020. *Colonial Migrants at the Heart of Empire.* University of California Press.

Gardini, Marco. 2020. "The Risk of Sliding Down." *American Ethnologist* 47 (3): 264–75.

Gerber, Julien-François. 2013. "The Hidden Consequences of Credit: An Illustration from Rural Indonesia." *Development and Change* 44 (4): 839–60.

Gerber, Julien-François. 2014. "The Role of Rural Indebtedness in the Evolution of Capitalism." *The Journal of Peasant Studies* 41 (5): 729–47.

Gerber, Julien-François. 2021. "Rural Indebtedness." In *Handbook of Critical Agrarian Studies,* edited by A. Haroon Akram-Lodhi, Kristina Dietz, Bettina Engels, and Ben M. McKay. Edward Elgar.

Ghosh, Jayati. 2023. "How Not to Deal with a Debt Crisis." *Social Europe.* January 16. https://www.socialeurope.eu/how-not-to-deal-with-a-debt-crisis.

Ghosh, Sahana. 2022. "Barbed Wire in an Agrarian Borderland." *Current Anthropology* 63 (3): 360–66.

Ghosh, Sahana. 2023. *Thousand Tiny Cuts: Mobility and Security across the Bangladesh-India Borderlands.* University of California Press.

Ghosh, Sahana. 2025. "Borderlands as Barracks: Constructing a National Geography of Security in India." *Cultural Anthropology* 40 (2): 221–48.

Gidwani, Vinay. 2008. *Capital, Interrupted: Agrarian Development and the Politics of Work in India.* University of Minnesota Press.

Gidwani, Vinay, and Priti Ramamurthy. 2018. "Agrarian Questions of Labor in Urban India: Middle Migrants, Translocal Householding and the Intersectional Politics of Social Reproduction." *The Journal of Peasant Studies* 45 (5–6): 994–1017.

Gilmore, Ruth Wilson. 2007. *Golden Gulag: Prisons, Surplus, Crisis, And Opposition in Globalizing California.* University of California Press.

Gilmore, Ruth Wilson. 2022. *Abolition Geography: Essays Towards Liberation.* Edited by Brenna Bhandar and Alberto Toscano. Verso.

Gilsenan, Michael. 1977. "Against Patron-Client Relations." In *Patrons and Clients in Mediterranean Societies,* edited by Ernest Gellner and John Waterbury. Duckworth.

Gilsenan, Michael. 1996. *Lords of the Lebanese Marches: Violence and Narrative in an Arab Society.* University of California Press.

Gomberg-Muñoz, Ruth. 2010. *Labor and Legality: An Ethnography of a Mexican Immigrant Network.* Oxford University Press.

Göransson, Markus Balázs, Lotta Hultin, and Magnus Mähring. 2020. "'The Phone Means Everything.' Mobile Phones, Livelihoods and Social Capital among Syrian Refugees in Informal Tented Settlements in Lebanon." *Migration and Development* 9 (3): 331–51.

Gordillo, Gastón R. 2014. *Rubble: The Afterlife of Destruction.* Duke University Press.

Gowayed, Heba. 2022. *Refuge: How the State Shapes Human Potential.* Princeton University Press.

Graeber, David. 2011. *Debt: The First 5,000 Years.* Melville House.

Grandia, Liza. 2012. *Enclosed: Conservation, Cattle, and Commerce Among the Q'eqchi' Maya Lowlanders.* University of Washington Press.

Green, W. Nathan. 2022. "Financing Agrarian Change: Geographies of Credit and Debt in the Global South." *Progress in Human Geography* 46 (3): 849–69.

Green, W. Nathan. 2025. "The Persistence of the Moneylender: How Informal Debt Deepens Financialization in the Cambodian Countryside." *The Journal of Peasant Studies* 52 (6): 1135–59.

Green, W. Nathan, and Jennifer Estes. 2019. "Precarious Debt: Microfinance Subjects and Intergenerational Dependency in Cambodia." *Antipode* 51 (1): 129–47.

Green, W. Nathan, and Jennifer Estes. 2022. "Translocal Precarity: Labor and Social Reproduction in Cambodia." *Annals of the American Association of Geographers* 112 (6): 1726–40.

Griffith, David. 1995. *Working Poor: Farmworkers in the United States.* Temple University Press.

Griffith, David. 2009. "Unions without Borders: Organizing and Enlightening Immigrant Farm Workers." *Anthropology of Work Review* 30 (2): 54–66.

Guérin, Isabelle, Santosh Kumar, and G. Venkatasubramanian. 2023. *The Indebted Woman: Kinship, Sexuality, and Capitalism.* Stanford University Press.

Guirguis, Laure, ed. 2020. *The Arab Lefts: Histories and Legacies, 1950s–1970s.* Edinburgh University Press.

Guyer, Jane I. 2012. "Obligation, Binding, Debt and Responsibility: Provocations about Temporality from Two New Sources." *Social Anthropology* 20 (4): 491–501.

Haddad, Bassam. 2012. *Business Networks in Syria: The Political Economy of Authoritarian Resilience.* Stanford University Press.

Haj, Samira. 1997. *The Making of Iraq, 1900–1963: Capital, Power, and Ideology.* State University of New York Press.

Hakim, Sam R., and Saad Andary. 1997. "The Lebanese Central Bank and the Treasury Bills Market." *Middle East Journal* 51 (2): 230–41.

Hall, Stuart. 1978. *Policing the Crisis: Mugging, the State, and Law and Order.* Macmillan.

Han, Clara. 2012. *Life in Debt: Times of Care and Violence in Neoliberal Chile.* University of California Press.

Han, Clara. 2020. *Seeing Like a Child: Inheriting the Korean War.* Fordham University Press.

Hanieh, Adam. 2013. *Lineages of Revolt: Issues of Contemporary Capitalism in the Middle East.* Haymarket Books.

Hann, Chris, and Keith Hart. 2011. *Economic Anthropology.* Polity.

Ḥannā, ʿAbdallāh. 1975. *al-Qaḍiyya al-zirāʿiyya wa-al-ḥarakāt al-fallāḥiyya fī Sūriyā wa-Lubnān.* Dār al-Fārābī.

Ḥannā, ʿAbdallāh. 1990. *al-ʿĀmmiyya wa-al-intifāḍāt al-fallāḥiyya fī Jabal Ḥawrān (1850–1918).* Ahālī li-al-Ṭibāʿa wa-al-Nashr.

Haralambous, Chloe Howe. 2020. "The Cause of the Refugee." *Boundary 2* 47 (4): 181–98.

Harootunian, Harry. 2019. *The Unspoken as Heritage: The Armenian Genocide and Its Unaccounted Lives.* Duke University Press.

Hartman, Saidiya V. 1997. *Scenes of Subjection: Terror, Slavery, and Self-Making in Nineteenth-Century America.* Oxford University Press.

Harvey, David. 2017. *Marx, Capital, and the Madness of Economic Reason.* Oxford University Press.

Haugbolle, Sune. 2010. *War and Memory in Lebanon.* Cambridge University Press.

Hermez, Sami. 2017. *War Is Coming: Between Past and Future Violence in Lebanon.* University of Pennsylvania Press.

Heyman, Josiah. 2001. "Class and Classification at the U.S.-Mexico Border." *Human Organization* 60 (2): 128–40.

Heyman, Josiah. 2022. "Border Walls and Passages: Effects on Labor Exploitation." In *The Routledge Handbook of the Anthropology of Labor.* Routledge.

Heyman, Josiah. 2024. "Rethinking Borders." *Journal of Borderlands Studies* 39 (3): 513–24.

Hinnebusch, Raymond A. 1989. *Peasant and Bureaucracy in Ba'thist Syria: The Political Economy of Rural Development.* Westview.

Hinnebusch, Raymond A. 1995. "The Political Economy of Economic Liberalization in Syria." *International Journal of Middle East Studies* 27 (3): 305–20.

Hinnebusch, Raymond, Atieh El Hindi, Mounzer Khaddam, and Myriam Ababsa. 2011. *Agriculture and Reform in Syria*. Lynne Rienner.

Hinnebusch, Raymond, and Tina Zintl. 2014. *Syria from Reform to Revolt, Volume 1: Political Economy and International Relations*. Syracuse University Press.

Hirschkind, Charles. 2020. *The Feeling of History: Islam, Romanticism, and Andalusia*. University of Chicago Press.

Ḥizb al-Shuyūʿī al-Lubnānī [Lebanese Communist Party]. 1973. *al-Barnāmij al-zirāʿī li-Ḥizb al-Shuyūʿī al-Lubnānī*. Dār al-Fārābī.

Hoag, Colin. 2022. *The Fluvial Imagination: On Lesotho's Water-Export Economy*. University of California Press.

Hokayem, Emile. 2013. *Syria's Uprising and the Fracturing of the Levant*. Taylor and Francis.

Holmes, Seth. 2013. *Fresh Fruit, Broken Bodies: Migrant Farmworkers in the United States*. University of California Press.

Holmes, Seth M., and Heide Castañeda. 2016. "Representing the 'European Refugee Crisis' in Germany and Beyond: Deservingness and Difference, Life and Death." *American Ethnologist* 43 (1): 12–24.

Horton, Sarah B. 2015. "Identity Loan: The Moral Economy of Migrant Document Exchange in California's Central Valley." *American Ethnologist* 42 (1): 55–67.

Horton, Sarah B. 2016. *They Leave Their Kidneys in the Fields: Illness, Injury, and Illegality among U.S. Farmworkers*. University of California Press.

Horton, Sarah B., and Josiah Heyman, eds. 2020. *Paper Trails: Migrants, Documents, and Legal Insecurity*. Duke University Press.

Inhorn, Marcia C., and Nancy J. Smith-Hefner. 2020. *Waithood: Gender, Education, and Global Delays in Marriage and Childbearing*. Berghahn Books.

İpek, Yasemin. 2025. *Crisiswork: Activist Lifeworlds and Bounded Futures in Lebanon*. Stanford University Press.

Iqbal, Basit Kareem. 2022a. "Economy of Tribulation: Translating Humanitarianism for an Islamic Counterpublic." *The Muslim World* 112 (1): 33–56.

Iqbal, Basit Kareem. 2022b. "Reprising Islamic Political Theology: Genre and the Time of Tribulation." *Political Theology*: 1–18.

Iqbal, Basit Kareem. 2025. *The Dread Heights: Tribulation and Refuge after the Syrian Revolution*. Fordham University Press.

Isaacman, Allen F., and Barbara S. Isaacman. 2013. *Dams, Displacement, and the Delusion of Development: Cahora Bassa and Its Legacies in Mozambique, 1965–2007*. Ohio University Press.

Ismail, Salwa. 2018. *The Rule of Violence: Subjectivity, Memory and Government in Syria*. Cambridge University Press.

ʿIṣmat, Riyāḍ. 1979. *al-Ṣawt wa-al-Ṣadā: dirāsa fī al-qiṣṣa al-sūriyya al-ḥadītha*. Dār al-Ṭalīʿa li-al-Ṭibāʿa wa-al-Nashr.

Jain, Priyanka, and Nivedita Jayaram. 2023. "The Intimate Subsidies of Left-Behind Women of Migrant Households in Western India." *Gender, Place & Culture* 30 (5): 638–56.

James, Deborah. 2014. *Money from Nothing: Indebtedness and Aspiration in South Africa*. Stanford University Press.

Janmyr, Maja. 2016. "Precarity in Exile: The Legal Status of Syrian Refugees in Lebanon." *Refugee Survey Quarterly* 35 (4): 58–78.

Janmyr, Maja. 2017. "No Country of Asylum: 'Legitimizing' Lebanon's Rejection of the 1951 Refugee Convention." *International Journal of Refugee Law* 29 (3): 438–65.

Janmyr, Maja. 2021. "Sudanese Refugees and the 'Syrian Refugee Response' in Lebanon: Racialised Hierarchies, Processes of Invisibilisation, and Resistance." *Refugee Survey Quarterly* 41 (1): 131–56.

Janmyr, Maja, and Lama Mourad. 2018. "Modes of Ordering: Labelling, Classification and Categorization in Lebanon's Refugee Response." *Journal of Refugee Studies* 31 (4): 544–65.

Jastrow, Otto. 2012. "The Shāwi Dialects of the Middle Euphrates Valley." *Encyclopaedia of Islam*. Brill.

Jayawardena, Kumari. 2015. *Class, Patriarchy and Ethnicity on Sri Lankan Plantations: Two Centuries of Power and Protest*. Orient BlackSwan.

Jegathesan, Mythri. 2019. *Tea and Solidarity: Tamil Women and Work in Postwar Sri Lanka*. University of Washington Press.

Johnson, Michael. 1986. *Class & Client in Beirut: The Sunni Muslim Community and the Lebanese State, 1840–1985*. Ithaca.

Joseph, Suad. 1983. "Working-Class Women's Networks in a Sectarian State: A Political Paradox." *American Ethnologist* 10 (1): 1–22.

Joseph, Suad. 1993. "Connectivity and Patriarchy among Urban Working-Class Arab Families in Lebanon." *Ethos* 21 (4): 452–84.

Joseph, Suad. 1994. "Brother/Sister Relationships: Connectivity, Love, and Power in the Reproduction of Patriarchy in Lebanon." *American Ethnologist* 21 (1): 50–73.

Joseph, Suad, ed. 2018. *Arab Family Studies: Critical Reviews*. Syracuse University Press.

Joseph, Suzanne E. 2013. *Fertile Bonds: Bedouin Class, Kinship, and Gender in the Bekaa Valley*. University Press of Florida.

Kadri, Ali. 2016. *The Unmaking of Arab Socialism*. Anthem.

Kaminer, Matan. 2024. *Capitalist Colonial: Thai Migrant Workers in Israeli Agriculture.* Stanford University Press.

Kandiyoti, Deniz. 1988. "Bargaining with Patriarchy." *Gender & Society* 2 (3): 274–90.

Kapadia, Karin. 2000. "Responsibility Without Rights: Women Workers in Bonded Labour in Rural Industry in South Asia." In *Disappearing Peasantries? Rural Labour in Africa, Asia, and Latin America,* edited by Jos E. Mooij, Deborah Bryceson, and Cristobal Kay. Intermediate Technology.

Karam, Jeffrey G., and Rima Majed, eds. 2022. *The Lebanon Uprising of 2019: Voices from the Revolution.* I. B. Tauris.

Kassamali, Sumayya. 2017. "Migrant Worker Lifeworlds of Beirut." PhD diss., Columbia University.

Kassamali, Sumayya. 2022. "Neoliberalism and Kafala." *The Public Source.* https://thepublicsource.org/neoliberalism-kafala.

Kassamali, Sumayya. 2025. "The Undercommons of Beirut." *Mashriq & Mahjar: Journal of Middle East & North African Migration Studies* 12 (2): 1–27.

Katz, Cindi. 2001. "Vagabond Capitalism and the Necessity of Social Reproduction." *Antipode* 33 (4): 709–28.

Katz, Friedrich. 1974. "Labor Conditions on Haciendas in Porfirian Mexico: Some Trends and Tendencies." *Hispanic American Historical Review* 54 (1): 1–47.

Kautsky, Karl. 1988. *The Agrarian Question Volume 1.* Zwan.

Kavak, Sinem. 2016. "Syrian Refugees in Seasonal Agricultural Work: A Case of Adverse Incorporation in Turkey." *New Perspectives on Turkey* 54: 33–53.

Kavak, Sinem, and Zeynep Ceren Eren Benlisoy. 2025. "Seasonal Migrant Farm Workers at the Nexus of Production and Social Reproduction in Contemporary Turkey." *Agriculture and Human Values* 42: 2473–91.

Khalaf, Sulayman. 1981. "Family, Village, and the Political Party: Articulation of Social Change in Contemporary Rural Syria." PhD diss., University of California, Los Angeles.

Khater, Akram. 2001. *Inventing Home: Emigration, Gender, and the Middle Class in Lebanon, 1870–1920.* University of California Press.

Khayyat, Munira. 2022. *A Landscape of War: Ecologies of Resistance and Survival in South Lebanon.* University of California Press.

Khneisser, Mona. 2024. "The Political Economy of 'Failure' in The World Bank-Funded Bisri Dam in Lebanon." *Development and Change* 55 (3): 351–74.

Kirk, Gabi. 2024. "Trains, Trees, and Terraces: Infrastructures of Settler Colonialism and Resistance in the Refaim Valley, Palestine-Israel." In *Gendered Infrastructures: Space, Scale, and Identity,* edited by Anu Sabhlok and Yaffa Truelove. West Virginia University Press.

Kochuyt, Thierry. 2009. "God, Gifts and Poor People: On Charity in Islam." *Social Compass* 56 (1): 98–116.

Koga, Yukiko. 2016. *Inheritance of Loss: China, Japan, and the Political Economy of Redemption after Empire.* University of Chicago Press.

Kohlbry, Paul. 2026. *Plots and Deeds: Agrarian Annihilation and the Fight for Land Justice in Palestine.* Stanford University Press.

Koselleck, Reinhart. 1988. *Critique and Crisis: Enlightenment and the Pathogenesis of Modern Society.* MIT Press.

Koselleck, Reinhart. 2005. *Futures Past: On the Semantics of Historical Time.* Columbia University Press.

Kosmatopoulos, Nikolas. 2011. "Toward an Anthropology of 'State Failure': Lebanon's Leviathan and Peace Expertise." *Social Analysis* 55 (3): 115–42.

Kosmatopoulos, Nikolas. 2024. *Master Peace: Lebanon's Violence and the Politics of Expertise.* University of Pennsylvania Press.

Kuruma, Samezō. 2025. *In Pursuit of Marx's Theory of Crisis.* Translated by Michael Schauerte. Haymarket Books.

Kwon, Heonik. 2008. *Ghosts of War in Vietnam.* Cambridge University Press.

Lange, Katharina. 2005. "'Shawaya': Economic Mélange, Pure Origins? Outsiders' and Insiders' Accounts of Tribal Identity in Northern Syria." In *Shifts and Drifts in Nomad-Sedentary Relations*, edited by Stefan Leder and Bernhard Streck. Ludwig Reichert Verlag.

Lange, Katharina. 2006. "Heroic Faces, Disruptive Deeds: Remembering the Tribal Shaykh on the Syrian Euphrates." In *Nomadic Societies in the Middle East and North Africa*, edited by Dawn Chatty. Brill.

Lange, Katharina. 2007. "Economic Change and Income-Generating Practices of Rural Youth in Northern Syria." In *Changing Values Among Youth: Examples from the Arab World and Germany,* edited by Elke Kaschl and Sonja Hegasy. Klaus Schwarz.

Lange, Katharina. 2012. "There Used to Be Terrible Disbelief": Mourning and Social Change in Northern Syria." In *Ethnographies of Islam: Ritual Performances and Everyday Practices,* edited by Baudouin Dupret, Thomas Pierret, Paulo G. Pinto, and Kathryn Spellman-Poots. Edinburgh University Press.

Lange, Katharina. 2014. "Producing (Tribal) History: Gendered Representations of Genealogy and Warfare in Northern Syria." *Nomadic Peoples* 18 (2): 34–52.

Lange, Katharina. 2015. "'Bedouin' and 'Shawaya': The Performative Constitution of Tribal Identities in Syria During the French Mandate and Today." *Journal of the Economic and Social History of the Orient* 58 (1–2): 200–235.

Lange, Katharina. 2019. "Submerged Memories: Memory, History, and Displacement Around Lake Asad, Syria." *Memory Studies* 12 (3): 322–35.

Lawson, Owain. 2021. "A National Vocation: Engineering Nature and State in Lebanon's Merchant Republic." *Comparative Studies of South Asia, Africa and the Middle East* 41 (1): 71–87.

Lawson, Owain. 2024. "Organised Abandonment in Lebanon's Litani River Basin." *Environment and Planning E: Nature and Space.*

Lazzarato, Maurizio. 2012. *The Making of the Indebted Man: An Essay on the Neoliberal Condition.* Translated by Joshua David Jordan. Semiotext(e).

Lear, Jonathan. 2009. *Radical Hope: Ethics in the Face of Cultural Devastation.* Harvard University Press.

Lemberg-Pedersen, Martin. 2019. "Manufacturing Displacement. Externalization and Postcoloniality in European Migration Control." *Global Affairs* 5 (3): 247–71.

Lenin, Vladimir I. 1974. *The Development of Capitalism in Russia.* Progress.

Lerche, Jens, and Alpa Shah. 2018. "Conjugated Oppression within Contemporary Capitalism: Class, Caste, Tribe and Agrarian Change in India." *The Journal of Peasant Studies* 45 (5–6): 927–49.

Levien, Michael, Michael Watts, and Yan Hairong. 2018. "Agrarian Marxism." *The Journal of Peasant Studies* 45 (5–6): 853–83.

Limbert, Mandana. 2010. *In the Time of Oil: Piety, Memory, and Social Life in an Omani Town.* Stanford University Press.

Lonergan, Steve, Jassim Al-Asadi, and Keith Holmes. 2023. *The Ghosts of Iraq's Marshes: A History of Conflict, Tragedy, and Restoration.* American University in Cairo Press.

Long, Katy. 2013. "When Refugees Stopped Being Migrants: Movement, Labour and Humanitarian Protection." *Migration Studies* 1 (1): 4–26.

López, Ann Aurelia. 2007. *The Farmworkers' Journey.* University of California Press.

López, Ann Aurelia. 2011. "NAFTA and the Campesinas Left Behind." *Anthropology Now* 3 (2): 35–40.

Love, Stephanie V. 2021. "The Poetics of Grievance: Taxi Drivers, Vernacular Placenames, and the Paradoxes of Post-Coloniality in Oran, Algeria." *City & Society* 33 (3): 422–43.

Love, Stephanie V. 2023. "Echoes of 'Dead' Colonialism: The Voices and Materiality of a (Post)Colonial Algerian Newspaper." *Journal of Linguistic Anthropology* 33 (1): 72–91.

Lubkemann, Stephen C. 2008. *Culture in Chaos: An Anthropology of the Social Condition in War.* University Of Chicago Press.

Ludden, David, ed. 2002. *Reading Subaltern Studies: Critical History, Contested Meaning and the Globalization of South Asia.* Anthem.

Mahmood, Saba. 2005. *Politics of Piety: The Islamic Revival and the Feminist Subject.* Princeton University Press.

Malkki, Liisa H. 1995a. *Purity and Exile: Violence, Memory, and National Cosmology Among Hutu Refugees in Tanzania.* University of Chicago Press.

Malkki, Liisa H. 1995b. "Refugees and Exile: From 'Refugee Studies' to the National Order of Things." *Annual Review of Anthropology* 24: 495–523.

Malkki, Liisa H. 1996. "Speechless Emissaries: Refugees, Humanitarianism, and Dehistoricization." *Cultural Anthropology* 11 (3): 377–404.

Martin, Keir. 2021. "Dependence." *The Open Encyclopedia of Anthropology.* https://www.anthroencyclopedia.com/entry/dependence.

Martin, Keir, Stale Wig, and Sylvia Yanagisako. 2021. "Battlegrounds of Dependence: Reconfiguring Labor, Kinship and Relational Obligation." *Focaal* 90: 1–10.

Martin, Keir, and Sylvia Yanagisako. 2020. "States of Dependence: Introduction." *Social Anthropology* 28 (3): 646–56.

Martiniello, Giuliano, and Julia Kassem. 2023. "The Corporate Food Regime and Lebanon: Machgara and Adverse Incorporation." *The Journal of Peasant Studies* 51 (5): 1–21.

Massaad, Barbara Abdeni. 2017. *Mouneh: Preserving Foods for the Lebanese Pantry.* Interlink.

Matar, Linda. 2013. "Twilight of 'State Capitalism' in Formerly 'Socialist' Arab States." *The Journal of North African Studies* 18 (3): 416–30.

Maurer, Bill. 2018. "Money Orders—and It's Done! Activating Theories of Money's Origins and Orders." *Money and Coinage in the Middle Ages,* edited by Rory Naismith. Brill.

Mazwi, Freedom, Paris Yeros, Praveen Jha, and Walter Chambati, eds. 2022. *Farming and Working Under Contract: Peasants and Workers in Global Agricultural Value Systems.* Columbia University Press.

McDowall, David. 1993. *A People Without a Country: The Kurds and Kurdistan.* Edited by Gerard Chaliand. Translated by Michael Pallis. Interlink.

McManus, Anne-Marie. 2022. "Al-Nuzuh: Displacement as Keyword." *Middle East Journal of Culture and Communication* 15 (4): 455–66.

McMichael, Philip. 2009. "A Food Regime Genealogy." *The Journal of Peasant Studies* 36 (1): 139–69.

McMichael, Philip. 2021. "Food Regimes." In *Handbook of Critical Agrarian Studies,* edited by A. Haroon Akram-Lodhi, Kristina Dietz, Bettina Engels, and Ben M. McKay. Edward Elgar.

Meliczek, Hans. 1986. "Land Settlement in the Euphrates Basin of Syria." *Ekistics* 53 (318/319): 202–12.

MENA Solidarity Network. 2025. "New Syrian Workers' Committees Launch Coordinated Protests at Mass Sackings of Government Employees." February 15. https://menasolidaritynetwork.com/2025/02/15/new-syrian-workers-committees-launch-coordinated-protests-at-mass-sackings-of-government-employees/.

Meneley, Anne. 1996. *Tournaments of Value: Sociability and Hierarchy in a Yemeni Town.* University of Toronto Press.

Mercy Corps. 2014. *Protect and Provide Livelihoods in Lebanon: Tomato Value Chain Assessment.* https://www.mercycorps.org/sites/default/files/2020-01/FINAL%20Mercy%20Corps%20Lebanon%20Tomato%20Value%20Chain-%20Branded.pdf.

Mezzadra, Sandro, and Brett Neilson. 2013. *Border as Method, or the Multiplication of Labor.* Duke University Press.

Mezzadri, Alessandra. 2020. "A Value Theory of Inclusion: Informal Labour, the Homeworker, and the Social Reproduction of Value." *Antipode* 53 (4): 1186–205.

Mezzadri, Alessandra, Sara Stevano, Lyn Ossome, and Hannah Bargawi. 2024. "The Social Reproduction of Agrarian Change: Feminist Political Economy and Rural Transformations in the Global South. An Introduction." *Journal of Agrarian Change* 24 (3): 1–18.

Mikdashi, Maya. 2022. *Sextarianism: Sovereignty, Secularism, and the State in Lebanon.* Stanford University Press.

Mincyte, Diana. 2023. "Rethinking Food Regime as Gender Regime: Agrarian Change and the Politics of Social Reproduction." *The Journal of Peasant Studies* 51 (1): 1–19.

Mitchell, Timothy. 2002. *Rule of Experts: Egypt, Techno-Politics, Modernity.* University of California Press.

Mittermaier, Amira. 2010. *Dreams That Matter: Egyptian Landscapes of the Imagination.* University of California Press.

Mittermaier, Amira. 2014. "Beyond Compassion: Islamic Voluntarism in Egypt." *American Ethnologist* 41 (3): 518–31.

Mittermaier, Amira. 2019. *Giving to God: Islamic Charity in Revolutionary Times.* University of California Press.

Mohanty, B. B., ed. 2016. *Critical Perspectives on Agrarian Transition: India in the Global Debate.* Routledge India.

Monroe, Kristin V. 2023. "Driving Across the Warscape: Syrian Cross-Border Taxi Drivers and the Politics of Mobility." *Environment and Planning C: Politics and Space* 41 (7): 1374–90.

Moreno-Lax, Violeta, and Martin Lemberg-Pedersen. 2019. "Border-Induced Displacement: The Ethical and Legal Implications of Distance-Creation through Externalization." *QIL QDI.* February 28. https://www.qil-qdi.org/border-induced

-displacement-the-ethical-and-legal-implications-of-distance-creation-through-externalization/.

Morgan, Jennifer L., and Alys Eve Weinbaum. 2024. "Introduction: Reproductive Racial Capitalism." *History of the Present* 14 (1): 1–19.

Moumtaz, Nada. 2021. *God's Property: Islam, Charity, and the Modern State.* University of California Press.

Mueggler, Erik. 2001. *The Age of Wild Ghosts: Memory, Violence, and Place in Southwest China.* University of California Press.

Mulder, Nicholas. 2022. *The Economic Weapon: The Rise of Sanctions as a Tool of Modern War.* Yale University Press.

Naff, Alixa. 1972. "A Social History of Zahle, the Principal Market Town in Nineteenth-Century Lebanon." PhD diss., University of California Los Angeles.

Narotzky, Susana. 2016. "Where Have All the Peasants Gone?" *Annual Review of Anthropology* 45 (1): 1–18.

Narotzky, Susana, and Gavin Smith. 2006. *Immediate Struggles: People, Power, and Place in Rural Spain.* University of California Press.

Nash, June C. 1993. *We Eat the Mines and the Mines Eat Us: Dependency and Exploitation in Bolivian Tin Mines.* Columbia University Press.

Nasr, Salim. 1978. "Backdrop to Civil War: The Crisis of Lebanese Capitalism." *Middle East Report* 73: 3–13.

Nassar, Jessy. 2025. "Commodified by Displacement: The Effects of Forced Displacement on Syrian Refugee Women in Lebanon's Agricultural Sector." *Migration Studies* 13 (1): mnae052.

Nassar, Jessy, and Nora Stel. 2019. "Lebanon's Response to the Syrian Refugee Crisis—Institutional Ambiguity as a Governance Strategy." *Political Geography* 70 (April): 44–54.

Natarajan, Nithya, and Katherine Brickell. 2022. "Credit, Land and Survival Work in Rural Cambodia: Rethinking Rural Autonomy through a Feminist Lens." *Journal of Agrarian Change* 22 (3): 473–88.

Ng, Emily. 2020. *A Time of Lost Gods: Mediumship, Madness, and the Ghost after Mao.* University of California Press.

Ngubane, Mnqobi. 2024. "Immigrant Farm Workers, Self-Exploitation and Social Reproduction: The Lesotho–South African Land-Labour Questions." *Review of African Political Economy* 183: 1–24.

Nguyen, Vinh. 2019. "Refugeetude: When Does a Refugee Stop Being a Refugee." *Social Text* 37 (2): 109–31.

Nietzsche, Friedrich Wilhelm. 1887. *The Genealogy of Morals.* Boni and Liveright.

Nixon, Rob. 2011. *Slow Violence and the Environmentalism of the Poor.* Harvard University Press.

Nucho, Joanne Randa. 2016. *Everyday Sectarianism in Urban Lebanon: Infrastructures, Public Services, and Power.* Princeton University Press.

Obeid, Michelle. 2019. *Border Lives: An Ethnography of a Lebanese Town in Changing Times.* Brill.

Obeid, Michelle. 2023. "Sovereignty at What Price? Existential Displacement at the Lebanese/Syrian Border." *Journal of the Royal Anthropological Institute* 29 (4): 784–801.

Obeid, Michelle, and Muzna Al-Masri. 2021. "Ethnographic Diaries: Capturing the Everyday in Crisis." *Rusted Radishes: Beirut Literary and Art Journal.*

O'Connor, James. 1981. "The Meaning of Crisis." *International Journal of Urban and Regional Research* 5 (3): 301–29.

O'Connor, James. 2001. *The Fiscal Crisis of the State.* Routledge.

Ojeilī, ʿAbd al-Salām. 1979. *al-Maghmūrūn.* Dār al-Sharq.

Oka, Rahul Chandrashekhar. 2014. "Coping with the Refugee Wait: The Role of Consumption, Normalcy, and Dignity in Refugee Lives at Kakuma Refugee Camp, Kenya." *American Anthropologist* 116 (1): 23–37.

O'Laughlin, Bridget. 2022. "No Separate Spheres: The Contingent Reproduction of Living Labor in Southern Africa." *Review of International Political Economy* 29 (6): 1827–46.

Ossome, Lyn, and Sirisha Naidu. 2021. "The Agrarian Question of Gendered Labour." In *Labour Questions in the Global South,* edited by Praveen Jha, Walter Chambati, and Lyn Ossome. Palgrave Macmillan.

Owen, David. 2020. *What Do We Owe to Refugees?* Polity.

Ozer, Yasemin. 2024. "Syrian 'Brokers of Care' and Lived Citizenship in Istanbul." *Citizenship Studies* 28 (6): 673–89.

Panosetti, Fadia, Taher Labadi, and Ahmad Heneiti. 2025. "Agrarian Questions in Global Palestine: Past, Present and Future." *The Journal of Peasant Studies*: 1–27.

Passerini, Luisa. 1987. *Fascism in Popular Memory: The Cultural Experience of the Turin Working Class.* Cambridge University Press.

Patnaik, Utsa, Sam Moyo, and Issa Shivji. 2011. *The Agrarian Question in the Neoliberal Era: Primitive Accumulation and the Peasantry.* Fahamu Books and Pambazuka Press.

Pearlman, Wendy. 2013. "Emigration and Power: A Study of Sects in Lebanon, 1860–2010." *Politics & Society* 41 (1): 103–33.

Pearlman, Wendy. 2018. *We Crossed a Bridge And It Trembled: Voices from Syria.* Custom House.

Peebles, Gustav. 2010. "The Anthropology of Credit and Debt." *Annual Review of Anthropology* 39 (1): 225–40.

Pelek, Deniz. 2019. "Syrian Refugees as Seasonal Migrant Workers: Re-Construction of Unequal Power Relations in Turkish Agriculture." *Journal of Refugee Studies* 32 (4): 605–29.

Pelek, Deniz. 2022. "Ethnic Residential Segregation among Seasonal Migrant Workers: From Temporary Tents to New Rural Ghettos in Southern Turkey." *The Journal of Peasant Studies* 49 (1): 54–77.

Perdigon, Sylvain. 2011. "Between the Womb and the Hour: Ethics and Semiotics of Relatedness Amongst Palestinian Refugees in Tyre, Lebanon." PhD diss., Johns Hopkins University.

Perdigon, Sylvain. 2015. "'For Us It Is Otherwise' Three Sketches on Making Poverty Sensible in the Palestinian Refugee Camps of Lebanon." *Current Anthropology* 56 (S11): S88–96.

Perdigon, Sylvain. 2018. "Life on the Cusp of Form: In Search of Worldliness with Palestinian Refugees in Tyre, Lebanon." *HAU: Journal of Ethnographic Theory* 8 (3): 566–83.

Pérez Niño, Helena, and Carlos Oya. 2021. "Contract Farming." In *Handbook of Critical Agrarian Studies,* edited by A. Haroon Akram-Lodhi, Kristina Dietz, Bettina Engels, and Ben M. McKay. Edward Elgar.

Perosino, Livia. 2024. "Deconstructing the Market: Agrarian Change and Social Differentiation in Jordan." *The Journal of Peasant Studies* 51 (5): 1102–19.

Perthes, Volker. 2006. *Syria under Bashar Al-Asad: Modernisation and the Limits of Change.* Routledge.

Petchesky, Rosalind, and Meena Alexander. 2014. "Introduction: Life and Debt." *Women's Studies Quarterly* 42 (1/2): 13–20.

Peteet, Julie. 1997. "Icons and Militants: Mothering in the Danger Zone." *Signs* 23 (1): 103–29.

Peteet, Julie. 2005. *Landscape of Hope and Despair: Palestinian Refugee Camps.* University of Pennsylvania Press.

Peteet, Julie. 2013. *Gender in Crisis: Women and the Palestinian Resistance Movement.* Columbia University Press.

Pfeifer, Karen. 1987. "The Fate of the Family Farm." *Middle East Report* 145: 45–47.

Picard, Elizabeth. 2002. *Lebanon, a Shattered Country: Myths and Realities of the Wars in Lebanon.* Holmes & Meier.

Picard, Elizabeth. 2005. "Trafficking, Rents, and Diaspora in the Lebanese War." In *Rethinking the Economics of War: The Intersection of Need, Creed, and Greed,* edited by Cynthia J. Arnson, I. William Zartman. Johns Hopkins University Press.

Pitt-Rivers, Julian. 2017. *From Hospitality to Grace: A Julian Pitt-Rivers Omnibus.* Edited by Giovanni da Col and Andrew Shryock. HAU Books.

Pitts, Graham Auman. 2016. "Fallow Fields: Famine and the Making of Lebanon." PhD diss., Georgetown University.

Povinelli, Elizabeth A. 2011. *Economies of Abandonment: Social Belonging and Endurance in Late Liberalism.* Duke University Press.

Prosnitz, Beth. 2023. "Indebtedness to Care: Land, Loans, and Love in Financializing Nepal." *The Journal of Peasant Studies* 51(2): 318–38.

Proudfoot, Philip. 2022. *Rebel Populism: Revolution and Loss Among Syrian Labourers in Beirut.* Manchester University Press.

Pursley, Sara. 2019. *Familiar Futures: Time, Selfhood, and Sovereignty in Iraq.* Stanford University Press.

Rabo, Annika. 1986. "Change on the Euphrates: Villagers, Townsmen and Employees in Northeast Syria." PhD diss., Stockholm University.

Rabo, Annika. 2008. "'Doing Family': Two Cases in Contemporary Syria." *Hawwa* 6 (2): 129–53.

Rabo, Annika. 2017. "Anthropological Methods and an Analysis of Memory: Migration, Past and Present in Raqqa Province, Syria." *Middle East Journal of Refugee Studies* 2 (1): 51–72.

Ragetlie, Rosalind, and Isaac Luginaah. 2023. "Masculinities in Context: How Food Insecurity Shapes Conjugal Dynamics in Northwestern Benin." *Canadian Journal of African Studies / Revue Canadienne Des Études Africaines* 57 (2): 349–68.

Rai, Pronoy. 2020. "Seasonal Masculinities: Seasonal Labor Migration and Masculinities in Rural Western India." *Gender, Place & Culture* 27 (2): 261–80.

Ramsay, Georgina. 2017. *Impossible Refuge: The Control and Constraint of Refugee Futures.* Routledge.

Ramsay, Georgina. 2020. "Time and the Other in Crisis: How Anthropology Makes Its Displaced Object." *Anthropological Theory* 20 (4): 385–413.

Rao, Smriti. 2021. "Labor and Social Reproduction." In *Handbook of Critical Agrarian Studies,* edited by A. Haroon Akram-Lodhi, Kristina Dietz, Bettina Engels, and Ben M. McKay. Edward Elgar.

Razavi, Shahra. 2009. "Engendering the Political Economy of Agrarian Change." *The Journal of Peasant Studies* 36 (1): 197–226.

Redfield, Peter. 2013. *Life in Crisis: The Ethical Journey of Doctors Without Borders.* University of California Press.

Reeves, Madeleine. 2014. *Border Work: Spatial Lives of the State in Rural Central Asia.* Cornell University Press.

Reumert, Anna. 2020. "Good Guys, Mad City: Etiquettes of Migration Among Sudanese Men in Beirut." *Mashriq & Mahjar: Journal of Middle East & North African Migration Studies* 7 (2): 48–69.

Reumert, Anna. 2023. "'Life Is a Gamble': Labors of Mobility, Risk, and Return between Sudan and Lebanon." *Cultural Anthropology* 38 (1): 113–41.

Reumert, Anna, Wendy Vogt, and Charles Piot. 2025. "Introduction: Bordering and the War on Migration." *American Ethnologist*, September 23. https://americanethnologist.org/online-content/introduction-bordering-and-the-war-on-migration-by-anna-simone-reumert-wendy-vogt-and-charlie-piot/.

Riachi, Roland, and Giuliano Martiniello. 2023. "Manufactured Regional Crises: The Middle East and North Africa under Global Food Regimes." *Journal of Agrarian Change* 23 (4): 792–810.

Richter, Gerhard. 2011. *Afterness: Figures of Following in Modern Thought and Aesthetics.* Columbia University Press.

Rignall, Karen E. 2021. *An Elusive Common: Land, Politics, and Agrarian Rurality in a Moroccan Oasis.* Cornell University Press.

Robson, Laura. 2023. *Human Capital: A History of Putting Refugees to Work.* Verso.

Roitman, Janet. 2005. *Fiscal Disobedience: An Anthropology of Economic Regulation in Central Africa.* Princeton University Press.

Roitman, Janet. 2013. *Anti-Crisis.* Duke University Press.

Rosenblatt, Nate, and David Kilcullen. 2019. "How Raqqa Became the Capital of ISIS." New America Foundation. http://newamerica.org/international-security/reports/how-raqqa-became-capital-isis/.

Rosenthal, Jill. 2023. *From Migrants to Refugees: The Politics of Aid along the Tanzania-Rwanda Border.* Duke University Press.

Roy, Arundhati. 1999. *The Greater Common Good.* India Book Distributor.

Ruijs, Marc. 2017. *Value Chain Analysis of (Greenhouse) Vegetables in Lebanon.* Wageningen Economic Research.

Saad, Dima. 2019. "Materializing Palestinian Memory: Objects of Home and the Everyday Eternities of Exile." *Jerusalem Quarterly* 80: 57–71.

Sa'ar, Amalia. 2004. "Many Ways of Becoming a Woman: The Case of Unmarried Israeli-Palestinian 'Girls.'" *Ethnology* 43 (1): 1–18.

Safieddine, Hicham. 2019. *Banking on the State: The Financial Foundations of Lebanon.* Stanford University Press.

Sahlins, Marshall. 1963. "Rich Man, Big-Man, Chief: Political Types in Melanesia and Polynesia." *Comparative Studies in Society and History* 5 (3): 285–303.

Sa'īd, 'Abdallāh Ibrāhīm. 1995. *Ashkāl al-milkiyya wa-anwā' al-arāḍī fī mutaṣarrifiyyat Jabal Lubnān wa-Sahl al-Biqā' 1861–1914: dirāsa muqārana fī al-tārīkh al-rīfī istināddan ilā wathā'iq aṣliyya*. Maktabat Baysān.

Said, Salam. 2018. "The Uprising and the Economic Interests of the Syrian Military–Mercantile Complex." In *The Syrian Uprising*, edited by Raymond Hinnebusch and Omar Imady. Routledge.

Sajadian, China. 2020a. "Critical Agrarian Studies." In *International Encyclopedia of Human Geography*, edited by Audrey Kobayashi. Elsevier.

Sajadian, China. 2020b. "The Agrarian Question in Lebanon Today: A View from a Camp in the Bekaa Valley." *Jadaliyya*, August 19. https://www.jadaliyya.com/Details/41585.

Sajadian, China 2022. "Rethinking Climate Refugees and the Syrian Refugee Crisis: An Agrarian Perspective of Displacement." *Arab Studies Journal* 30 (2): 74–81.

Sajadian, China. 2023. "The Drowned and the Displaced: Afterlives of Agrarian Developmentalism across the Lebanese-Syrian Border." *Mashriq & Mahjar: Journal of Middle East & North African Migration Studies* 10 (1): 9–43.

Sajadian, China. 2024. "Reproductive Binds: The Gendered Economy of Debt in a Syrian Refugee Farmworker Camp." *Journal of Agrarian Change* 24 (3): 1–23.

Sajadian, China. 2025a. "The Hidden Abodes of Agricultural Production: Notes from the Lebanese-Syrian Border." *Dialectical Anthropology* 49 (3): 489–97.

Sajadian, China. 2025b. "Fragmented Foodways: Visualizing Seasonal Labor among Syrian Farmworkers in Lebanon." *Anthropology News*, August 25. https://www.anthropology-news.org/articles/fragmented-foodways-visualizing-seasonal-labor-among-syrian-farmworkers-in-lebanon/.

Salamandra, Christa. 2004. *A New Old Damascus: Authenticity and Distinction in Urban Syria*. Indiana University Press.

Salamandra, Christa. 2013. "Sectarianism in Syria: Anthropological Reflections." *Middle East Critique* 22 (3): 303–6.

Salamandra, Christa, and Leif Steinberg, eds. 2015. *Syria from Reform to Revolt, Volume 2: Culture, Society, and Religion*. Syracuse University Press.

Saleh, Elizabeth. 2017. "A Tangled Web of Lies: Reflections on Ethnographic Fieldwork with Syrian Turkmen Women on the Side of a Road in Beirut." *Contemporary Levant* 2 (1): 55–60.

Saleh, Zainab. 2020. *Return to Ruin: Iraqi Narratives of Exile and Nostalgia*. Stanford University Press.

Salem, Sara. 2020. *Anticolonial Afterlives in Egypt: The Politics of Hegemony*. Cambridge University Press.

Ṣalībā, ʿAzīz. 1999. *Tārīkh al-ḥaraka al-niqābiyya fī al-Biqāʿ bayna al-ʿummāl wa-al-muzāriʿīn wa-al-ʿummāl al-zirāʿiyyīn (1908–1998)*. Dār al-Fārābī.

Ṣalībā, ʿAzīz. 2004. *al-Biqāʿ fī al-tārīkh wa-al-minṭaqa*. Dār al-Fārābī.

Ṣāliḥ, Niḍāl al-. 1999. *al-Mughāmara al-thāniya: dirāsāt fī al-riwāya al-ʿarabiyya*. al-Manshūrāt al-Ittiḥād al-Kuttāb al-ʿArab.

Salinas, Cristina. 2018. *Managed Migrations: Growers, Farmworkers, and Border Enforcement in the Twentieth Century*. University of Texas Press.

Salloukh, Bassel. 2005. "Syria and Lebanon: A Brotherhood Transformed." *Middle East Report* 236: 14–21.

Salloukh, Bassel, Rabie Barakat, Jinan S. Al-Habbal, Lara W. Khattab, and Shoghig Mikaelian. 2015. *The Politics of Sectarianism in Postwar Lebanon*. Pluto.

Salti, Nisreen. 2019. "No Country for Poor Men: How Lebanon's Debt Has Exacerbated Inequality." *Carnegie Middle East Center*. https://carnegie-mec.org/2019/09/17/no-country-for-poor-men-how-lebanon-s-debt-has-exacerbated-inequality-pub-79852.

Sanyal, Kalyan. 2007. *Rethinking Capitalist Development: Primitive Accumulation, Governmentality and Post-Colonial Capitalism*. Routledge India.

Sanyal, Romola. 2017. "A No-Camp Policy: Interrogating Informal Settlements in Lebanon." *Geoforum* 84: 117–25.

Sanyal, Romola. 2018. "Managing Through Ad Hoc Measures: Syrian Refugees and the Politics of Waiting in Lebanon." *Political Geography* 66: 67–75.

Sargent, Adam. 2019. "Moral Economies of Remuneration: Wages, Piece-Rates, and Contracts on a Delhi Construction Site." *Anthropological Quarterly* 92 (3): 757–85.

Sarkis Fernández, Diana. 2015. "Trabajar con el corazón. Trabajo, capital y economías morales en la agricultura Siria." PhD diss., University of Barcelona.

Sarkis Fernández, Diana. 2020. "'Amnarjaʿ La Wara (We Are Going Backwards)': Economic Reform and the Politics of Labour in Agrarian Syria." *The Journal of Peasant Studies* 49 (2): 363–80.

Sato, Noriko. 1997. "'We Are No More in Bondage, We Are Peasants': Memory and the Construction of Identity in the Syrian Jazirah." *Journal of Mediterranean Studies* 7 (2): 195–217.

Saxton, Dvera I. 2021. *The Devil's Fruit: Farmworkers, Health, and Environmental Justice*. Rutgers University Press.

Sayigh, Rosemary. 1979. *Palestinians: From Peasants to Revolutionaries: A People's History*. Zed Books.

Sayigh, Rosemary. 1981. "Encounters with Palestinian Women Under Occupation." *Journal of Palestine Studies* 10 (4): 3–26.

Schmeding, Annika. 2023. *Sufi Civilities: Religious Authority and Political Change in Afghanistan*. Stanford University Press.

Schneider, Jane, and Peter Schneider. 2005. "Mafia, Antimafia, and the Plural Cultures of Sicily." *Current Anthropology* 46 (4): 501–20.

Schuster, Caroline E. 2014. "The Social Unit of Debt: Gender and Creditworthiness in Paraguayan Microfinance." *American Ethnologist* 41 (3): 563–78.

Schuster, Caroline E . 2015. *Social Collateral: Women and Microfinance in Paraguay's Smuggling Economy*. University of California Press.

Scott, David. 2004. *Conscripts of Modernity: The Tragedy of Colonial Enlightenment*. Duke University Press.

Scott, David . 2014. *Omens of Adversity: Tragedy, Time, Memory, Justice*. Duke University Press.

Scott, James C. 1977. *The Moral Economy of the Peasant: Rebellion and Subsistence in Southeast Asia*. Yale University Press.

Scott, James C. 1985. *Weapons of the Weak: Everyday Forms of Peasant Resistance*. Yale University Press.

Scott, James C. 1992. *Domination and the Arts of Resistance: Hidden Transcripts*. Yale University Press.

Scott, James C. 1998. *Seeing Like a State: How Certain Schemes to Improve the Human Condition Have Failed*. Yale University Press.

Scott-Smith, Tom. 2024. *Fragments of Home: Refugee Housing and the Politics of Shelter*. Stanford University Press.

Seikaly, Sherene. 2015. *Men of Capital: Scarcity and Economy in Mandate Palestine*. Stanford University Press.

Selby, Jan. 2019. "Climate Change and the Syrian Civil War, Part II: The Jazira's Agrarian Crisis." *Geoforum* 101: 260–74.

Selby, Jan, Omar S. Dahi, Christiane Fröhlich, and Mike Hulme. 2017. "Climate Change and the Syrian Civil War Revisited." *Political Geography* 60: 232–44.

Sender, Hannah. 2024. "Making Rent: How Forced Migrant Families Access Private Rental Housing in the Biqa' Valley, Lebanon." *Environment and Urbanization 36* (2): 401–417.

Seremetakis, C. Nadia. 2019. *Sensing the Everyday: Dialogues from Austerity Greece*. Routledge.

Sethi, Aarti. 2018. "The Life of Debt in Rural India." PhD diss., Columbia University.

Shah, Alpa, and Jens Lerche. 2020. "Migration and the Invisible Economies of Care: Production, Social Reproduction and Seasonal Migrant Labour in India." *Transactions of the Institute of British Geographers* 45 (4): 719–34.

Shaikh, Anwar. 2016. *Capitalism: Competition, Conflict, Crises*. Oxford University Press.

Shanin, Teodor. 2009. "Chayanov's Treble Death and Tenuous Resurrection: An Essay about Understanding, about Roots of Plausibility and about Rural Russia." *The Journal of Peasant Studies* 36 (1): 83–101.

Sharpe, Christina. 2016. *In the Wake: On Blackness and Being*. Duke University Press.

Shevchenko, Olga. 2008. *Crisis and the Everyday in Postsocialist Moscow*. Indiana University Press.

Singerman, Diane. 1995. *Avenues of Participation: Family, Politics, and Networks in Urban Quarters of Cairo*. Princeton University Press.

Smilianskaia, Irina Mikhailnova. 1972. *al-Ḥaraka al-fallāḥiyya fī Lubnān: al-niṣf al-awwal min al-qarn al-tāsiʿ ʿashar*. Translated by ʿAdnān Jāmūs. Dār al-Fārābī.

Sowers, Jeannie, John Waterbury, and Eckart Woertz. 2013. "Did Drought Trigger the Crisis in Syria?" *Footnote*, September 12. https://footnote.co/did-drought-trigger-the-crisis-in-syria.

Srouji, Samer. 2005. "Capturing the State: A Political Economy of Lebanon's Public Debt Crisis 1992–2004." MA thesis, Institute of Social Sciences.

Stack, Carol B. 1983. *All Our Kin: Strategies for Survival in a Black Community*. Basic Books.

Starn, Randolph. 1971. "Historians and 'Crisis.'" *Past & Present* 52: 3–22.

Steedly, Mary Margaret. 2019. *Hanging without a Rope: Narrative Experience in Colonial and Postcolonial Karoland*. Princeton University Press.

Stel, Nora. 2020. *Hybrid Political Order and the Politics of Uncertainty: Refugee Governance in Lebanon*. Routledge.

Stoler, Ann Laura, and Karen Strassler. 2000. "Castings for the Colonial: Memory Work in 'New Order' Java." *Comparative Studies in Society and History* 42 (1): 4–48.

Strassler, Karen. 2009. *Refracted Visions: Popular Photography and National Modernity in Java*. Duke University Press.

Striffler, Steve. 2002. *In the Shadows of State and Capital: The United Fruit Company, Popular Struggle, and Agrarian Restructuring in Ecuador, 1900–1995*. Duke University Press.

Striffler, Steve. 2007. "Neither Here nor There: Mexican Immigrant Workers and the Search for Home." *American Ethnologist* 34 (4): 674–88.

Sukarieh, Mayssoun, and Nur Arafeh. 2023. "Breaking the Cycle: Toward a New Imaginary of the Food System in Lebanon." Carnegie Middle East Center. https://carnegie-mec.org/2023/07/03/breaking-cycle-toward-new-imaginary-of-food-system-in-lebanon-pub-90110.

Sur, Malini. 2021. *Jungle Passports: Fences, Mobility, and Citizenship at the Northeast India-Bangladesh Border.* University of Pennsylvania Press.

Sykes, Karen M., and Christine Jourdan. 2020. "Bridewealth and the Autonomy of Women in Melanesia." *Oceania* 90 (3): 178–93.

Tabler, Andrew. 2018. "A Tale of Six Tribes: Securing the Middle Euphrates River Valley." Washington Institute of Near East Affairs. https://www.washingtoninstitute.org/policy-analysis/view/a-tale-of-six-tribes-securing-the-middle-euphrates-river-valley.

Takriti, Abdel Razzaq, and Hicham Safieddine. 2022. "Arab Socialism." In *The Cambridge History of Socialism*, edited by Marcel van der Linden. Cambridge University Press.

Tamari, Salim. 1983. "The Dislocation and Re-Constitution of a Peasantry: The Social Economy of Agrarian Palestine in the Central Highlands and the Jordan Valley, 1960–1980." PhD diss., University of Manchester.

Tarnowski, Stefan. 2022. "Struggling with Images: Revolution, War, and Media in Syria." PhD diss., Columbia University.

Taussig, Michael. 1980. *The Devil and Commodity Fetishism in South America.* University of North Carolina Press.

Taylor, Elizabeth. 1984. "Egyptian Migration and Peasant Wives." *MERIP Reports* 124.

Thomas, Deborah A. 2019. *Political Life in the Wake of the Plantation: Sovereignty, Witnessing, Repair.* Duke University Press.

Thompson, E. P. 1978. "Eighteenth-Century English Society: Class Struggle without Class?" *Social History* 3 (2): 133–65.

Thompson, Elizabeth. 2000. *Colonial Citizens: Republican Rights, Paternal Privilege, and Gender in French Syria and Lebanon.* Columbia University Press.

Thomson, William, Cynthia Gharios, and Rami Zurayk. 2022. "From Silk to Concrete: Exploring the Socio-Spatial Aspects of the Agrarian Question(s) in Mount Lebanon." *The Journal of Peasant Studies* 50 (4): 1613–35.

Thorleifsson, Cathrine. 2016. "The Limits of Hospitality: Coping Strategies among Displaced Syrians in Lebanon." *Third World Quarterly* 37 (6): 1071–82.

Ticktin, Miriam. 2011. *Casualties of Care: Immigration and the Politics of Humanitarianism in France.* University of California Press.

Traboulsi, Fawwaz. 2007. *A History of Modern Lebanon.* Pluto.

Trouillot, Michel-Rolph. 2020. "The Odd and the Ordinary: Haiti, the Caribbean and the World." *Vibrant: Virtual Brazilian Anthropology* 17: 1–7.

Tsikata, Dzodzi A. 2006. *Living in the Shadow of the Large Dams: Long Term Responses of Downstream and Lakeside Communities of Ghana's Volta River Project*. Brill.

Tucker. 2021. "Shifting Approaches to Women and Gender in Labor, Politics and Society." *Middle East Report* 300.

Turkmani, Nur, and Kanj Hamade. 2020. *Dynamics of Syrian Refugees in Lebanon's Agriculture Sector.* Issam Fares Institute for Public Policy and International Affairs. https://www.aub.edu.lb/ifi/Pages/publications/research_reports/2019-2020/20200215-dynamics-of-syrian-refugees-in-lebanon-agriculture-sector.aspx.

Turner, Cal, and Sara Van Horn. 2024. "How US 'Foreign Aid' Has Helped Destabilize Haiti: Interview with Jake Johnson." *Jacobin*. https://jacobin.com/2024/03/us-foreign-aid-destabilize-haiti.

Turner, Lewis. 2015. "Explaining the (Non-)Encampment of Syrian Refugees: Security, Class and the Labour Market in Lebanon and Jordan." *Mediterranean Politics* 20 (3): 386–404.

Ushakin, Sergej Aleksandrovič. 2009. *The Patriotism of Despair: Nation, War, and Loss in Russia*. Cornell University Press.

Veltmeyer, Henry, and Raul Delgado Wise. 2016. *Agrarian Change, Migration and Development*. Fernwood.

Verdery, Katherine. 2003. *The Vanishing Hectare: Property and Value in Postsocialist Transylvania*. Cornell University Press.

Verdery, Katherine. 2013. *The Political Lives of Dead Bodies: Reburial and Postsocialist Change*. Columbia University Press.

Vignal, Leila. 2012. "Syria: Anatomy of a Revolution." *La Vie Des Idées / Books and Ideas*, September 21. http://www.booksandideas.net/Syria-Anatomy-of-a-Revolution.html.

Wacquant, Loïc. 2010. "Crafting the Neoliberal State: Workfare, Prisonfare, and Social Insecurity." *Sociological Forum* 25 (2): 197–220.

Walia, Harsha. 2021. *Border and Rule: Global Migration, Capitalism, and the Rise of Racist Nationalism*. Haymarket Books.

Wedeen, Lisa. 2019. *Authoritarian Apprehensions: Ideology, Judgment, and Mourning in Syria*. University of Chicago Press.

Weeks, Kathi. 2011. *The Problem with Work: Feminism, Marxism, Antiwork Politics, and Postwork Imaginaries*. Duke University Press Books.

Weiss, Hadas. 2021. "Social Reproduction." *The Open Encyclopedia of Anthropology*. https://www.anthroencyclopedia.com/entry/social-reproduction.

Weiss, Hadas. 2022. "Social Reproduction as the Reproduction of Capitalism." *Focaal* 2022 (93): 105–11.

Weist, Katherine M. 1995. "Development Refugees: Africans, Indians and the Big Dams." *Journal of Refugee Studies* 8 (2): 163–84.

White, Ben, and Hanny Wijaya. 2022. "What Kind of Labour Regime Is Contract Farming? Contracting and Sharecropping in Java Compared." *Journal of Agrarian Change* 22 (1): 19–35.

Wilder, Gary. 2015. *Freedom Time: Negritude, Decolonization, and the Future of the World.* Duke University Press.

Wilder, Gary. 2022. *Concrete Utopianism: The Politics of Temporality and Solidarity.* Fordham University Press.

Williams, Elizabeth R. 2023. *States of Cultivation: Imperial Transition and Scientific Agriculture in the Eastern Mediterranean.* Stanford University Press.

Wilson, Alice. 2023. *Afterlives of Revolution: Everyday Counterhistories in Southern Oman.* Stanford University Press.

Winchell, Mareike. 2016. "After Servitude: Bonded Histories and the Encumbrances of Exchange in Indigenizing Bolivia." *The Journal of Peasant Studies* 45 (2): 453–73.

Winchell, Mareike. 2017. "Economies of Obligation: Patronage as Relational Wealth in Bolivian Gold Mining." *HAU: Journal of Ethnographic Theory; Chicago* 7 (3): 159–83.

Winchell, Mareike. 2022. *After Servitude: Elusive Property and the Ethics of Kinship in Bolivia.* University of California Press.

Wintour, Patrick. 2019. "Thousands of Syrian Refugees Could Be Sent Back, Says Lebanese Minister." *The Guardian*, June 15. http://www.theguardian.com/world/2019/jun/15/thousands-of-syrian-refugees-could-be-sent-back-says-lebanese-minister.

Wise, Raúl Delgado. 2010. "The Migration-Development Nexus: A Marxist Class Perspective." In *Imperialism, Crisis and Class Struggle,* edited by Henry Veltmeyer. Brill.

Wise, Raúl Delgado. 2022. "The Migration-Development Nexus under Scrutiny." In *Handbook on Migration and Welfare,* edited by Markus M. L. Crepaz. Edward Elgar.

Yaghi, Zeead. 2025. *Pathways Towards Food Sovereignty in Lebanon.* Arab Reform Initiative, September 12. https://www.arab-reform.net/publication/pathways-towards-food-sovereignty-in-lebanon/.

Yassīn, Bou Ali. 1985. *Al-Idīyulujīyā Wa al-Ādab Fī Surīya: 1967–1973.* Damascus.

Yassin-Kassab, Robin, and Leila Al-Shami. 2016. *Burning Country: Syrians in Revolution and War.* Pluto.

Yurchak, Alexei. 2005. *Everything Was Forever, Until It Was No More: The Last Soviet Generation.* Princeton University Press.

Zaloom, Caitlin, and Deborah James. 2023. "Financialization and the Household." *Annual Review of Anthropology* 52: 399–415.

Zani, Leah. 2019. *Bomb Children: Life in the Former Battlefields of Laos.* Duke University Press.

Zuntz, Ann-Christin. 2021. "Refugees' Transnational Livelihoods and Remittances: Syrian Mobilities in the Middle East Before and After 2011." *Journal of Refugee Studies* 34 (2): 1400–422.

Zuntz, Ann-Christin. 2023. "Human Routers: How Syrian Refugee Brokers Build the Infrastructure of Displacement." *Cultural Anthropology* 38 (4): 517–40.

Zuntz, Ann-Christin, Mackenzie Klema, Shaher Abdullateef, Esraa Almashhor, Salim Faisal Alnabolsi, Sinem Sefa Akay, et al. 2022. "Syrians' Only Option–Rethinking Unfree Labour Through the Study of Displaced Agricultural Workers in the Middle East." *Journal of Modern Slavery: A Multidisciplinary Exploration of Human Trafficking Solutions* 7 (2): 9–32.

Zurayk, Rami. 2011. *Food, Farming, and Freedom: Sowing the Arab Spring.* Just World Books.

Zurayk, Rami. 2013. "Civil War and the Devastation of Syria's Food System." *Journal of Agriculture, Food Systems, and Community Development* 3 (2): 7–9.

Index

Note: An italicized page number indicates a figure on the corresponding page.

Stanford Studies in Middle Eastern and Islamic Societies and Cultures

Lara Deeb and Sherene Seikaly, editors

Colorblind: Racial Thinking and Cultural Production in Modern Iran and the Diaspora 2026
AMY MOTLAGH

The State of Lebanon: Popular Politics and Institution Building in the Wake of Independence 2026
ZIAD M. ABU-RISH

Plots and Deeds: Agrarian Annihilation and the Fight for Land Justice in Palestine 2026
PAUL KOHLBRY

Race and the Question of Palestine 2025
LANA TATOUR AND RONIT LENTIN, EDITORS

Dust That Never Settles: Literary Afterlives of the Iran-Iraq War 2025
AMIR MOOSAVI

The Revolution Within: Islamic Media and the Struggle for a New Egypt 2025
YASMIN MOLL

Unruly Labor: A History of Oil in the Arabian Sea 2024
ANDREA WRIGHT

The Incarcerated Modern: Prisons and Public Life in Iran 2024
GOLNAR NIKPOUR

Elastic Empire: Refashioning War Through Aid in Palestine 2023
LISA BHUNGALIA

Colonizing Palestine: The Zionist Left and the Making of the Palestinian Nakba 2023
AREEJ SABBAGH-KHOURY

On Salafism: Concepts and Contexts 2023
AZMI BISHARA

Revolutions Aesthetic: A Cultural History of Ba'thist Syria 2022
MAX WEISS

Street-Level Governing: Negotiating the State in Urban Turkey 2022
ELISE MASSICARD

Protesting Jordan: Geographies of Power and Dissent 2022
JILLIAN SCHWEDLER

Media of the Masses: Cassette Culture in Modern Egypt 2022
ANDREW SIMON

States of Subsistence: The Politics of Bread in Contemporary Jordan 2022
JOSÉ CIRO MARTÍNEZ

Between Dreams and Ghosts: Indian Migration and Middle Eastern Oil 2021
ANDREA WRIGHT

Bread and Freedom: Egypt's Revolutionary Situation 2021
MONA EL-GHOBASHY

Paradoxes of Care: Children and Global Medical Aid in Egypt 2021
RANIA KASSAB SWEIS

The Politics of Art: Dissent and Cultural Diplomacy in Lebanon, Palestine, and Jordan 2021
HANAN TOUKAN

The Paranoid Style in American Diplomacy: Oil and Arab Nationalism in Iraq 2021
BRANDON WOLFE-HUNNICUTT

Screen Shots: State Violence on Camera in Israel and Palestine 2021
REBECCA L. STEIN

Dear Palestine: A Social History of the 1948 War 2021
SHAY HAZKANI

A Critical Political Economy of the Middle East and North Africa 2020
JOEL BEININ, BASSAM HADDAD, AND SHERENE SEIKALY, EDITORS

Showpiece City: How Architecture Made Dubai 2020
TODD REISZ

For a complete listing of titles in this series, visit the Stanford University Press website, www.sup.org.